Reframing Syrian Refugee Insecurity through a Feminist Lens

Reframing Syrian Refugee Insecurity through a Feminist Lens

The Case of Lebanon

Jessy Abouarab

LEXINGTON BOOKS
Lanham • Boulder • New York • London

Published by Lexington Books
An imprint of The Rowman & Littlefield Publishing Group, Inc.
4501 Forbes Boulevard, Suite 200, Lanham, Maryland 20706
www.rowman.com

6 Tinworth Street, London SE11 5AL, United Kingdom

British Library Cataloguing in Publication Information Available

The hardback edition of this book was previously catalogued by the Library of Congress
as follows:

Library of Congress Cataloging-in-Publication Data
Names: Abouarab, Jessy, 1982- author.
Title: Reframing Syrian refugee insecurity through a feminist lens : the case of Lebanon
    / Jessy Abouarab.
Description: Lanham : Lexington Books, [2020] | Includes bibliographical references
    and index.
Identifiers: LCCN 2020005968 (print) | LCCN 2020005969 (ebook) |
    ISBN 9781793613912 (cloth) | ISBN 9781793613936 (paper) |
    ISBN 9781793613929 (epub)
Subjects: LCSH: Women refugees—Syria—Social conditions. | Women refugees—
    Lebanon—Social conditions. | Political refugees—Syria—Social conditions. | Political
    refugees—Lebanon—Social conditions. | Feminist theory. | Transnationalism. |
    Syria—History—Civil War, 2011—-Refugees—Lebanon. | Lebanon—Emigration
    and immigration—Social aspects. | Lebanon—Social conditions.
Classification: LCC HV640.5.S97 A245 2020 (print) | LCC HV640.5.S97 (ebook) |
    DDC 956.9104/231—dc23
LC record available at https://lccn.loc.gov/2020005968
LC ebook record available at https://lccn.loc.gov/2020005969

I humbly dedicate this book to the memory of my beloved father.

Contents

Acknowledgments

I could not have produced this book without the many inspiring friends and colleagues who have profoundly influenced my academic life and work. I wish to express my sincere gratitude to Susanne Zwingel for her limitless patience, invaluable guidance, and constructive criticism. I am equally indebted to Harry Gould, Eric Lob, and Dennis Wiedman for their conscientious supervision, thought-provoking discussions, and enriching advice that have greatly expanded my knowledge. A special thank you to Mark Padilla. Your Photovoice research to promote policy dialog among street-based drug users in Santo Domingo motivated me to adapt your method and enrich this research with an innovative grounded approach. Thank you, Yesim Darici for welcoming me to the Center for Women's and Gender Studies. I am further grateful for all the opportunities that you, Victoria Burns, MIchaela Moura, and Tamara Erbant provided me to grow as a scholar in a center that I am honored to call my second home. A special thank you to the many good friends at Florida International University who encouraged and supported me in my efforts the past six years. Sophia Younis, Nicolas Terradas, Onur Erpul, Zenel Garica, and Bibek Chand I am inspired by your strength, energy, and dedication to our friendship.

I am also grateful to my friends and colleagues in Lebanon, whose dedication to the Syrian refugee crisis in Lebanon is a constant source of motivation and difficulty to do good by others. I wish to thank Malak Rahal, the first of many humanitarian experts and Lebanese constituents who agreed to invest their time, energy, and wisdom in enriching this book. I have learned so much from our discussions, and I hope that your voices are heard and reflected adequately within this manuscript.

Finally, I cannot thank enough my extended family in Lebanon, whose love and kindness are my pillar. A special thank you to my extra ordinary mother, Wedad Zard, perfect sister, Julie Abouarab, amazing brothers, Norman Abouarab, Raymond Abouarab, and loving siblings in-law, Oscar Yamin, Katya Segovia, for being my rock and always encouraging me to finish what I have started. I would like to thank the amazing Antoinette Hernani, Hala Atwi, and my precious nephews, Edgar, Anthony, and Julian for your unconditional love and unwavering support that made me the privileged and proud person that I am today.

Introduction

For more than half a century, international norms dedicated to the protection of refugees have proliferated, yet their role in alleviating war's negative impacts on human life remains limited. Many issues and people are silenced due to narrow security approaches that focus on either abstract threat prevention and refugee control or macro-level refugee protection and humanitarian aid. As such, this book investigates the inherently political concept of "security" as it permeates the forced migration case of Syrian refugees in Lebanon. There are various levels of (in)security construction, management, and implications that are contextually relevant to refugeeism, which can be defined as "a movement of populations between existing and autonomous juridical states."[1] Sociocultural, historical, religious, and institutional experiences all play a significant role in how a state appropriates, translates, and reformulates discourses into local context.[2] One finds that global discourses differ from local attitudes that shape host states' perceptions and policy practices toward incoming refugees. Underlying factors, such as geopolitics and biased cultural influence on strategic policy planning, significantly inform this research, affect social perceptions, and subsequently impact how policies are to be declared and implemented. Identity politics is particularly relevant for exploring silenced bodies such as Syrian refugees, who experience multidimensional and (dis)continuous insecurities in Lebanon.

Communities are products of historical and social contingencies that shape specific cultural identities, reflecting individual and collective security interests and practices. Lebanon has a long history with Syria, in which political and sectarian conflicts have altered the fabric of its society, influencing attitudes, opinions, and politics both internally and on a regional scale. Although the diversity of Lebanese political opinions is often vast, it seems that most Lebanese public and social outlets now have one commonality: "The Syrian displaced persons have no place in our home country."[3] Even when many Lebanese citizens witnessed similar displacement during recent wars, some of them question the legitimacy of Syrian refugees being forced to flee their home country, willingly disregarding the widely televised human atrocities occurring in Syria. The Lebanese anxieties projected in public statements and policy reports focus solely on repressing and resisting an overwhelming number of Syrian asylum seekers. The main goal of focusing on such views is to prevent Syrian foreigners from posing further damage to the already destabilized Lebanese state. As such, the Lebanese anxieties portray Syrian refugees as needy at best, and as a problem or a liability at worst, creating an impasse for residing Syrians to settle and integrate.

My consideration for this study derives from me being a Lebanese American female with a long-standing interest in social justice, women's rights, and gender equality. My interest in Syrian women's rights and refugee protection in Lebanon materialized in 2015 during a family visit. During that time, Lebanese media outlets and local politicians highlighted the burdens that Lebanon was enduring due to the increasing Syrian refugee influx. On the one hand, the host state's public discourse of masculinized threats, such as Syrian men committing crimes and terrorist attacks in several Lebanese towns, legitimized their ad hoc aggressive practices of stripping Syrians of refugee status, disqualifying them from being fully integrated. On the other hand, humanitarian agencies' feminizing depictions of "passive" Syrian refugees, such as vulnerable women and children living in impoverished areas, accorded Syrians a de facto refugee status, qualifying them for international protection and assistance.

Anti-Syrian sentiments lingering from previous periods of occupation in Lebanon persist to this day. This fact was evident throughout my field research in Lebanon, during which a substantial number of Lebanese families expressed dislike for the Syrian presence. Despite the change of Syrians' status in the country from an occupying force to a group of forced migrants, many Lebanese nationals still perceive them as a threat to the country's security, economy, and demographic structure. Prior to the refugee crisis, Syrians were perceived as an extension of the occupying army of the Assad regime.

My father, General Said Abouarab, was a Lebanese Army officer who fought for Lebanon's stability his entire life. He witnessed several wars, deterred several coups d'états, and even took bullets and missiles that marked his body while safeguarding his country from foreign and domestic threats. His resilience was not extinguished even when the Syrian army took over the Ministry of Defense in October 1990, marching all the way to his office that still had the residue of a missile blast from a few weeks earlier. My father outwardly welcomed the new Syrian occupiers, all the while protecting other Lebanese patriots by shredding all sensitive documents and keeping a low profile until the end of his service. My mother, like many Lebanese mothers, was the unknown soldier[4] whose resilience saved many people's lives while, at the same time, protecting four children from bombshells and Syrian captivity. My mother, siblings, and I were internally displaced for almost a year, but privileged for having strong family support, informal networks, and allies who sheltered us until the end of the Lebanese Liberation War in 1990. Although I was very young at the time, this experience lingered with my family in the form of various health problems and psychological traumas that forced us to migrate in the early 1990s to the United States of America for a year.

The fact is that the Lebanese Civil War was one of the most gruesomely convoluted long-term conflicts, lasting fifteen years from 1975 to 1990.[5] The collective memory of modern Lebanese society mostly blames the actions of Palestinian refugees for the start of the Lebanese sectarian Civil War, during which a person's identity card served as a potential death warrant. Checkpoints spread across the country where "people would often be shot on the spot if their documents revealed the 'wrong' sort of sectarian affiliation."[6] It is important to note that sectarianism in Lebanon still shapes the way the country functions in that Lebanon suffers from a chronically unstable political system that is gendered and path-dependent. Founded on sensitive political, religious, and sectarian balances, Lebanon bases one's communal identity on tribal allegiance as opposed to equality and rights, where yesterday's warlords remained in power as today's leading political figures.[7]

Coming from a Christian-Catholic-Maronite family, I was socialized in an all-French Christian school with anti-Syrian leanings, not knowing and yet fearing the "other." I became highly involved in anti-Syrian occupation student organizations and local resistance efforts. I witnessed Syrian soldiers arresting several of my friends in street protests, harshly interrogating and torturing them. Later in 2001, I began pursuing my bachelor's degree in political science at the American University of Beirut (AUB). This experience allowed me to be submerged in a diverse group of academics and was significantly different from the protective anti-Syrian culture I was accustomed to. Not only did I learn a great deal about the intricacies of Lebanese politics and street cultures, I also became more aware of the complexities within the Lebanese sects and the divergent views of Syria's role in Lebanon. Accordingly, I took part in political arguments within safe student spaces about the Syrian presence in Lebanon, while avoiding voicing anti-Syrian opinions too publicly for fear of Syrian retaliation.

Before AUB, I always thought that all Lebanese people wanted the Syrian presence out of the country. Nevertheless, attending a diverse campus with a plethora of religious sects challenged some of my subconscious beliefs, assumptions, and prejudices related to the occupying Syrian presence. With time, I formed close and meaningful relationships with many Syrian students from different religious backgrounds. I regularly engaged them in heated political and religious discussions about Lebanese, Syrian, and regional dynamics. On the one hand, I witnessed the lack of political justice and the often-intersecting impacts of sociocultural discrimination that hinder Lebanese citizens from overcoming previous conceptions of Syria. On the other hand, I had the privilege of participating in community engagements and cultural awareness exercises that strengthened my rapprochement toward the Syrian "other." These experiences allowed me to connect with the "other" on an empathetic level and appreciate the common humanity within the diverse Lebanese-Syrian communities by differentiating politics and government activities from respective individuals' views and religious beliefs.

Still, conversations about the gendered power relations and the daily challenges of the conflict were nonexistent at that time. I always felt that most research and policies sidelined women's matters and agency for the sake of other issues that deemed more important when discussing government activities and people's experiences during that time. Being privileged enough to later travel, live abroad, and experience the world, my conceptions of race, class, ethnicity, nationality, and faith matured. Having meaningful conversations about gender, religion, and other multiple identities that affect people's everyday experiences enhanced my perception of the interrelatedness of world politics. I came to understand how backgrounds and cultures (re)shape one's identity, values, and beliefs, influencing the type of topics a person feels suitable to discuss.

After spending many years away from the region's torments, I found myself back in Lebanon in 2015 for a family visit, encountering a million and some Syrian refugees officially registered with the United Nations High Commissioner for Refugees (UNHCR).[8] During that time, I was asked to help organize and facilitate a municipal electoral campaign for a relative. My attempt barely lasted one night before I realized that his anti-Syrian rhetoric shifted from the Syrian government of Bashar al-Assad to the Syrians displaced in Lebanon, scapegoating al-Assad's reign. It was surprising to me how quickly and easily political rhetoric changes in order to sustain the parochial interests of certain political groups. A few years back, I remember that same relative catechizing about the duty of Syria to host and assist their displaced Lebanese "brothers" during the 2006 Lebanese–Israeli war. As circumstances shifted with now millions of Syrians seeking refuge in Lebanon, his position switched to considering them a risk and a burden not welcomed in the country. Ironically, to this day, most of the employees he hires are Syrians who can be paid lower wages with no legal benefits. This situation mirrors many other Lebanese employers taking advantage of the Syrian crisis for personal gain while simultaneously expressing disdain for the Syrian refugee presence.

This personal experience motivated me to critically question the current Syrian refugee crisis in Lebanon. The former Lebanese resilience, strength, and optimism for ending the Syrian occupation of Lebanon shifted to marginalizing claims of Syrian refugees becoming a never-ending occupying menace. The very mixed feelings and experiences that most Lebanese have had with Syrians in their country, generally as occupiers, was the impetus for my research exploring the web of power relations that permeates today's contentious Syrian refugee (in)security management and impact.

NOTES

1. Judith Butler and Gayatri Chakravorty Spivak, *Who Sings the Nation-State?: Language, Politics, Belonging* (London, England: Seagull Books, 2007), 6.

2. Sally Engle Merry, *Human Rights and Gender Violence: Translating International Law into Local Justice* (Chicago, IL: University of Chicago Press, 2009), 3.

3. Human Rights Watch, *Our Homes Are Not for Strangers: Mass Evictions of Syrian Refugees by Lebanese Municipalities* (April 20, 2018), https://www.hrw.org/report/2018/04/20/our-homes-are-not-strangers/mass-evictionssyrian-refugees-lebanese-municipalities.

4. Svetlana Alexievich, *The Unwomanly Face of War: An Oral History of Women in World War II* (New York: Random House, 2017), 5.

5. Hassan Krayem, "The Lebanese Civil War and the Taif Agreement," in *Conflict Resolution in the Arab World: Selected Essays*, ed. Paul Salem (Beirut, Lebanon: American University of Beirut, 1997), 411–36.

6. "Lebanon 'Moves Right Way' on ID," *BBC News* (February 24, 2009), http://news.bbc.co.uk/2/hi/middle_east/7906125.stm.

7. Maja Janmyr, "Precarity in Exile: The Legal Status of Syrian Refugees in Lebanon," *Refugee Survey Quarterly* 35, no.4 (2016): 58–78.

8. "Refugees From Syria: Lebanon," *UNHCR* (March 2015, 6), http://reliefweb.int/report/lebanon/refugees-syria-lebanonmarch-2015.

Chapter 1

Understanding the Syrian Refugee Crisis in Lebanon

RESEARCHER'S BACKGROUND AND POSITIONING

As the principal investigator, I am both an insider and an outsider. Despite being born in Lebanon, I was privileged to live abroad and possess dual citizenship in the United States of America, a land that I could call home. Being both physically and culturally detached from the daily Lebanese intricacies made me conscious of the gender differences between Lebanon and America. It was these types of spaces that made me both an insider and an outsider to the Syrian refugee crisis in Lebanon, in need of constant reflexivity to determine how this research should be conducted and for whom it is intended.

This book is, at its core, a personal project aiming to explore the gendering of Syrian refugee (in)securities in the case of Lebanon. Although the diversity of Lebanese political opinions is often vast, it seemed that most Lebanese public and social outlets differed from my personal opinion in that they believed "The Syrian displaced persons have no place in our home country."[1] I had many Lebanese friends who questioned the legitimacy of Syrian refugee claims of being forced to flee their homes, oblivious of the widely televised human atrocities that were happening in Syria, even though not long ago, they witnessed, like I did, similar challenges during the many wars. Unlike me, however, their projected anxieties focused on how to deter Syrian residents from taking over Lebanon. This positionality geared me toward planning and conducting a bottom-up exploration in accordance with the everyday refugee (in)security practices that are the subject of this study. A participatory research approach including people who have lived through such experiences enriches this research by fundamentally questioning and rethinking previously established top-down knowledge.

No matter how well-intentioned, without collaborating with local enthu-
siasts in a truly participatory way, this research runs the risk of missing out
on some of the inner dynamics of the securitization and protection of Syrian refugees. The research process detailed in this book enabled Lebanese
coresearchers to step back cognitively from their familiar routines and power
relationships, questioning and rethinking established gendered structures and
rhetoric contributing fruitful knowledge-generating narratives. Though the
five Lebanese volunteers assisting Syrian refugees included as research participants in this study were not the main objects of inquiry, their interaction
and knowledge of their surroundings enrich this research. That is why it is
important to highlight their positioning as coresearchers, emphasizing their
background and expertise. The coresearchers' life experiences within both
Lebanese and Syrian refugee communities put them at a unique advantage
of being privileged to understand the intricacies and perceptions within both
groups. Even though the participants come from different Lebanese social
upbringings, all of them come from a relatively privileged college background and working-class setting, where the Syrian refugee presence in their
country does not threaten their livelihood (in)directly. As a matter of fact,
three of the co-researchers' livelihood (in)directly improved due to working
with the Syrian refugee population across Lebanon.

Most of the participants acknowledged that their Lebanese community
(sub)consciously pressured their perceptions of the Syrian crisis as a threat
to the overall Lebanese society, even though they believed that the media
and official rhetoric (un)intentionally simplified the complex dynamics of
the Syrian crisis in Lebanon. The coresearchers' views of the Syrian refugee
situation were essential for the process of knowledge production, for they
promised a new and different take on the subject under study by elaborating their own opinions and experiences. Their collaborative input provided
important contributions to the study by voicing the complex realities of Syrian refugees' different daily (in)securities, while, at the same time, recognizing their anxieties as Lebanese citizens toward the Syrian presence within
their communities.

THE GENDERED CASE OF LEBANON

Forced migration due to warfare is a traumatic experience with depth and
breadth that pose significant challenges to interweaving affected groups, such
as refugees, neighboring host states, and humanitarian agencies. Contrary to
popular perception, most global forced migration occurs between developing
countries with contiguous borders.[2] Moreover, a massive and sudden inflow
of refugees embodies tremendous security and sociopolitical concerns for

hosting communities. For example, triggered by the ongoing war in Syria, millions of Syrian nationals sought refuge in neighboring countries such as Lebanon, a nation populated by roughly five million people. Capturing the unique dynamics of this South-South forced migration case, in which Syrian refugees now make up nearly one-third of Lebanon's population, is a thought-provoking research task. Although Lebanese authorities made tremendous efforts in containing the refugee crisis, their attention has primarily focused on direct short-term solutions such as providing their most vulnerable Lebanese citizens with shelter and food while attempting to secure their borders against the influx of new refugees.[3] This narrow, traditional security framework prioritizes national security of the state first, citizen security second, and the security of refugees last in a genderless, overgeneralized manner. Under the guise of sovereignty, state-centric structures for addressing forced displacement and the lack of a commonly agreed-upon international legal framework are severe obstacles for addressing both short- and long-term refugee insecurities. Concurrently, generalized research on the host state security–refugee protection nexus—what the study refers to as *"refugee (in)security"*—and how it matters in global politics limits us from critically examining the gaps within the (en)gendered politics of Syrian forced migration into Lebanon.

It is critical to note that women are mostly absent from this type of refugee (in)security framework.[4] The Lebanese government and international agencies seem to provide little-to-no relief to the majority of officially registered refugees: Syrian women escaping the horrors of war. Moreover, since women and men distinctly experience (in)securities spatially and by gender,[5] refugee women are doubly marginalized due to their refugee status and gender. In particular, public policies play a huge part in delineating Syrian refugee women's ability to secure their life without discriminatory labels that might constrain and marginalize them as unwelcomed displaced persons that threaten the host state's stability.[6] Under international law, being recognized as a refugee signifies that the international community and government agencies should strive to ensure the empowerment of the acknowledged groups of people for equal access to education, healthcare, safety, shelter, and most importantly, gender-sensitive employment opportunities. Still, refugee integration and assimilation processes are state-dependent, manifesting asymmetrically within populations, with women often being subjected to greater adversity than others. These dynamics thus necessitate an empirically motivated gender lens to meaningfully examine how the Syrian refugee crisis is exacerbated in the case of Lebanon, and how it profoundly impacts Syrian refugee women.

As such, this book is both a process and a product, whereby Syrian refugee insecurity is (en)gendered and experienced. Here, the term "gender" possesses a dual meaning: it is a matter not only of difference but also of inequality. First, this research defines gender as a social construction of being perceived as a male or a female. Secondly, gender shapes the structural system of privileging male behaviors that can feminize or masculinize diverse groups of asylum seekers, which is what the study refers to as *"gender(ing)."*[7] Accordingly, this study uses a gender lens to highlight the current dyadic construction of Syrian refugees as either men/masculine, framed as a security threat, or women/feminine, depoliticized with no agency, in which the meaning of one is dependent on the meaning of the other.[8] By exploring this dyadic social construction and cultural representation of Syrian refugees and their gendered performance in the case of Lebanon, this research aims to disrupt the perceived dichotomy of refugees within the schemes of refugee insecurity, providing a space for productive dialogue across disciplines. The transnational politics of forced migration requires a multileveled initiative under a gender lens to better explore these gaps within the divergent perceptions and practices of Syrian refugee insecurity in the case of Lebanon soundly and ethically.[9] Thus, this book explores the questions of how refugee security norms get defined, how they are managed, and how they impact local contexts, for women particularly.

AN ALTERNATIVE UNDERSTANDING
OF A REFUGEE CRISIS

Gendered power relations are everywhere in global politics, and "whenever they are not recognized, the silence is loud."[10] That is why understanding these dynamics is essential when contextualizing the different (re)productions of Syrian refugee security strategies and protection mechanisms in the case of Lebanon. With so much attention going toward the need for both international aid to protect refugees and national security concerns to assure state stability, a gender lens would provide a more in-depth exploration of how the plight of Syrian women does not seem to receive the necessary attention that it so desperately needs. This research thus draws on feminist critiques of security studies and refugee protection regimes to enhance the efficiency of refugee protection efforts, while also accommodating host states' security concerns in a constructive way. It aims to shed light on the challenges faced by Syrian refugees in Lebanon, most of whom are women who seem to be silenced the most throughout the different stages of refugee (in)security. Considering the absence of extensive South-South forced migration studies, I chose Lebanon's case of the Syrian refugee crisis because it adds value to the general debate on security construction and gender norm translation in refugee governance mechanisms.

In this context, incorporating a gender dimension into analyzing the nuances of security norms' construction and implementation can improve our understanding of how these norms are formed and internalized, as well as shed light on their local impact. A feminist read on the refugee protection regime unearths many issues and gives voice to people who have been marginalized by traditional security and refugee protection methods. The study uses cross-disciplinary tools, such as expert interviews, in-depth longitudinal cultural theme analysis, and a participatory method called Photovoice, to understand the multileveled challenges of the refugee crisis in Lebanon, in which Syrian refugee insecurity is gendered and experienced. These tools contribute methodologically to the understanding of how gender plays into an increasingly securitized refugee migration and how this, in turn, affects Syrian women's experiences and resilience efforts in the case of Lebanon.

The study is significant in a refugee security context, in which (inter)national decisions impact diverse groups of refugees for the rest of their lives. Accordingly, the book's approach gives a much more applied assessment, expanding the literature on security studies, refugee governance, and norm translation. It offers an alternative theoretical and methodological understanding of what it means to be a refugee in a neighboring Middle Eastern country where refugee crises have been extensive and protracted. Although there has been much scholarly attention to refugee security studies and protection mechanisms, little research has focused on the views and perspectives of silenced stakeholders, especially neighboring host communities and refugees themselves. Accordingly, this book responds to feminists' call for implementing a multileveled research approach that closes the gap between theoretical knowledge and practical solutions. This transnational feminist research fills an empirical and methodological void in International Relations scholarship. It sheds light on how the gendering of refugee (in)security is multilayered, continually shifting through processes of construction, interpretation, and application with an array of political, humanitarian, socioeconomic, and security complications. Due to its transnational focus, this book equips both academics and practitioners with the necessary skills to understand complex social phenomena, questioning existing paradigms and structures that tend to homogenize, objectify, and discriminate silenced bodies such as Syrian women.

STRUCTURE OF THE TEXT

The following chapter traces the shift of geopolitical and Lebanese social attitudes toward Syrian refugees by highlighting important critical junctures in the Lebanese-Syrian relationship. It then explores the official Lebanese sensitivities toward the term "refugee" in general, and Syrians in Lebanon specifically. Lastly, it analyzes the political implications of explicit and implicit changes in security practices right after the last significant political juncture post-2014. It also highlights the aggressive and regulative refugee control methods that bolstered the role of local authorities and municipalities to legitimize ad hoc and, at times, illegal actions furthering securitized practices across Lebanon.

Chapter 3 analyzes the contextual dynamics, tension, and resistance that shape and are shaped by specific refugee crisis response plans between collaborating political institutions with distinct visions and goals. Specifically, the focus will be on two core institutions: the Lebanese government and the UNHCR. Lebanon is used as an example of a sovereign developing state overwhelmed with refugees, while the UNHCR is the leading international organization responsible for refugees' protection. Although roles played by other UN agencies and regional organizations to reduce statelessness and protect refugees are important, the UNHCR plays a significant role in the case of Lebanon, where most response projects are either funded or implemented through the UNHCR. A longitudinal comparison of consecutive Syrian Crisis Response Plans (LCRPs) and its triangulation with other primary sources highlights the transformation of Lebanon's Syrian refugee crisis management. This chapter thus brings to view the power dynamics between two collaborating bodies of different knowledge claims and approaches to managing the Syrian crisis.

Chapter 4 explores how gender (in)security norms are applied on the ground. It highlights the gendered impact on refugees' (in)security practices in general, and on Syrian women specifically. Photovoice methodology was utilized by local Lebanese volunteers to increase the visibility of the Syrian refugee crisis by recording and reflecting on the refugees' realities through pictures and voice. This participatory action research approach transforms our understandings of the daily Syrian refugee anxieties and resilience efforts in ways that extend beyond the narrow policies that hinder contextual contributions to general knowledge. It elaborates on the local volunteers' important contributions to the study by voicing their views of different Syrian refugees' daily insecurities, while, at the same time, recognizing their anxieties as Lebanese citizens toward the Syrian presence within their communities.

The concluding chapter explores the local repercussions of the Syrian refugee crisis in Lebanon due to the imposition of restrictive policies on the entry, movement, and residence of Syrians in Lebanon after December 2014. It provides a synthesis by discussing the importance of re-framing Syrian refugee insecurity through a feminist lens by situating gender within critical scholarship in the fields of security studies, refugee protection regimes, and norm translation. It explores what seems to be a vicious cycle of insecurities across Lebanon due to inadequate Syrian refugee management practices. The chapter concludes with a discussion of the benefit of including an interdisciplinary feminist framework and research methods as strategies to further our knowledge of multilayered social phenomena with structural and gendered implications.

NOTES

1. Human Rights Watch, "Our Homes Are Not for Strangers: Mass Evictions of Syrian Refugees by Lebanese Municipalities." April 20, 2018, https://www.hrw.org/report/2018/04/20.

2. Dilip Ratha and William Shaw, "South-South Migration and Remittances." *The World Bank* (2007), p. 2.

3. Mark Manly, "UNHCR's Mandate and Activities to Address Statelessness in Europe." *European Journal of Migration and Law* 14, no. 3 (2012): 261–77.

4. Elisabeth Olivius, "Constructing Humanitarian Selves and Refugee Others: Gender Equality and the Global Governance of Refugees." *International Feminist Journal of Politics* 18, no. 2 (2016): 276.

5. Lene Hansen, "The Little Mermaid's Silent Security Dilemma and the Absence of Gender in the Copenhagen School." *Millennium: Journal of International Relations* 29, no. 2 (2000): 285–306.

6. Sue Lautze, and John Hammock, *Saving Lives and Livelihoods: The Fundamentals of a Livelihood Strategy* (Medford, MA: Feinstein International Famine Center, Tufts University, 1997).

7. Jane Freedman, *Gendering the International Asylum and Refugee Debate* (Palgrave Macmillan, 2015), 19.

8. Freedman, *Gendering the International Asylum and Refugee Debate*, 19.

9. Amitav Acharya, "The Limitations of Mainstream International Relations Theories for Understanding the Politics of Forced Migration" (Lecture, Centre for International Studies, Oxford University, October 27, 2008). Karen Jacobsen and Loren B. Landau, "The Dual Imperative in Refugee Research: Some Methodological and Ethical Considerations in Social Science Research on Forced Migration." *Disasters* 27, no. 3 (2003): 185–206. Alexander Betts, *Forced Migration and Global Politics* (New York, NY: John Wiley & Sons, 2009).

10. J. Ann Tickner and Laura Sjoberg, "Feminism," in *International Relations Theory, Discipline and Diversity*, 3rd ed., ed. Tim Dunne, Milja Kurki, and Steve Smith (Oxford: Oxford University Press, 2013), 209.

Chapter 2

Lebanese-Syrian (In)Security Practices

SECURITIZATION OF REFUGEES

Traditionally, security concerns focus on sovereign states as unitary actors that need to secure themselves from any form of threat in order to survive. These sovereign states focus on reinforcing their territorial boundaries through hard military control and deterrence practices toward any perceived incoming threat.[1] Within an "anarchic" state-based system, many host states construct asylum seekers in security discourses, mostly portraying incoming refugees as opportunistic masculine threats to their national security and socioeconomic stability. As such, speech acts are influential in the construction and legitimization of specific security measures toward a specific issue or a group.[2] However, speech acts are not the only form of action that constructs security frameworks. Complex security activities are also made up of countless local everyday practices—"patterned ways of doing things"[3] that are socially developed through learning and training—that tend to get overlooked in mainstream research on security studies.[4]

Unlike habits, practices do not need extensive repetition to be acquired. The process of securitization could be linked to routinized practices of security professionals as well as "anchoring" practices, which means that a certain body would define their own set of strategies for action over others by setting new standards for "good" or "bad" domestic policies. As such, routinized or anchoring practices create a set of dynamics that enable local perceptions and anxieties to flourish or diminish.[5] Accordingly, these "mundane bureaucratic practices,"[6] drawn from everyday politics, inform how a host society's "conduct of unease" can direct the security norms and expectations toward a homogenized group of Syrian refugees. The routinized practices of security professionals, bureaucrats, and police reinforce counterintuitive "conditional

15

hospitality" through the reproduction of securitized issues and rules.[7]
Through hyper-regulated border control measures and visa requirements,
practices such as these possess a co-constitutive structural power that silence
refugees' insecurities and inhibit the different groups of asylum seekers from
accessing much needed essential services.

In truth, this concept of "securitization" is all about perception and interpretation, in which security is a "self-referential practice."[8] Securitization
theory highlights the fact that "security threats" are socially constructed,
subjective, and relatively dependent on the observer and their intersectional
background. Threats do not exist independently from the discourses that mark
them as such.[9] When constructed, perceived threats produce local practices
that would "[demand] urgent and immediate attention, as well as the use of
extraordinary measures to counter this threat."[10] The inaccurate construction
of refugees as a security burden legitimizes extraordinary measures taken
to protect a false community identity of the insecure "Us" (citizens) from
the dangerous visualized "Other" (a foreign threat).[11] As a political act, the
securitization of refugees as distant "others" transforms them into matters of
security rather than humanity, legitimizing strict border security mechanisms
on the entry and status determination of asylum seekers.[12] These generalized constructions of identity gradually reinforce statist assumptions about
the importance of securitizing citizenship and immigration control, framing
the humanitarian identity of the host state as a vulnerability it cannot afford.
Sovereign host states thus politicize, via political speeches, media representation, provocative images, and local practices, the threat of refugees obtaining
legal status as a measure to protect their national security, welfare, and, most
importantly, identity.[13]

Still, security norms are not static. These norms are continuously
(re)interpreted, localized, and contextualized, forming organized and meaningful behaviors that create a variety of accepted practices that lead to a
variety of outcomes.[14] Moreover, security practices tend to be contextually relative due to different viewers' interests. Practices engage with their
respective environments and objects, whether those are natural, cultural, or
political. Consequently, practices of adoption, resistance, and opposition to
refugee migration transform universal norms, such as human rights, into
securitized state practices of controlling refugee migration, legitimizing ad
hoc discriminatory agendas in the name of sovereignty. Highlighting the
role of such security practices in the case of Lebanon can reveal processes
of securitization that might not be shown when focusing solely on generalized security discourse or speech acts. By bridging theories into an empirical case, this chapter will explore why and how Lebanese security practices
changed the host state's physical environment as well as the discursive social
idea of hosting Syrian refugees within its communities. The local Lebanese

perceptions and practices, in turn, explain how national interest forms and justifies exceptional mechanisms of refugee deterrence with counterproductive consequences in the case of Syrian refugee women.

With the growing international refugee crisis, geopolitics and biased social attitudes play instrumental roles in shaping refugee (in)security construction with (en)gendered practices. The Middle East, specifically Lebanon, has a long history of political and sectarian conflicts that have not only altered the fabric of its communities but also influenced the local attitudes, opinions, and policies toward hosting refugees from neighboring countries. Several recent publications have examined Lebanon's lack of commitment to international refugee law.[15] Still, most scholars have not longitudinally traced the political junctures that led to the current Lebanese securitization practices toward the recent influx of Syrian asylum seekers. Lebanese perceptions of the Syrian refugee population and the increasing social tensions between both communities depend upon historical and bureaucratic factors. With this in mind, this chapter first examines four significant political junctures in the gendered Lebanese-Syrian relationship. Second, it explores Lebanon's sensitivities toward the term "refugee" and the consistent legitimization of its rejection of the 1951 Refugee Convention. Third, it analyzes Lebanon's securitized refugee management practices that ostracize Syrian refugees in general. Finally, this chapter provides further detail on the systemic gender discrimination that the Lebanese polity already imposes on its citizens, which doubly marginalizes Syrian refugee women.

CRITICAL JUNCTURES IN THE
LEBANESE-SYRIAN RELATIONS

Historical critical junctures are relatively short periods of time that lead to ideational changes within the policy fabric, as well as organizational changes that generate "self-reinforcing path-dependent processes."[16] A wide range of scholarship often refers to these instances as "turning points," "paradigm shifts," "crises," and "unsettled times." Such crises develop due to "change agents" contesting the existing status quo and attempting to (re)design policies that were once upheld.[17] Internal and external changes can trigger new path-dependent practices that constrain state behavior to become qualitatively different from previous norms and interests, ultimately affecting policy-making.[18] These changes would co-create lasting effects on the "choices made during [those] critical junctures in history," closing off different paths during that time frame.[19]

In the case of Lebanon, contemporary political history has been defined by many interrelated factors that affected not only its internal structure but also its role within the region. Religion, which is believed to be one of the corner-stones of the country's sociopolitical fabric, played a significant role in shaping Lebanese dynamics, as different sects, mainly Maronite, Sunni, Shiite, Druze, and Greek Orthodox, developed into the primary social organizations maintaining political security. Most importantly, identity politics led to communal favoritism over individual rights, causing resentment and alienation between the different Lebanese subcommunities. Lebanon's sectarian stability depends on "the ability of communal elites to sustain the power-sharing agreement and maintain control" over their respective constituents.[20]

Since its independence, Lebanon's eighteen religious sects paved the way for a confessional power-sharing system that was further institutionalized under the *Ta'if* Accord after the end of the Civil War in 1989.[21] The *Ta'if* Accord—a regional summit brokered in the city of *Ta'if*, Saudi Arabia—incorporated in the Lebanese Constitution a more confessional distribution (a system of government that is a de jure mix of religion and politics) of political power among the main religious groups. The three dominant ethnoreligious sects (Maronite Christians, Sunni Muslims, and Shiite Muslims) took the leading positions, with the office of the president assigned to a Christian Maronite, that of the prime minister to a Sunni Muslim, and the Speaker of the National Assembly to a Shiite Muslim.[22]

Meanwhile, the legacy of the Civil War and repeated foreign occupation kept the Lebanese polity deeply fragmented.[23] During that time, both Israel and Syria had a heavy military presence within the country. Syria maintained a strong foothold along the eastern Mediterranean coast as well as a strategic role in Lebanon's protracted war with Israel, while Israel held its ground in Southern Lebanon.[24] Many Lebanese citizens resented their so-called Syrian "brothers" for leaving their government pathologically fragmented and too weak to stand against foreign occupation.[25] Even to this day, Syrian refugees suffer from Syria's domination over Lebanon as Lebanese nationals continue to resent the fact that their country cannot agree on any major political decisions without the Assad regime's blessing. As long as the two countries do not officially demarcate their common border, Lebanon legally remains a hostage of Syria's geopolitical ambitions such that the Lebanese-Syrian gendered relationship can never reach equal terms. The convoluted history between these two countries has thus, up to this point, prevented the establishment of a healthy formal relationship between two sovereign states.

Despite that fact, there have been nuanced shifts within the Lebanese-Syrian relationship due to several critical junctures that transformed interstate relations. The critical junctures in question led to the redesigning of policies that Lebanon once upheld toward residing Syrian refugees. As such, it is imperative to trace four critical junctures within Lebanese-Syrian relations that (in)directly led to today's changes in Lebanese policy practices toward

Critical Junctures in the Lebanese Syrian Rapport

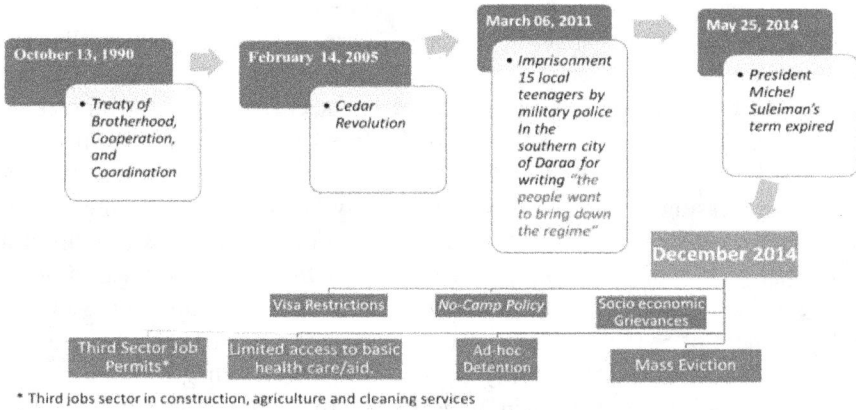

October 13, 1990
• Treaty of Brotherhood, Cooperation, and Coordination

February 14, 2005
• Cedar Revolution

March 06, 2011
• Imprisonment 15 local teenagers by military police In the southern city of Daraa for writing "the people want to bring down the regime"

May 25, 2014
• President Michel Suleiman's term expired

December 2014

Visa Restrictions | No-Camp Policy | Socio economic Grievances

Third Sector Job Permits* | Limited access to basic health care/aid. | Ad-hoc Detention | Mass Eviction

* Third jobs sector in construction, agriculture and cleaning services

Figure 2.1 Lebanese-Syrian Relations and Syrian Refugee (In)Security Practices.
Source: Photo by Author.

Syrians residing within the country. The information contained in figure 2.1 summarizes the critical junctures that will be examined in further detail in the following sections.

First Juncture: 1990–2005

On October 13, 1990, the Lebanese Civil War came to an end when favorable regional and international developments overlapped with the anguished internal parties' desire for reconciliation.[26] This political juncture guaranteed Syria's custodianship over Lebanon, as mandated by American and European authorities after the Lebanese Civil War, securing a free Syrian hand in internal Lebanese politics.[27] As a consequence, Lebanese-Syrian relations were cast in "brotherhood" terms.[28] This "special" relationship strengthened with its inclusion in the *Ta'if* Accord[29] and was further institutionalized, later on, through a formal treaty in 1991—the Treaty of Brotherhood, Cooperation, and Coordination between the Syrian Arab Republic and the Lebanese Republic. This treaty streamlined what could be perceived as a gendered relationship between both countries, in which Lebanese security and foreign policy objectives became dependent on Syria's well-being. Accordingly, Article 3 of the Treaty of Brotherhood interconnected Lebanese security with Syria's well-being, a matter that caused great concern to many Lebanese politicians at that time, as they feared that they would become hostage to Syrian maneuvers within the region: "The interdependence of the security of the two countries shall require that Lebanon shall not, under any circumstances, be made a source of threat to the security of Syria."[30] This article called for wide-ranging security cooperation between both countries to eliminate what they deemed as a threat with perceivable gendered effects.

After the establishment of the Treaty of Brotherhood, Syrian intelligence dominated the security operations across Lebanese territories, legally entitling it to scrutinize any Lebanese resident for "security reasons." In practice, Syrian security agencies in Lebanon had a free hand to pursue any perceivable threat to its regime, withholding from all Lebanese constituents the freedom of expressing concerns or opposition to Syria's control.[31] Adding further to Lebanese concerns, Article 4 of the treaty set an ambiguous timeline for Syria's slow withdrawal from Lebanon, stating that "after the institution of political [. . .] the Syrian and Lebanese Governments shall decide on the redeployment of Syrian forces."[32] Subsequently, the Alawite regime in Syria subordinated the Lebanese polity by not allowing it self-governance. This "brother-sister" metaphor shown in the above articles extended beyond rhetoric, affecting relations between both states on political and social levels.[33]

With boots on the ground, Syria turned Lebanon into a police state, *"Dawlat al-Mukhabarat,"* targeting any person or political group who resisted it.[34] Syria acted as a colonial administrator in Lebanon, bolstering post-war pro-Syria Lebanese parties with political and financial rewards, encouraging these parties to preserve the status quo.[35] Additionally, anti-Syria Lebanese parties were banned, and top Lebanese positions were manipulated by Syrian agents.[36] Few prominent Lebanese political figures were lucky enough to flee the country in order to avoid the fate of many others who were imprisoned, or assassinated due to their anti-Syrian stands.[37] Lebanon became dependent on the "big brother," stuck in a then-low-intensity conflict with Israel and not able to conduct independent negotiations without Syria's "blessings."[38] From the widespread physical presence of Syrian military checkpoints to the establishment of Syrian-operated detention facilities, the signs of Syria's dominion over Lebanon became visible in the majority of Lebanese citizens' daily lives.[39]

On a socioeconomic level, the Treaty of Brotherhood virtually subcontracted Lebanon to the Syrian economy such that Syrians were able to work in Lebanon and acquire significant remittances.[40] A labor agreement was then made in 1994, legalizing the status of approximately 900,000 Syrian workers in Lebanon, which resulted in the capital flight of what is estimated as millions of dollars from Lebanon being added daily to the Syrian economy.[41] The Syrian presence in Lebanon was further magnified by arbitrary practices such as the 1994 naturalization decree that granted Lebanese citizenship to hundreds of thousands of pro-Syria Arab foreigners residing in Lebanon.[42] This discretionary power over naturalization allowed pro-Syria political elites to bestow foreigners with Lebanese citizenship as an instrument to develop political clienteles.[43]

Second Juncture: 2005–11

The visible reign of Syria over Lebanon lasted until 2005, when the Cedar Revolution pushed for the withdrawal of Syrian troops from Lebanese territories. The Cedar Revolution came fifteen years after the end of the Lebanese Civil War and almost five years after Israeli troops' withdrawal from Southern Lebanon. This political juncture, triggered by the assassination of late Lebanese prime minister Rafic Hariri on February 14, 2005, was led by several anti-Syrian Lebanese factions blaming the Assad regime for his death.[44] However, even after the Syrian military withdrawal in 2005, Syrian oversight continued to influence Lebanese politics. With the presence of strong Syrian allies, such as Hezbollah, the long-standing political, economic, and social ties between both countries constituted a vast network of influence within Lebanese polities. The void that the Syrian military withdrawal left triggered an increase in violence with several car bombs, explosions, and assassination attempts on a number of "anti-Syrian intellectuals and politicians," mostly blamed on the Syrian regime.[45] This was coupled with submissive behaviors and continuous expectations from pro-Syria Lebanese politicians for Syria to lead the country.[46]

Despite Syria's political influence in Lebanon, Lebanese officials continued attempts to forge a formal relationship with Syria—a move that was substantiated by the establishment of the first Syrian embassy in the country in December 2008.[47] Additionally, Lebanon's then-president, Michel Suleiman, conducted the first state visit to Syria and forged the agreement to establish formal relations between both countries.[48] This significant act hindered the days of undiluted Syrian hegemony over Lebanon such that Lebanon as a state became formally acknowledged by Syria as sovereign. The frequency of diplomatic tactics and formal relations between Lebanon and Syria thus increased after 2008. However, informal intimidation tactics and assassination attempts against anti-Syrian political and security personnel were visibly recorded during that time.[49]

The departure of Syria's direct control left a security and political void in Lebanon. The Lebanese political process was at a stalemate, characterized by unwillingness from the major political elites to reach a shared vision of the future trajectory of Lebanon.[50] Also, Israel's thirty-three-day attack in July 2006 was more extensive, reaching deeper into Northern Lebanon than ever before. The death and destruction in several Lebanese cities, towns, and villages empowered pro-Syrian Hezbollah to gain popularity within many local communities. By acquiring a reputation for being a legitimate political actor fighting Israel with the aid of the Assad regime, Hezbollah gained direct control of most of the Lebanese intelligence infrastructure, which made sure anti-Syrian maneuvers were thwarted.[51] Meanwhile, no real efforts were made by either state to officially delineate the borders between Syria and Lebanon. This was mostly due to the disputed issue of the *Shebaa* farms, which Israel claimed was Syrian land. Not having the borders officially delineated kept Lebanon's claim over its southern territory with Israel unresolved.[52]

Third Juncture: 2011–14

Fast-forwarding to March 6, 2011, Syria was rocked by anti-regime demonstrations calling for President Assad's impeachment, creating room for ongoing domestic turmoil in Syria, and impacting Lebanese domestic affairs. Most notably, four Syrian brothers who were opposition activists in Lebanon vanished just after distributing flyers protesting their current government in front of the Syrian embassy in Beirut.[53] Human Rights Watch condemned the act, fearing that Lebanon was "back to doing Syria's dirty job."[54] Meanwhile, at the onset of the 2011 crisis in Syria, Lebanon maintained an "open-door policy"—a policy of welcoming all incoming Syrians without exception, committing to the Treaty of Brotherhood between both countries.[55] Then on June 11, 2012, an official Lebanese declaration called for establishing a policy of neutrality toward the Syrian conflict under the banner of a "dissociation policy seeking not to be involved in the Syrian conflict and maintaining neutrality in international institutions."[56] This course of action, albeit lauded by the international community and various human rights organizations, did not stem from the Lebanese government's genuine willingness to practice its humanitarian obligations.[57] In actuality, it was the lack of policy that resulted from an amalgam of conflicting opinions that crippled the Lebanese political establishment. During this period of political deadlock, deep divisions in the Lebanese government prevented any attempt to put this policy of dissociation into practice.[58]

Meanwhile, Michel Suleiman's pro-Syrian presidency maintained the polarized Lebanese political spectrum and kept the Lebanese Army and United Nations Interim Force in Lebanon (UNIFIL) away from safeguarding the blurry and porous Lebanese border with Syria. As a result, the Lebanese open border policy sustained until the end of his presidency in 2014. While President Suleiman remained loyal to previous agreements with the Syrian Assad regime, the border between both countries was left open to virtually any Syrian fleeing the war simply because the Lebanese government was too divided to formulate an effective strategy to regulate the influx of refugees into the country.[59] The rift between national political parties, those that were pro-Syrian regime and those opposing it, prevented Lebanon from responding earlier to the Syrian refugee crisis.[60] This practice of inaction and the lack of strategic vision led to the fragmentation of the entire Syrian refugee population across Lebanese territory. Accordingly, the geographical dispersal of Syrians within Lebanon mostly followed a sectarian pattern, in which Sunnis mostly resided in heavily populated Sunni regions and the predominantly Christian and Shiite areas welcomed Syrian Christians and Alawites.[61]

Moreover, the Lebanese government failed to fight corruption and reach a consensus over a united foreign policy related to Hezbollah's military involvement in the Syrian war.[62] Hassan Nasrallah declared in April 2013 that Hezbollah would be giving Syria "a hand," stating that "Syria is the backbone of the resistance and we [Hezbollah] will not sit with our hands crossed."[63] With the active participation of Hezbollah in the well-known clearing operation in *al-Qusayr* in Syria, this event marked the official start of Hezbollah's military intervention in the Syrian war.[64] Since then, all other Lebanese political parties voiced their fears and disapproval of Hezbollah sending an increasing number of its militants to Syria, complaining that the organization was putting Lebanon in danger by interfering in a foreign war. Still, the mainstream political climate in Lebanon positioned itself as neutral with an "open-door policy," in solidarity with the Syrian refugee community. It inconsistently advocated for aiding "displaced" persons with the hope that the Syrian crisis would soon end and that the hosted communities would soon return to their homeland.[65]

While many Lebanese nationals believed that the Syrian crisis was temporary and that the Assad reign would endure,[66] the Labor Agreement stayed in a place, allowing Syrians to work in Lebanon without any actual restrictions.[67] As such, the lack of governmental initiative to deter the increasing influx of incoming Syrians triggered an outcry among the Lebanese public, who complained about the competition in the business and labor sectors. Even though the Lebanese government maintained a very permissive position toward Syrian refugees on its territory due to a sociopolitical paralysis,[68] the local attitude toward the integration of the Syrian labor force in Lebanon shifted in the following years.

Fourth Juncture: Post-2014

On May 25, 2014, pro-Syria president Michel Suleiman's term expired, and Lebanon had no president, creating a new political juncture. Consequently, a self-appointed parliament[69] further exacerbated Lebanon's presidential stalemate, failing (for the forty-fifth time) to elect a president in three consecutive years.[70] It should be noted that presidential elections in Lebanon do not depend solely on domestic politics. Regional powers and several external factors, such as the Syrian crisis, critically influenced local dynamics, creating a power vacuum with new instabilities and opportunities that galvanized different forces at work. As a result of this political paralysis, a security gap allowed hundreds of thousands of Syrians to enter the country without official supervision. At that time, there was a rise in militancy belonging to the self-described Islamic State and allied factions threatening populated areas. More than a dozen terrorist attacks were directed at sectarian targets. Hundreds of foreign and local fighters, claiming loyalty to either ISIS, *Jabhat al-Nusra*, or the Free Syrian Army, attacked several Lebanese Army posts within heavily Sunni-populated Lebanese towns to reinforce the Syrian opposition against the Assad regime and its Lebanese allies.[71]

Moreover, without a strong Lebanese presidential figure to support the continuance of the Assad regime, the initial mood in the Lebanese public sphere which had called for a stance of solidarity with their Syrian "brothers" quickly shifted.[72] In June 2014, the presidential elections in Syria occurred with President Bashar el-Assad, winning with a landslide majority of 88 percent of the votes.[73] This event led to tens of thousands of Syrians marching toward their embassy in Beirut chanting pro-regime slogans in solidarity with Bashar el-Assad.[74] However, with the Syrian crisis increasing in intensity, turning into a full-fledged war, not only did domestic actors clash but the Syrian crisis also resulted in (in)direct military interventions and political confrontations from Lebanese factions competing in a protracted international war of proxies.[75] Gruesome war methods—such as sieges, starvation, and chemical attacks—were publicly criticized by various Lebanese factions who blamed local political groups such as Hezbollah for being too invested in the "external" Syrian armed struggle.[76] The condemning attitudes concerning the Syrian conflict did not diminish with the continuous bloodshed and increased human suffering in Syria, which pushed millions of Syrians to forcibly leave the country in search for asylum."[77] Alas, the once feeble number of 7,088 registered refugees in Lebanon in March 2012 skyrocketed to more than one million refugees in March 2014, legitimizing local calls for securitizing the influx of Syrians to the country.[78]

By the end of 2014, Lebanon, with an area of 10,452 square kilometers (4,036 square miles) and a population of roughly 5 million, hosted approximately 1.2 million registered displaced Syrians, almost one-third of the overall Lebanese population.[79] Figure 2.2 illustrates how the absorption of such an influx proved to be extremely strenuous for Lebanese governmental institutions, which already suffered from shortages in delivering essential services to its domestic sphere.

With the Syrian government's threats of confiscating millions of properties from Syrians who had fled, failing to register their estates properly and on time, the odds of Syrians being "trapped" in Lebanon increased precariously with no viable way to return. In fact, a new decree introduced by the Assad regime called Law 10, also known as "Absentees law," could be a means to reinforce the discriminatory gendered relations between the Syrian state and its outcasts, in which millions of refugees could lose their lands, legitimizing the government's seizure of such assets and threatening to change Syria's

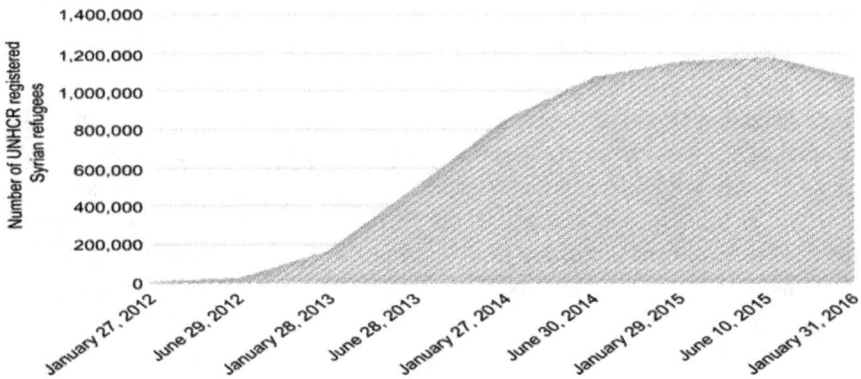

Figure 2.2   UNHCR Registered Syrian Refugees (2016). UNHCR.

demographic.[80] Even though the legislation was not yet in effect, it still allows the Baathist government to confiscate properties of millions of displaced Syrians unless they prove ownership with the Ministry of Local Administration within thirty days. This type of structural violence not only punishes the millions who have opposed the Assad government by denying them their rights to their land but also threatens Lebanon's demography by silencing displaced Syrians' claims as outcasts not able to ever go back to their lands. Meanwhile, this same law rewarded mainly the Alawite and Christian pro-Assad communities in taking over the confiscated Sunni Muslims' properties.[81]

The rapid increase of Syrians registering as refugees with the UNHCR (between 2013 and 2014) led to a shift in Lebanese attitudes toward the then perceived "Syrian refugee burden." As a reaction to previous Syrian aggressions when occupying Lebanon, the reevaluation of the "Brotherhood" relationship enshrined in the Treaty of Brotherhood, Cooperation, and Coordination between Lebanon and Syria came under scrutiny.[82] The perception of patriarchal kinship to Syria and its population turned to a perception of either a masculinized burden of a terrorist threat coupled with political instabilities or a feminized burden that drowned the country with unaffordable socioeconomic insecurities, leaving all odds manifesting against Syrian refugees in Lebanon. According to one news article, the Lebanese patriarch Bechara Boutros al-Rahi accused Syrian refugees of "snatching (the Lebanese people's) daily bread from their mouths, throwing them into a state of poverty and deprivation."[83] In fact, his statement was an echo of the long-standing fear of hosting a large number of refugees, especially Syrian refugees who threaten Lebanon's security and burden its sluggish economy, taking jobs or straining Lebanon's public services.[84] As such, the following section explores the long Lebanese history with forced migration and the reasons behind the host state's distrust over accommodating a large number of refugees, Syrians especially.

LEBANON'S SENSITIVITY TOWARD
THE WORD "REFUGEE"

Since Lebanon functions under a weak quasi-democracy in the Middle East, the constant influx of people into the country is one of its greatest concerns.[85] From the day it took its independence, the history of the country is closely intertwined with forced migration and refugees. This section proceeds with the various empirical findings that highlight Lebanon's sovereign practices of refugee exclusion. It revisits some crucial issues elaborated in the previous section that lead to the imposition of restrictive gendered policies on the entry, residence, and movement of Syrian refugees in Lebanon.

In effect, Lebanon never passed any national legislation pertaining to the status of refugees on its territories. According to the UNHCR, Lebanon hosts a great number of Iraqis, Syrians, and Palestinians, among others.[86] Some are considered as guests; others are viewed as threats. Still, Lebanon does not have an official refugee law, thus forced migrants are treated as economic migrants and temporary foreign visitors.[87] Even though more than 145 states have ratified the Convention Relating to the Status of Refugees, Lebanon, like several other countries in the region, is not a signatory. A sovereign state's exclusive control over its territory is well established in international law, securing its right to grant or deny asylum to foreign persons coming to its territory.[88] Conventionally, universal obligations on states ensure that no asylum seeker loses their basic rights and benefits when fleeing persecution. However, no sovereign state, including Lebanon, seems to be legally obligated to accept asylum seekers. Rather, it is nonbinding humanitarian concerns that encourage sovereign states to host those in need of asylum. As a customary practice, issues relating to the concept of *non-refoulement*, such as residency permits and the right to work, are under the host state's discretion. Consequently, the reality of domestic exclusionary practices could be warranted for any security threat justified by state authorities. Additionally, Lebanon's unimpressive human rights track-record on issues of prolonged detentions, arbitrary arrests, and forced deportations fostered a favorable environment for political manipulation and legitimization of its exclusionary power practices.[89] Accordingly, many loopholes and realpolitik encouraged overwhelmed Lebanon to securitize incoming refugees' entry, threatening them with penalization and repatriation.

Still, once asylum seekers are inside Lebanese territory, Lebanon has a duty to treat those foreigners humanely without repatriating them to states in which they would face persecution. We find in the Constitution's Preamble that "Lebanon is a founding and active member of the United Nations Organization, committed to its Charter and the Universal Declaration of Human Rights," thus warranting individual freedom of opinion, equality, right to access work, and own property.[90] Lebanon's Constitution takes pride in the Lebanese forefather of the Declaration of Human Rights, Charles Malek, stating that the country embodies all human rights principles without exception in any sector and scope. Lebanon is, additionally, a signatory of numerous human rights treaties and conventions that contain provisions relating to refugees' protection, including "The International Covenant on Civil and Political Rights (ICCPR) (1966), the International Covenant on Economic, Social, and Cultural Rights (ICESCR) (1966), and the 1965 International Convention on the Elimination of All Forms of Racial Discrimination (ICERD)."[290] Accordingly, nondiscrimination of refugees—access to education, work, and housing—are enshrined in most of the above treaties, which Lebanon already endorses.

In this respect, Lebanon seems to be fully engaged in the social construct of collective sovereign states' efforts toward human rights, ratifying the norms of previously agreed-upon covenants that are deemed universally essential for human security, especially for prohibiting refoulement. Consequently, internationally guaranteed human rights—what became known as human security: *"freedom from want"* and *"freedom from fear"* that ranged from personal to socioeconomic and political security—ensured that Lebanon, as a sovereign state, secures a minimum of individual autonomy and preserves the right of foreign individuals residing within the country to be protected when fleeing their home state.[91] In addition, once Lebanon as a host state accepts foreign citizens, it is theoretically required to provide them with basic human rights and duties, including freedom of thought, of movement, and freedom from any degrading treatment toward a person's liberty.[92] However, according to an expert interviewee from the Lebanese Ministry of Social Affairs, "the only legal mandate you have is toward the Lebanese citizens. In relation to Syrian refugees you have some type of Sharia courts even in some informal settlements and [. . .] 90% of the Syrian refugees are Sunnis and Dar Al-Fatwa is managing the religious aspect of the presence of them through the Cheikh."[93] This statement exemplifies how, in practice, Lebanon's intricate translation processes of its commitment to the global discourse of human rights in effect deny de facto Syrian refugees from legally accessing adequate government assistance and protection.[94] The expert interviewee's misguided statement about Lebanon's mandate is legally wrong. It dodges Lebanon's international responsibility to provide refugees their basic right to security, liberty, and freedom of movement by relinquishing the Lebanese government's duty toward non-citizens to unaccountable self-interested third parties, such as Dar Al-Fatwa, with sectarian ambitions deepened by historical events and the social make-up of the country.

As discussed in the previous section, Lebanon suffers from a chronically unstable political system that it is gendered and path-dependent. Founded on

sensitive political, religious, and sectarian balances, Lebanon bases citizenship on one's communal identity and tribal loyalty as opposed to equality
and individual rights.[95] Each refugee group is perceived differently according to the many criteria that enter the equation, including, but not limited to
their race, their social status, but mainly their religious affiliation. The discriminatory Lebanese nationality law and penal code reinforces the numerous
personal status laws that engender long-standing sectarian patriarchal social
norms. Lebanese authorities often promote this judicial pluralism as essential
to protecting the sectarian diversity within the confessional system of the
country. In practice, the multiplicity of laws deterred Lebanese citizens from
intermingling across religious groups for fear of losing their religious identity
or further complicating key aspects of their lives, such as marriage, divorce,
child custody and education, and death.

The sectarian sensitivities present within the country created a space for
refugee groups belonging to privileged sects to gain better treatment than others. For example, through history, Christian Armenian refugees in Lebanon
fully integrated without having to assimilate. Other than Armenia, Lebanon
is the only country that guarantees its Armenian community both parliamentary and ministerial representation.[96] Armenians enjoy anomalous communal
autonomy, preserving their identity, administering their private schools that
are taught in both Arabic and Armenian, and regulating their personal status
through their own religious courts.[97] Christian Palestinians enjoy similar
rights whereby Lebanese citizenship was given to most of them.[98] However,
when it came to the resettlement of Sunni Muslim Palestinian refugees, it
was, and still is, a controversial issue. In fact, the perceived impact their
settlement would have had on the sectarian balance of the country created a
feeling of insecurity, even within the government, which resulted in barring
Palestinian refugees from employment in the public sector, limiting them
from acquiring permits to work in the private sphere, or even buying properties. The Lebanese government, dominated then by Maronite Christians,
justified its discriminatory laws and practices that would hegemonize the
entire Palestinian refugee population as instigators of war, objectifying the
Palestinian refugees' presence as a security threat of overcrowded, volatile,
and ungoverned spaces.[99] Meanwhile, Christian micro-communities enjoyed
prosperity, political representation, and communal autonomy, while the
Sunni Palestinians have languished as an underclass, abandoned to political
and sectarian marginalization.[100]

The Palestinian Refugee Case

When it first started, the Palestinian refugee presence in Lebanon provoked
deep communal, political, and ideological divisions.[101] Still, official Lebanese

statements have always rejected their permanent settlement, which is commonly known as *"tawteen"* in Lebanon.[102] The inherent fears related to Palestinian refugees and their permanent residence in Lebanon, by both officials and citizens, was legally manifested in Lebanon's refusal to join the 1951 Refugee Convention. Lebanon's attempt to shield itself from the prospects of permanently settling Palestinian refugees in Lebanon further justified these measures as a supportive move to the forcibly displaced Palestinians' "Right of Return."[103] This advocacy was complemented with the denial of legal integration and assimilation of most Palestinians within the Lebanese fabric. Even when the Civil War ended, all local factions supported the amended Lebanese Constitution of September 21, 1990, that introduced a new provision in the Preamble, Section I stating that "there shall be no segregation of the people on the basis of any type of belonging, and no fragmentation, partition, or settlement of non-Lebanese in Lebanon."[104] Even though the provision established a rule of no segregation, it still made sure that the only people not to be segregated were Lebanese, while clearly stating that non-Lebanese, such as the Palestinians residing within the country cannot settle permanently.

On another note, Lebanese mistrust of Palestinians residing within their country transcends sectarian fears. It goes back all the way to 1969, when the Lebanese skirmishes with the Palestinian Liberation Organization (PLO) operating within the country ended with the Cairo agreement between Yasser Arafat, heading the PLO, and General Emile Bustani, the Lebanese military commander.[105] In effect, this agreement legitimized the PLO's presence and its right to fight Israel from within Lebanon.[106] The primary objective behind Lebanon's endorsement was to sideline itself from the Arab–Israeli conflict, while still advocating for the Palestinian cause. However, this led to a failed attempt to establish a system of cooperation between both parties and did not prevent the PLO's threat to Lebanon's sovereignty.[107] This agreement counterintuitively granted militant Palestinians the right to use the refugee camps on Lebanese territory as ungoverned militarized bases, establishing autonomous regulatory institutions for Palestinians living inside formally acknowledged refugee camps.[108] Consequently, this agreement created space for Palestinian institutions to develop in Lebanon, the outcome of which was called "a state within the state." The PLO's heavy presence in major strategic areas within Lebanon aggravated existing sectarian tensions between Lebanese factions.[109] Historical accounts demonstrated the aggression and the taking up of arms by Palestinian refugees, targeting Lebanese nationals and political parties.[110] Taking over west Beirut, the PLO took part in the Lebanese Civil War, where "thousands of Palestinians became both victims and victimizers."[111] As a result, till this day, Lebanon characterizes refugees, such as the Palestinians, as "ticking time bombs," and, ever since, Lebanese security and intelligence forces consistently targeted Palestinian refugee formal settlements within the country.[112]

Memorandum of Understanding between Lebanon and the UNHCR

Advancing to September 2003, Lebanon signed a Memorandum of Understanding (MoU) with the UNHCR, defining each party's role concerning incoming refugees. Accordingly, the UNHCR's primary responsibility in Lebanon was to support the host state in registering incoming applicants, issuing them temporary residency permits, providing protection and assistance until the UNHCR finds a durable solution for de facto refugees.[113] Initially, Lebanon had maintained a gentleman's agreement with the UNHCR, relying on its operations within the Lebanese territory to adjudicate asylum applications, deciding who is eligible for protection as de facto refugees.[114] The UNHCR strengthened its position within the country by taking over the responsibility of being the primary provider to Syrians refugees from the host state.[115] On the one hand, this lenient approach provided space for a significant increase in refugees from different nationalities to enter and settle in Lebanon, triggering a series of local and international security concerns. On the other hand, the MoU contained some gendering structural measures that would shortly bring about its demise. The MoU clearly states that Lebanon is "no country of asylum"; rather, it is a "transit country" due to its sociopolitical considerations and concerns. It goes as far as defining the term "asylum seeker" as a "person seeking asylum in a country other than Lebanon," making Lebanon a transitionary state and not a permanent one.[116] After all, the MoU was only utilized to shift refugee management responsibilities from the state, which is supposed to be the primary duty-bearer to the UN agency.[117]

The MoU stipulated that, as part of its responsibilities, the UNHCR is tasked with processing applications from asylum seekers, granting refugee certificates that would be valid for two years (eligible for renewal). Meanwhile, the Lebanese government was tasked with only tolerating de facto refugee presence temporarily while making sure that Lebanese citizens' rights are prioritized.[118] The agreement allowed the UNHCR to secure short-term solutions by providing the registered de facto refugees basic assistance and protection while expecting that the UNHCR would resettle those registered to third countries within that period.[119] Accordingly, the UN agency was compelled to formalize this compromised arrangement with the Lebanese government, struggling when attempting to regulate the main aspects of what is an obvious case of refugee protection with the lack of any encouraging national refugee law.[120] In the case of permit expiration, Lebanese authorities had the legal right to take necessary action against any illegal resident, defeating, in the first place, the purpose of temporarily hosting those fleeing their home country to seek protection.[121]

Although the international community criticized these shortcomings, the MoU between Lebanon and UNHCR was at first considered a positive preliminary step for protecting registered de facto refugees within the country. For the first time, the Lebanese government recognized those de facto refugees' semi-legal presence in Lebanon by offering them temporary residency permits.[122] Still, the MoU clearly stated that Lebanon was a "transit country." Accordingly, the temporary legal residency permits introduced by the Lebanese government only curtailed UNHCR's capacity to continuously ensure that residing Syrians would register their detailed information, hence preventing undocumented threats to public safety. It is important to note that there were a few thousand asylum seekers in Lebanon when it passed its responsibility for managing refugees' registration, healthcare, education, and livelihood assistance to the UNHCR. The MoU was only considered as a first step, a basis in defining Lebanon's limited obligations concerning asylum seekers, with no solid national response strategy that could manage a large influx of refugees. The MoU's failure worsened the UNHCR's position, such that as of 2014, the heavy Syrian presence in Lebanon forced the Lebanese government to shift its policy practices to reduce the number of Syrians within its territory. This move profoundly affected UNHCR's ability to implement its already compromised international protection mandate and placed its jurisdiction under the direct supervision of the Ministry of Social Affairs (MoSA). The justification for this, according to a MoSA expert interviewee, was: "Now we have a totally different approach; [. . .] All NGOs, all organizations, whether international regional or local partners, have to communicate with the Ministry of Social Affairs and get its approval before proceeding [with any action on Lebanese ground]."[123]

The Syrian Refugee Case

In 2014, with the Syrian crisis underway, the connotations of the word "refugee" worsened. When almost 30 percent of Lebanon's population was made up of Syrian refugees, it is only normal that Lebanese constituents were concerned that the large Syrian presence within the country threatened its security and stability. The sudden overpopulation severely strained the country's stability, affecting nearly all Lebanese sectors: the security, infrastructure, economy, health, education, labor, and environment, ultimately endangering the already delicate Lebanese social fabric.[124] Accordingly, refugee movements to Lebanon have been referred to by the Lebanese government as crises of displacement not to be governed by law but by ad hoc security practices.[125] These decisions were attempts to emphasize the fact that Syrian refugees are not recognized as such, but rather as "temporary displaced persons" (a legally loaded term that is vaguely defined) who are expected either to resettle in third countries or to return to their homeland as soon as the security and political conditions there settle down.[126]

Lebanese domestic attitudes and laws did not help displaced Syrians, let alone undocumented illegal residents, who were left with few legal recourses.[127] The Lebanese public feared the creation of another space for Syrians that would engender a state within the state.[128] Shared concerns of Syrian refugees exacerbating the deteriorating Lebanese economic, security, infrastructural, and social structures brought public outcry over residing Syrians being implicated in security threats in Lebanon. For example, numerous attacks against the Lebanese Army and the bombings of several Lebanese regions were planned and executed by radical Syrians posing as refugees.[129] Accordingly, the attention and care the international organizations, especially the UNHCR, provided to Syrians generated local resentment toward perceived Syrian opportunists who were "living in better conditions than we are."[130] The feeling of anti-Syrian resentment was reinforced by earlier perceptions of who the incoming Syrians previously represented (the Assad regime). As former members of the Syrian regime, incoming Syrians could not escape the Lebanese collective bitterness toward them that dated back to the Syrian occupation with boots on the ground.[131] Therefore, more problems, uncertainties, and dangers became correlated with the term "refugee," silencing most Syrians who lost homes, jobs, and personal assets. Moreover, different political actors in Lebanon have also focused on demonizing the Syrian refugee population, marginalizing them further in the pretext that these "Sunni" refugee masses pose a threat to Lebanese sectarian (im)balance.[132] Therefore, hostile sentiments and aggressive attitudes toward the unwanted displaced Syrians is no more than a symptom of the much deeper geopolitical sectarian relationship between the two countries.[133]

This increase of local anxieties could be seen with the appointment of President Michel Aoun in 2016, whose tenure began with a promise that "displaced Syrians would quickly return to their homeland and abstain from turning refugee camps into security hubs."[134] This president came with a lot of anti- Syrian occupation baggage from the Civil War. As a matter of fact, in 1989, General Aoun unsuccessfully led a liberation war against the Syrian Army that abated his attempt to gain sovereign control of the Lebanese coastline. He shelled the Baabda Presidential Palace and the Lebanese Ministry of Defense in Yarze, pushing him into exile in France. General Aoun only returned to Lebanon eleven days after the withdrawal of Syrian troops from the country, on May 7, 2005. Still, the anti-Syrian anxieties within Lebanon expanded beyond the fact of having historical issues with Syrians in the country or not. An echoing statement, later made by Lebanon's Sunni prime minister, Mr. Saad Hariri, further exemplifies this argument. He stated: "Today if you go around most of the host communities, there is a huge tension between the Lebanese and the Syrians. . .I fear civil unrest."[135] In example of how these fears were translated into discriminatory practices, a 2015 study showed that a 60 percent increase in crime in Beirut was directly related to the refugee population, while as of 2011, 26 percent of the prison population was of Syrian nationality.[136] These growing negative perceptions of Syrian refugees in Lebanon facilitated Lebanon's General Security Officers' (GSO), who have questionable capacities and training in knowing how and when to identify justifiable humanitarian cases, abuse of power in vilifying Syrian refugees. Their mandate tends to focus on combating crimes and potential cases of terrorism, giving them room to verbally abuse potential refugee victims while interrogating, discriminating, and putting them in harm's way.

SOVEREIGNTY THROUGH EXCLUSION

The increase in the number of refugees in Lebanon and the resulting challenges led to a "re-ordering of national politics and relations vis à-vis hosting Syrians,"[137] thickening the once-"thin" boundaries that separated these two neighboring countries. A series of governmental ad hoc restrictions marked, for the first time in Lebanon's history, an extensive filtering system for Syrians entering Lebanese territories. In late 2014, the Lebanese government shifted its official stance toward hosting Syrian refugees from "No Policy" to a security framework that would formalize the flow and aid to incoming Syrians, limiting their legal rights and socioeconomic welfare.[138] The previous open-door policy, commended for its leniency, was completely reversed, negatively affecting the UNHCR's initiative to oversee the distribution of aid and services related to Syrian de facto refugees across the country. [139,140] In fact, the increasing role that the Lebanese government played post-2014 forced the UNHCR to step down from leading the international refugee protection mandate, barring it from registering more refugees and stripping thousands of residing Syrians of their legal status. As a result, the tenuous cooperation between the host state and the humanitarian organization led to fluctuating and complicated state practices that were unfavorable for accommodating Syrian refugees within the country.[141]

As Lebanon did not formally extend asylum to de facto Syrian refugees residing within the country, international organizations, the UNHCR particularly, were not capable of deterring harassment, xenophobic violence, detention, and forced deportation from local "security" agencies toward refugees. These exclusionary practices, complemented by the UNHCR's limited role in Syrian refugee crisis management, were further fueled by the Lebanese collective memory of Syrian domination. Local Lebanese authorities and security agencies legitimized ad hoc discrimination under the guise of fighting terrorism and preserving the Lebanese sectarian identity balance. In a careful effort to deter Syrians from being legally admitted into the country, "standard" bureaucratic practices were used to reject temporary residency applications that were perceived to be either incomplete or filed by opportunists falsely claiming refugee status.

On another note, the legitimate unparalleled refugee burden faced by Lebanese communities hosting Syrians rendered it impossible for Lebanese government agencies to provide the necessary aid and assistance that is already subject to intra-Lebanese sectarian calculations.[142] While Lebanon's humanitarian budget decupled between the beginning of the crisis and 2015, the expansion of aid funding led to a change in the refugee management approach. The UNHCR found itself having to negotiate any assistance terms with semi-functional government agencies that have competing interests. In other words, international aid was no longer limited to the UNHCR's role to lead Syrian refugee operations. Instead, most international aid went to financing the Lebanese government's "budget support" and a plethora of nongovernmental organizations that were issue-oriented and whose missions came with the risk of corruption and fraud.[143] Research has shown that the Transparency International's 2016 Corruption Perceptions Index scored Lebanon with 28 over 100, labeling it as "plagued, untrustworthy and badly functioning."[144]

In theory, most donated funds necessitated approval from the semi-functioning Lebanese authorities to ensure that the disbursement and procurement of funds did not jeopardize the country's security and interests. In actuality, Lebanese public institutions were unwilling and insufficiently trained to properly assess the needs of the diverse groups that make up the Syrian refugee population. Male-controlled institutions prioritized gender-blind policies to safeguard national interests, worsening the Syrian refugee experiences within host communities. As a result of these interweaving factors, ad hoc exclusionary policies popped up across the country, tightening Lebanese visa and border policies toward Syrians, rejecting the creation of any formal refugee settlements, and limiting refugee mobility within the country—three sectors that will be developed in the following subsections.[145]

Visa Restrictions and Border Control

In 2015, the Lebanese government began implementing a series of restrictions that made it increasingly challenging for Syrians both to enter the country and to obtain a temporary residency visa, the time frame for which became even shorter—ranging from one day to a year at most.[146,147] However, Lebanon's visa entry requirements and practices favored the relatively privileged 'displaced' Syrians over the financially disadvantaged ones, depicting the former as depoliticized, immobile, and passive, when in reality this was a means to increase local spending, investments, and economic growth in the country. The visa dilemma worsened on May 6, 2015, when the male-dominated Lebanese government issued a ministerial policy paper demanding the suspension of official registration of Syrian refugees, closing officially its border with Syria.[148] For the first time in Lebanon's history, this decree introduced a visa system for Syrians, hindering the majority of residing Syrian de facto refugees (women and children) from obtaining legal status and accessing adequate housing, employment, and protection. As stated by a MoSA expert interviewee, the policy established three primary objectives for managing the Syrian displacement into Lebanon, dictated by security concerns:[149]

1. Reduce the number of Syrians registered with the UNHCR as de facto refugees through border control.
2. Bolster security in the country to keep the displaced population under control.
3. Reinforce local stability by prioritizing Lebanese industries, vulnerable communities, and infrastructure.

In practice, this decree only bolstered Lebanon, a non-signatory state to the Principle of Non-Refoulment of the 1951 Refugee Convention, to (en)gender refugee insecurities through arbitrary arrests, torture, mass eviction, and de facto refoulment of perceived Syrian refugee threats.[150]

According to the expert interviewee of MoSA, this was an erroneous governmental approach focused on stopping the official registration of Syrian refugees at a certain exact number.[151] Surprisingly, the expert interviewee's opinion echoed humanitarian criticisms toward the malfunctioning of the new refugee policies introduced by the Lebanese government. Such policies imposed significant restrictions on the UNHCR's ability to properly manage Syrian refugees in Lebanon, let alone successful integration. In fact, according to the new governmental rules, all Syrians registered with UNHCR had to sign a pledge that revoked their right to work in the country.[152] Some refugees were even asked to sign other legal documents stating that they were obliged to return to Syria as soon as their residency papers expired.[153]

In the Lebanese state system that perpetuates a male-dominated, clan-based political order, the majority of Syrian refugees were denied any genuine prospect of obtaining legal status and were constantly threatened with forcible deportation back to Syria. Dismissive governmental rhetoric, such as the announcement from Lebanese minister of social affairs Rashid Derbas, declared that "the cessation of asylum is final because Lebanon can no longer bear anymore. [. . .] Lebanon does not deserve more burdens, and there are countries closer to them [Syrian refugees] to which they can resort."[154] Despite such aggressive rhetoric toward residing Syrians, the Lebanese government had neither the means to efficiently close its border nor the will to refrain from further exploiting the cheap informal labor and humanitarian aid that amplified due to the Syrian crisis. Instead of prioritizing official efforts to demarcate and close the porous border between both states, Lebanese government regulatory practices further exploited already-residing Syrians by charging a $200 USD fee for residency permit renewals per person.

These newly introduced bureaucratic procedures were so "onerous and expensive that it became challenging for people to meet the [residency] requirements."[155] For the first time in Lebanese-Syrian relations, different (il)legal entities dealing with refugees, whether they be local authorities or informal security actors, took charge in securitizing Syrian identification and residency in Lebanon under the guise of preserving law and order. The existing million-or-so residing Syrians were examined regularly by the various (il)legal security agencies to verify that their registration with the UNHCR was legal and up to date.[156] And when Syrian nationals were not able to pay the residency renewal fee bi-annually, they were thus subjected to removal from the UNHCR's "displaced person" list and liable for deportation.

Within this law and order Lebanese structure, the General Security (GS) Directorate was the main intelligence agency that oversees visa issuance, as well as management of Syrian displacement within the country. In fact, Article 17 of the 1962 Lebanese law on the entry and exit of foreign nationals gave the GS virtually unrestricted judicial police power to arrest, detain, and deport suspicious foreigners.[157] Rather than using civilian immigration employees, this deterrent law empowered self-interested security personnel in military uniforms to process immigration statuses within Lebanon. The GS was responsible for controlling all foreigners' legal status in the country, including Syrians' residency. Following the 2015 adaptation of the ministerial policy paper decree,[158] the GS limited the lawful acquisition of residency by Syrian refugees, barring them from obtaining most of the seven visa categories provided for incoming foreigners: tourist, business, real estate ownership, student, transit, medical treatment, or legal sponsorship visa—better known as the Kafala system.[159] Without providing documented proof of hotel bookings or medical treatment appointments certified by MoSA upon entry, displaced Syrians would only qualify for two visa types to legally reside in Lebanon up to six months, eligible for renewal: the Kafala system or the de facto refugee registration with the UNHCR. Both visas required annual residency renewal fees, stipulating that Syrians over the age of fifteen had to pay around 200 USD per person bi-annually to keep their de facto refugee-status legal.

Concurrently, these steps guaranteed GS officers arbitrary control over foreigners' legal statuses and the entitlement to revoke the residency permits of Syrians who (re)enter their home country, disallowing them any protective "privilege."[160] Issues such as increasing mobility restrictions imposed upon Syrians wishing to return home for a quick visit could result in the termination of their refugee status and legal right to (re)enter Lebanon, preventing family reunification.[161] Meanwhile, vengeful threat tactics, such as pretrial detention and biased interrogation practices, helped security agencies to deter most Syrians from filing complaints against Lebanese citizens, police officers, or security personnel for fear of losing their already limited legal status.[162]

Kafala System

Kafala visas belong to a system constructed around the model of employer-sponsorship for foreign laborers.[163] Under the Kafala system, an individual employer (*kafeel*) would undertake all financial and legal responsibility for the migrant they sponsor. In the case of Lebanon, the employer controls the entry and residency rights of their employee in the country with the impunity to confiscate their passports as a way to limit their freedom of movement for any security reason.[164] The migrant worker (*makfoul*) would thus become totally dependent on their employer to renew their residency and provide them with income. This disguised modern-day slavery system of withholding a person's official documentation leaves the employee vulnerable to all sorts of exploitation and abuse, such as being barred from "enter[ing] the country, transfer[ing] employment nor leave[ing] the country for any reason without first obtaining explicit written permission from the kafeel."[165,166] While the confiscation of employees' passports arguably violates Article 36 of the Lebanese Foreigner's Law, which stipulates that any foreigner found on Lebanese ground without valid proof of identity is subject to fines and imprisonment, most employers have no qualms about such practices given that they are not liable for penalization. Police, army, and General Security officers have the right to detain any foreigner who cannot prove that they are in the country legally, even if employers are the ones responsible for the missing documents.[167]

Despite the restrictions and risks associated with this system, Kafala visas became largely sought after by Syrians in the Lebanese context. A new dynamic emerged in which Lebanese citizens would only sponsor Syrians who could afford to informally compensate them for it.[168] The Kafala system thus granted relatively financially privileged Syrian nationals the ability to live a relatively decent life on a quid-pro-quo basis. However, most displaced Syrians were not so privileged as to qualify for the Kafala visa system and

were forced to work informally to sustain their livelihoods. The majority of
Syrians residing in Lebanon could barely afford the fees for residency permit
issuance, let alone renewal, to remain lawfully employed in the country.[169]
One of the few options available to them was to resort to registering as de
facto refugees with the UNHCR.

Syrian Refugees Registered through the UNHCR

Registration under the UNHCR provides Syrian de facto refugees with a distinct set of limited rights and duties in Lebanon. It is important to note that
prior to the Syrian conflict Lebanon allowed a great number of displaced male
Syrians to mostly worked and resided in the country under informal agreements, meaning that they were never required to provide any official documentation as proof of work or residency. However, after the dramatic increase
of the Syrian refugee working population, unfair job competition with cheaper
labor costs skyrocketed within the Lebanese job market. As such, the informal
jobs that Syrians once qualified for—like construction, sanitation management, and agribusiness—expanded to other positions that were once formally
reserved only for Lebanese employees, jeopardizing the Lebanese labor force
and exacerbating the exploitation of Syrians' working conditions.[170]

Officially, unlike the Syrians sponsored in the Kafala system, Lebanon
only allowed those registered with the UNHCR access to basic aid and health
care without the right to work legally. In fact, Syrians could only register with
the UNHCR and qualify for aid if they provided legal documentation con-
firming their identity, local residence, and pledging not seek employment.[171]
As such, Syrians who wished to formally work in Lebanon had to relinquish
their registration with the UNHCR that guaranteed them some humanitarian
aid in order to be eligible for one of the three employment positions available
to them: solid waste management, construction, and agribusiness.[172] In reality, these positions always fell outside the formal job market, with Lebanese
employers evading taxes by avoiding formal hiring agreements, contracts,
and payroll documentation with their Syrian employees.

With the implementation of the 2015 ministerial policy paper decree, Lebanese security measures toward residing Syrians hardened so that refugees
who failed to provide the required legal documentation were given a morato-
rium of up to ten days to secure it, after which their stay became illegal. It is
crucial to note that all mandatory documents underwent lengthy bureaucratic
processes, requiring municipal notarization and signatures from Lebanese
officials, both of which were often challenging to acquire, time-consuming,
and expensive. Based on UNHCR calculations, these processes were realisti-
cally unaffordable for most Syrian refugees, who were often unable to meet
the registration requirements.[173] Also, the UNHCR's registration documents

did not necessarily grant automatic residency permits given that they were subject to governmental approval through the GS. Consequently, refugees registered with the UNHCR before 2015 only obtained temporary legal status depending on the GS's discretion.[174] As for Syrians informally registered in Lebanon after 2015, the UNHCR could guarantee them little protection, legal aid, or assistance.[175] A lack of information-sharing between the UNHCR and Lebanon resulted in increased restrictions from the host government and local communities upon UN operations within the country.[176] As a consequence, (il)legal securitized practices left Syrian refugees in a legal limbo with the constant fear of arrest, apprehension, and forced deportation.

Undocumented Syrian Refugees

Those Syrians who could neither afford a sponsorship through the Kafala system nor gather the necessary documents to register with the UNHCR fell under the category of illegal residency. The lack of identity proof or legal documents resulting from the bombing and burning of their homes hindered many Syrians from obtaining official registration with the UNHCR, adding to the overall number of illegal residents in Lebanon.[177] Furthermore, a deficit in humanitarian funding increased Syrians' vulnerability to debt and poverty, leaving many of them unable to register or renew their residency. The UNCHR estimated that the percentage of Syrian refugee households lacking valid residence permits rose from "9 percent in January 2015 to 61 percent in July 2015."[178] In fact, this number increased to 70 percent, and approximately 700,000 Syrians were undocumented and socially marginalized by January 2016.[179]

Moreover, most newborn Syrian children could not be legally registered as the UNHCR only enrolled those born in Lebanon with a valid birth certificate—a document that is bureaucratically almost impossible to acquire for non-Lebanese persons—and at least one parent already registered.[180] Both Syrian and Lebanese nationality regulations are predominately paternalistic—jus sanguinis,[181] meaning that a child's citizenship is attainable only via paternal lineage.[182] Therefore, most Syrian children in Lebanon unable to acquire their father's nationality (either because the father was an illegal resident or just not present at birth) end up stateless, lacking a fundamental legal recognition of nationality, let alone proof of identity,[183] which violates the Convention of the Rights of the Child that Lebanon endorses.[184] These stateless children became legal ghosts, unregistered and unsensitized to both Lebanese and Syrian governments' cumbersome legal impositions, restrictions, and problematic procedures for proper integration or eventual repatriation.

All in all, though Lebanese officials continuously reassure their commitment to the "safe" return of Syrians to their home country, the precarious legal status of two-third of Syrian refugees in Lebanon, who either lost their

legal residency or were born stateless within the country, is further complicated by the fact that different governmental agencies apply the rules at their
discretion, not under a unified rule of law.[185] Such sporadic, ad hoc decisions
allow various (il)legal security agencies to revoke expired residency documents and strip undocumented Syrians of their fundamental rights, leading
to further marginalization and refugee exploitation under the pretext of safeguarding national security.[186]

A No-Camp Policy

Another form of sovereignty through exclusion is Lebanon's long-standing
ban on formal refugee settlements. Historically, the formal establishment of
Palestinian refugee camps (PRCs) was blamed for bringing the country to
the fragile state of security it finds itself in today. Based on previous experiences with being unable to regulate PRCs, the Lebanese government refused
to build new refugee camps as primary settlements for "displaced" Syrians.
Permanent shelters were banned as local communities worried that such initiatives might encourage Syrians to settle in their area indefinitely. In 2013,
the Ikea Foundation's project "Better Shelters," which donated easily trans-
portable shelters that had solar panels on the roof and could be put up in four
hours, was directly shut down by Lebanese authorities to curb the possibility
of establishing permanent Syrian settlements.[187] As such, Lebanese authorities prohibited the construction of durable homes, threatening to demolish
any concrete structures that might entice Syrians to permanently settle in the
Informal Tented Settlements (ITSs).

Historically, ITSs existed long before the Syrian crisis, mostly in agricultural, rural, and mountainous areas in Lebanon. In fact, versions of such
settlements have been used by nomadic peoples residing at the outskirts
of privately owned agricultural land for centuries. Several seasonal tribal
migrant workers and their extended families, locally known as "*Bedouin
el Arab*," and which the UNHCR refer to as "nomadic and border populations,"[188] have always migrated back and forth between their home communities in Syria and rural areas in Lebanon.[189] Prior to the Syrian conflict,
Bedouin men would cultivate Lebanese farmland and work on construction
sites, whereas women and children over the age of five worked in Lebanese
households as well as in camps, collecting fruit and vegetables during harvest
season.[190] On weekends, Bedouins roamed different villages' plazas (*Midan*)
and restaurants, selling toys, gum, and even reading people's fortunes. At
the end of the agribusiness season, most Bedouins would go back to their
respective towns near or across state borders, having collected enough money
to move to a warmer, more economically viable place with work and school
opportunities.

However, with the crisis dynamics unfolding in Syria, increasing numbers of Syrian Bedouins and their extended families were compelled to permanently reside in Lebanon out of fear of being persecuted or recruited for a war in Syria they did not wish to partake in. As housing possibilities in Lebanon became very limited and the government objected to the construction of official and semi-formal camps, Syrians were scattered across the country, occupying spaces such as rental apartments, garages, and unfinished buildings, with some living on the streets.[191] As a consequence, ITSs proliferated in Northern Lebanon and in the Bekaa Valley, increasing in size and form to hazardously accommodate, other than the Bedouins, the ever-growing number of incoming Syrians in unsafe and exploitative conditions.[192] Aside from having feeble housing structures and poor sanitation, susceptible to extreme weather conditions in the mountainous and arid open spaces, Syrians had to live in longer-term informal camps, maintaining very low standards of living during the harsh winters in rural Lebanon. The Lebanese no-camp regulations enticed various local agencies to enforce ad hoc rules, carry out security checks, and ensure that no concrete semi-structures over 3 feet erected in any Syrian ITS, increasing the frequency of local harassment.[193] Additionally, landowners' predatory relationships with their Syrian tenants depended mostly on informal rental arrangements with frequent threats of eviction when renters were unable to pay.[194]

Consequently, the fear of being evicted, detained, and deported engendered long-term physical restrictions on ITS structures and dynamics that were once part of the Bedouin culture. With their presence becoming very noticeable to the host populace and municipalities, these informal spaces forced Syrian refugees residing in ITSs into a "state of anonymity and marginality that in itself is also confining [. . .] not only physically but also at the level of cognition, emotions, and temporality."[195] As ITS dynamics changed, different interdependent privileged bodies, such as municipalities, landowners, and Syrian *shawish*—a masculine word used to refer to Syrian men informally supervising ITSs—took the role of gatekeepers, controlling, monitoring, and disciplining residing Syrian families in the informal refugee camps.[196]

The Lebanese Armed Forces (LAF) and other intelligence officers systematically raided several ITSs, apprehending terrorist suspects and deterring any perceivable potential threats with the aim of maintaining law and order.[197] Accordingly, reports stated that the LAF arrested Syrians in ITSs for "alleged national security offenses, with human rights risks during pretrial, detention, and interrogation."[198] Military detention centers replaced the feeble housing structures that were viewed as shelters, housing terrorists and other criminal suspects with de facto Syrian refugees and other small-crime detainees in overcrowded spaces. Meanwhile, if any complaint against military conduct was voiced, the military penchant and court judgment over-rode civilian appeals. In clear violation of Article 13.3 of the International Convention on Civil and Political Rights (ICCPR),[199] several cases showed that military courts did not announce the justifications behind their declared judgments, thus enabling unlawful military trials, ad hoc detention, and negligent care.[200]

Curfews and Checkpoints

Coordination between local municipalities and the Lebanese central government security forces varied spatially and by sects. While many Sunni Muslims in Lebanon were more tolerant toward the majority of Syrian refugees, local Shiite, Druze, and Christian Lebanese communities did not share the same enthusiasm toward the majority of Syrian incomers, most of whom were Sunnis.[201] The sectarian and political deadlock occurring in Lebanon was amplified by the lack of coherent national strategies for addressing the Syrian influx, leaving different (il)legal local bodies to take matters into their own hands. Local municipalities were left to manage the refugee status quo in their respective communities, expanding their jurisdiction by including checkpoint strategies for monitoring and regulating the sudden refugee influx into their areas. As a direct result, most municipalities increased their police taskforces, which were not recognized by the central government as "official" security service providers, to enforce curfews and supervise Syrian refugees. In fact, there were no standard operational policies for the Lebanese municipal police. Their accountability measures and recruitment standards, such as background checks and proof of no criminal history, were neither certified nor based on professional police training before individuals assumed duty and carried firearms.[202]

In addition, the different municipalities' contradictory policies toward Syrians depended on specific areas of residence. Most of these policies were the fruits not only of local decision-makers but also of popular stances toward residing Syrians, with some areas being more welcoming and others, more hostile. An important example of the hostility Syrians faced from some Lebanese communities, condemned by international authorities for its unethical and antagonistic element, was the decision of 252 out of 1,108 municipalities to impose curfews on Syrian de facto refugees after nightfall.[203] It is crucial to note that under Article 12 of the ICCPR there is no legal basis for municipalities to impose curfews on a specific community while exempting others.[204] In that respect, the biased policies of illegal curfews and evictions that the 252 Lebanese municipalities imposed on Syrian residents reinforced the hostilities between both Lebanese and Syrian communities.[205]

SYSTEMIC DISCRIMINATION OF SYRIAN
WOMEN: A DOUBLE TRAGEDY

It is important to highlight that Syrian women are not isolated from the various types of insecurities mentioned previously, as they form the majority of the officially registered de facto refugees in Lebanon.[206] By September 2018, while women comprised 52.3 percent of all Syrians registered with the UNHCR, and a significant 23.8 percent of those women were adults aged eighteen to fifty-nine, most Syrian males registered in Lebanon were either children or elderly, with only 18.2 percent being working adults aged eighteen to fifty-nine. Therefore, around 58 percent of registered Syrian refugees were dependents most probably falling under the guardianship of the adult female majority. In support of this idea, in 2017, the UN reported that females headed 19 percent of Syrian refugee households in Lebanon without a husband or other adult male relative being present.[207] These women were either widows, divorced, or ones whose husbands did not register, went missing, sought asylum in other countries, or worse, died.[208]

Given the context in which women have a lesser social and legal status, they often also have insufficient capital, support, and legal backing to protect themselves without a male guardian. The Vulnerability Assessment of Syrian Refugees in Lebanon (VASyR), jointly produced by the UNHCR, the World Food Program, and UNICEF, states that "female-headed households were less food secure, had worse diets, adopted severe coping strategies more often and had higher poverty levels [and were] almost twice as likely as male-headed households to live in informal settlements, and were less likely to have legal residency."[209] This implies that Syrian women are more likely than any other group to suffer the consequences of restrictive Lebanese no-camp policies, visa renewal processes, curfews, and checkpoints, even if those policies were gender-neutral and did not specifically target women.[210]

Traditionally stigmatized, Syrian women seeking refuge in Lebanon are paradoxically subjected to double discrimination: first as refugees, and again as women. A news report made by Al Jazzera stated that Syrian women refugees are not only fighting for survival, but they are also in constant conflict with their own communities. One Syrian widow named Fatima told the news agency that

> every time I voice my opinion on how to improve the aid distribution in the camp, the Syrian men in the village shut me up. Because I am a woman, I am being told my opinions are worthless even though I am more educated than most of them. [. . .] They say I am too open and too manly because I leave the house and speak out, even though my clothing has nothing to do with openness.[211]

With so much attention going toward patriarchal national security concerns to assure state stability, the plight of Syrian women does not receive the necessary consideration that it so desperately needs. A deeper examination of the gendered Lebanese institutions that restrict women's access to justice, rights, and empowerment opportunities is necessary to expose some of the discrimination that women generally endure in Lebanon in association to their gender. When female Lebanese citizens endure such inequalities, it is natural to expect that Syrian women's agency and decision-making authority over their life choices would be similarly undermined, if not worse. The types of discrimination that women in Lebanon face provide an idea of the least of what Syrian women residing within the country endure. As such, the following subsections will explore the various gendered realities that women in Lebanon brave through daily.

Absence of Female Political Participation

Commonly, including female political participation enables women in politics as agents of change to further the rights of Syrian women refugees by strengthening and promoting their efforts both in refugee protection processes and in community empowerment initiatives at the local level, as well as in the linkages between the two. Still, as structural hierarchies exclude Lebanese women from sensitive political and judicial positions, men have always occupied the highest positions of public administration in Lebanon, such as the Constitutional Council and the Supreme Judicial Council.[212] At the level of the executive branch, there has been a total absence of women ministers in Lebanon. Until 2017, only 3 percent of Lebanon's parliament members were female, most of whom were basically figureheads, either the daughters, wives, or sisters of a renowned male politicians who either died, were assassinated, or could no longer run for office themselves.[213] These "elected" women legislators had little-to-no agency in any Lebanese decision-making process. In fact, none of the female politicians were able to actively ameliorate women's legal position in Lebanon while serving on parliamentary committees.

One comprehensive strategy proposed by the Lebanese government to address gender discrimination and promote gender equality was to increase women's political participation because it was believed that excluding their voices would produce limited knowledge and harmful practices.[214] A Ministry of Women's Affairs was established in 2016, however, it was counterintuitively headed by a man (Jean Ogasapian) whose mission to include a 30 percent female quota for the parliamentary election of 2018 utterly failed when only 6 women out of the 128 members won.[215] These newly elected female politicians did not contribute any positive change in women's roles, abilities, and status in Lebanese society, as they only reflected existing patriarchal institutions.[216] The six female parliamentary members also came from an elitist upper class, which means that they were unable to identify with the distinct insecurities experienced by the vast majority of Lebanese women. Consequently, their attention to Syrian women residing in Lebanon could only project their fellow male politicians' homogenized stance toward the perceived gendered burden that Syrians pose, leading to further objectification of female Syrian refugees.

The Discriminatory Citizenship Law

In 2016, as another tactic to become more inclusive toward women, the newly established Ministry of Women's Affairs announced that November 4 would henceforth be known as National Women's Day in Lebanon.[217] This date was chosen because on November 4, 1952, Lebanese women attained the rights to vote and to pass on their citizenship to their children, even while their legislative rights in Lebanon barely existed.[218] However, as per the 1960 Lebanese Citizenship and Naturalization Law, Lebanese women's right to pass on citizenship to their children was retracted for cases in which the children were fathered by foreigners. This citizenship law prohibited Lebanese women married to non-Lebanese nationals from passing their citizenship not only to their foreign spouses but also to their own children.[219] Though Article 7 of the Lebanese Constitution affirms gender equality, the main public justification for such a xenophobic and misogynistic law was the fear of opportunistic Palestinian men taking advantage of the situation and marrying Lebanese women in order to gain citizenship. Hypocritically, while Lebanese women were deprived of the opportunity to pass their citizenship on to their significant others, official Lebanese ad hoc executive orders provided undisclosed male foreigners who had enough status or funds to obtain Lebanese citizenship.[220]

As for non-Lebanese women with illegal status, the official Lebanese procedures did not allow them to complete the birth registration process for their newborn babies without attempting risky measures such as bribery, forgery, and identity theft.[442] The "Good Practice Paper" published by the UNHCR stated that the process usually involved several legal steps, such as paying fees, acquiring a hospital-certified birth notification letter, reviewing a state's official civil registry, and paying fines in cases of any delinquency or late registration.[221] Referring to the "Good Practice Paper," many Syrian parents were misinformed or incapable of undergoing the whole six-step process, which had lasting effects on their children's eligibility to register and enroll in school or access other state services.[222] Consequently, it was extremely challenging for any Syrian family to prove the identity of their newly born children and provide accredited parental links upon their eventual return to Syria through official borders. Moreover, a MoSA expert interviewee reiterated that "unless the crisis ends, people [Syrians] will not go back there, and these people [non-registered Syrian children] do not exist," making it a double tragedy.

Draconian Personal Status Laws

Till this date, Lebanon does not have a civil code to regulate issues such as divorce, property rights, or the care of children. Instead, different religious courts administered distinct personal status laws that often-issued rulings that violated women's rights with little governmental oversight. On November 3, 2015, the Committee on the Elimination of Discrimination against Women expressed serious concerns in its concluding observations on Lebanon about the country's delay in adopting relevant amendments. The Committee commented that the current personal status laws could lead to various forms of discrimination against women, engendering long-standing sectarian patriarchal norms within their respective religious sects and between the different religious denominations.[223] Without a modern set of civil laws, social customs and religious courts that rule on family matters treated women as inferior to men. Seen as family guardians, men held greater power over their wives and children.[224] They were perceived as the ones responsible for their children with regard to finances, health, travel, and consent for marriage.[225] As of 2017, the Global Gender Gap Index ranked Lebanon 135th out of 144 in a consistent decline in the Middle East and North Africa (MENA) region, with only Syria and Yemen lagging further behind.[226]

Unchecked patriarchal religious courts discriminated against Lebanese women, treating them as second-class citizens with insufficient oversight and accountability from the Lebanese government. Gender-based discrimination in inheritance, job opportunities, and education were a few of the unfortunate events that most Lebanese men never had to deal with. The fact is that preserving the family's honor and reputation was perceived as the responsibility of the head of the household, typically a man. In Arab culture, most men worked in public spheres while women occupied private spheres.[227] Therefore, it was only natural that Arab men considered it their right to control the public access of their female family members, stripping women of any state accountability pivotal to their freedom. Additionally, Lebanese court procedures discriminatorily dismissed women's claims against gender-based violence for lack of evidence.[228]

Furthermore, most women in Lebanon were not financially independent. Syrian women, especially, could not afford legal or material assistance during protracted legal proceedings, making them vulnerable to cases of arrest without bail as punishment for defending themselves against any type of abuse. As for the case of child custody, the majority of personal status laws in Lebanon legally assured children to a familial male guardian without visitation rights for the mother in cases of spousal separation, divorce, or death. As such, in Sunni Muslim gendered practices—which made up most of the Syrian population residing in Lebanon—"guardianship in the absence of a child's father did not pass to its mother. Instead, custody was granted to another male member of the father's family."[229] Consequently, depending on their sect, officially registered Syrian women had to abide by their respective discriminatory personal laws, making them particularly vulnerable to inadequate protection measures from all sorts of abuse, harassment, and exploitation due to their gender and status of being second-class residents.

Meanwhile, opportunist landlords, security agents, faith-based officials, and community members, among many others, took advantage of Syrian women's position of being either widowed or unmarried with no male guardians to protect them.[230] As for the ones who crossed the borders illegally, their status in the country was compromised and their insecurities were far worse. Without a residency permit, undocumented Syrian women were threatened, abused, sometimes violated, and potentially arrested with no consideration for their gendered insecurities. According to the expert from Justice without Borders, the Lebanese government's social service providers and the police did not provide immunity to illegal residents for immigration law violations. In that respect, Syrian refugee women who attempted to file a complaint and prosecute those accused of gender-based violence were subject to further abuse, harassment, detention, and potential deportation.[231]

SYNTHESIZING (IN)SECURITY PERCEPTIONS AND PRACTICES

As explored in the first section of this chapter, the long common history between Lebanon and Syria, traced briefly through four critical junctures (the end of the Lebanese Civil War in 1990; the assassination of Prime Minister Rafic Hariri in 2005; the start of the Syrian Civil War in 2011; and the Syrian refugee drastic influx in Lebanon in 2014), (en)gendered intolerant and exclusionary Lebanese social attitudes toward Syrian refugees. The collective fear and grand narratives of Syrians being a constant threat essentialized Syrian refugees' identity as a danger to Lebanon's stability, (re)producing simplistic, somewhat harmful readings of what both parties' insecurities entailed. The chapter illuminated how Lebanese insecurity discourse and bodily threats toward residing Syrians were mostly framed as individualizing ad hoc state security practices of managing illegal foreigners and national threats.[232] Counterintuitively, such practices simultaneously (re)produced a collective fear that required (il)legal bodies to step up and use ad hoc securitized measures in deterring any perceivable menace to their local communities.

The second part of this chapter explored the official Lebanese sensitivities toward the term "refugee," as well as published attitudes toward Syrians residing in Lebanon. Lebanese collective memory influenced the subjectivity of official Lebanese statements and practices of explicitly and/or implicitly homogenizing diverse groups of Syrians as an occupying threat. Even though several Sunni communities within Lebanon asymmetrically welcomed fellow Sunni Syrians, the official conception of refugee insecurity led to Lebanon's exclusionary practices that (en)gendered visa restrictions and border control, no-camp policy, curfews, and checkpoints. Hostile sentiments and attitudes toward Syrian refugee (in)security translated into a range of ad hoc security mechanisms that reproduced gender hierarchies and hegemonies between the Syrian refugees and Lebanese communities depending on the location and demographics of where they reside.

The third section of this chapter discussed Lebanon's sovereignty through exclusionary practices, highlighting the intersectional power hierarchies that asymmetrically (re)shaped most Lebanese sectarian communities' political, cultural, religious, and socioeconomic attitudes toward hosting Syrian refugees. On the one hand, Syrians were blamed for the string of economic woes, including mismanagement, corruption, and increasing debt, that Lebanon was experiencing under the weight of hosting large numbers of refugees.[233] On the other hand, Syrian refugees were often homogenized in official Lebanese rhetoric and practices, perceived as a masculine sectarian to Lebanon's public and troubling the confessional consociationalism system of power-sharing that already bred a lack of trust in hosting Syrian refugees. With the Sunni ISIS faction threatening the northern Lebanese-Syrian border, the prospects of a spillover effect across Lebanon increased, especially in Christian and Shiite areas.

In that respect, sectarianism plays an important role when exploring the different communities' struggles with socioeconomic degradation. Densely populated Sunni areas in Lebanon were more concerned with the economic devastation that led to acute radicalization and extremism.[234] Most notably, in the heavily Sunni-populated *Ain el Helweh* refugee camp in Sidon, terrorist cells mobilized and run by Palestinian militant Bilal Badr actually engaged in sporadic clashes with the Lebanese Army, legitimizing the Lebanese fear of Syrians becoming involved in terrorist activities across the country.[235] As a reaction to Sunni terrorist turbulence, the Lebanese Army Forces and General Security began issuing laws to evict and relocate some informal settlements, prohibiting any camp formation without prior official written consent.[236] These exclusionary practices, in turn, justified Lebanese measures of exceptional mechanisms to deter Syrian refugees' insecurities with counterproductive consequences. In order to secure and preserve their Lebanese communities' sectarian identity, Lebanese government officials provided deportation buses to certain antagonistic non-Sunni Lebanese villages to send the "unwanted" back to nearby Syrian villages by the border.[237] As such, several Lebanese communities requested their deportation, sending Syrian men, women, and children back to the same country that, not long ago, dominated Lebanon for thirty years.

As exposed in the final section of this chapter, Lebanese domestic regulations and security practices possessed a co-constitutive power of silencing and structurally objectifying Syrian women's insecurities. Women were not isolated from all types of structural and ad hoc relational insecurity practices performed within the host country. The invisibility of the majority of the "unwanted" refugees generalized Syrian women insecurities as part of the abstract security threat, forcing the women to live in remote rural areas with feeble housing structures, limited aid, and exploitative living conditions. By overgeneralizing the million and some Syrian intruders, the systemic bias against women within Lebanese polity added to Syrian women's tragedy of being associated to the gendered Lebanese perceptions of Syrian refugees as a masculine threat. The general perception that women held a peripheral role in crisis situations worsened the insecurities, such as legal and economic strife, gender-based violence (GBV), and psychosocial scarring, that Syrian refugee women endured in their new realities. At the same time, Syrians' intersectional identity rarely (re)produced collective, self-contained referential objects.[238] Even though Syrian women and children's identities and agencies were often erased in public discourses, some were better positioned than others depending on the location in which they resided. By alternating between the bureaucratic gender-blind humanitarian prioritization of refugee protection and the securitized Lebanese ad hoc stratification of masculinized refugee threats, painful refugee policy practices (en)gendered a compromised crisis response plan that will be further examined in the following chapter.[239]

NOTES

1. Alexander Wendt, *Social Theory of International Politics* (Cambridge University Press, 1999), 1.

2. Barry Buzan, *People, States & Fear: An Agenda for International Security Studies in the Post-Cold War Era* (Colchester, England: ECPR Press, 2008), 36.

3. Emanuel Adler and Vincent Pouliot, "The Practice Turn in International Relations: Introduction and Framework." *International Studies Association 49th Annual Convention*, San Francisco, 2008, 2629.

4. Adler and Pouliot, "The Practice Turn in International Relations," 2629.

5. Philippe Bourbeau, "The Practice Approach in Global Politics." *Journal of Global Security Studies* 2, no. 2 (2017): 170–82.

6. Didier Bigo, "Security and Immigration: Toward a Critique of the Governmentality of Unease." *Alternatives* 27, no. 1_suppl (2002): 63–92.

7. Sarah Gibson, "Abusing Our Hospitality: Inhospitableness and the Politics of Deterrence." *Mobilizing Hospitality: The Ethics of Social Relations in a Mobile World* (2007): 159–77.

8. Barry Buzan, Ole Wæver, and Jaap De Wilde, *Security: A New Framework for Analysis* (Harvard: Lynne Rienner Publishers, 1998), 25.

9. Alison Gerard and Sharon Pickering, "Gender, Securitization and Transit: Refugee Women and the Journey to the EU." *Journal of Refugee Studies* 27, no. 3 (2014): 338–59.

10. Mark McDonald, "Securitization and the Construction of Security." *European Journal of International Relations* 14, no 4 (2008): 563–87.

11. Wilmott Annabelle Cathryn, "The Politics of Photography: Visual Depictions of Syrian Refugees in UK Online Media." *Visual Communication Quarterly* 24, no. 2 (2017): 67–82.

12. Scott D. Watson, "Manufacturing Threats: Asylum Seekers as Threats or Refugees." *Journal of International Law & International Relations* 3 (2007): 100.

13. Jef Huysmans, *The Politics of Insecurity: Fear, Migration and Asylum in the EU* (Routledge, 2006), 46.

14. Elizabeth Olivius, "Governing Refugees through Gender Equality: Care, Control, Emancipation." *Doctoral dissertation, Umeå universitet,* 2014, 44.

15. Maja Janmyr, "Precarity in Exile: The Legal Status of Syrian Refugees in Lebanon." *Refugee Survey Quarterly* 35, no. 4 (2016): 58–78.

16. Giovanni Capoccia and R. Daniel Kelemen, "The Study of Critical Junctures: Theory, Narrative, and Counterfactuals in Historical Institutionalism." *World Politics* 59, no. 3 (2007): 341–69.

17. David Nachmias and Chava Nachmias, "Content Analysis," in *Research Methods in the Social Sciences*, ed. Edward Arnold (London, England, 1976), 132–9.

18. Edward Anthony Koning, "The Three Institutionalisms and Institutional Dynamics: Understanding Endogenous and Exogenous Change." *Journal of Public Policy* 36, no. 4 (2016): 639–64.

19. Nils A. Butenschøn, "Arab Citizen and the Arab State: The 'Arab Spring' as a Critical Juncture in Contemporary Arab Politics." *Democracy and Security* 11, no. 2 (2015): 111–28.

20. Jaulin Thibaut, "Citizenship, Migration, and Confessional Democracy in Lebanon." *Middle East Law and Governance* 6, no. 3 (2014): 250–71.

21. Rola El-Husseini, *Pax Syriana: Elite Politics In Postwar Lebanon* (Syracuse University Press, 2012), 38.

22. Thibaut, "Citizenship, Migration, and Confessional Democracy in Lebanon," 250–71.

23. Rola El-Husseini, *Pax Syriana,* 38.

24. Scott Preston, "The Confessional Model and Sectarian Politics: Lessons from Lebanon and the Future of Iraq," Honors Theses, 2281, 2013.

25. Augustus Richard Norton, "Lebanon After Ta'if: Is the Civil War Over?" *Middle East Journal* 45, no. 3 (1991): 457–73.

26. Krayem Hassan, "The Lebanese Civil War and the Taif Agreement." *Conflict Resolution in the Arab World: Selected Essays* (1997): 411–35.

27. Fawwaz Traboulsi, *A History of Modern Lebanon* (Pluto Press, 2007), 245.

28. Marie-Joëlle, Zahar, "Peace by Unconventional Means: Lebanon's Ta'if Agreement." *Ending Civil Wars: The Implementation of Peace Agreements* (2002): 567–97.

29. The English Translation of the Ta'if Accord can be retrieved from: https://www.un.int/lebanon/sites/www.un.int/files/Lebanon/the_taif_agreement_english_version_.pdf.

30. The English Translation of the Ta'if Accord can be retrieved from: https://www.un.int/lebanon/sites/www.un.int/files/Lebanon/the_taif_agreement_english_version_.pdf.

31. Erik Husem, "The Syrian Involvement in Lebanon: An Analysis of the Role of Lebanon in Syrian Regime Security, From Ta'if to the Death of Hafiz al-Assad (1989–2000)," *FORSVARETS FORSKNINGSINSTITUTT (FFI) Norwegian Defence Research Establishment* (2002), https://admin.ffi.no/no/Rapporter/02-03005.pdf.

32. "Treaty of Brotherhood, Cooperation, and Coordination Between the Syrian Arab Republic and the Lebanese Republic." *United Nations—Treaty Series* (1992), 154, https://peacemaker.un.org/sites/peacemaker.un.org/files/LBSY_910522_TreatyBrotherhoodCooperationCoordination.pdf.

33. Diane Riskedahl, "The Sovereignty of Kin: Political Discourse in Post-Ta'if Lebanon." *PoLAR: Political and Legal Anthropology Review* 34, no. 2 (2011): 242.

34. Marius Deeb, *Syria's Terrorist War on Lebanon and the Peace Process* (Springer, 2003), 4.

35. Farid El Khazen, "Political Parties in Postwar Lebanon: Parties in Search of Partisans." *Middle East Journal* 57, no. 4 (2003): 605–24.

36. Dib Kamal, *Warlords and Merchants: The Lebanese Business and Political Establishment* (Ithaca Press, 2004). Husem, "The Syrian Involvement in Lebanon."

37. El Khazen, "Political Parties in Postwar Lebanon," 605–24.

38. Kail C. Ellis, "Lebanon: The Struggle of a Small Country in a Regional Context." *Arab Studies Quarterly* (1999): 5–25.

39. Daniel Meier, "Lebanon: The Refugee Issue and the Threat of a Sectarian Confrontation." *Oriente moderno* 94, no. 2 (November 18, 2014): 382–401.

40. Meier, "Lebanon," 382–401.

41. Volker Perthes, "From Front State to Backyard? Syria and the Risks of Regional Peace," in *Economic and Political Impediments to Middle East Peace* (London, England: Palgrave Macmillan, 2000), 225–40.

42. Thibaut, "Citizenship, Migration, and Confessional Democracy in Lebanon," 250–71.

43. Ibid., 250–71.

44. Riskedahl, "The Sovereignty of Kin," 234.

45. Meier, "Lebanon," 382–401.

46. Leila Tarazi Fawaz, *An Occasion for War: Civil Conflict in Lebanon and Damascus in 1860* (University of California Press, 1994).

47. Riskedahl, "The Sovereignty of Kin," 233–50.

48. Ian Black, "Syria and Lebanon to Establish Diplomatic Relations." *The Guardian* (October 14, 2008), https://www.theguardian.com/world/2008/oct/14/syria-lebanon.

49. Samia Nakhoul, "Analysis: Killing of Security Chief Raises Fears for Lebanon." *Reuters Beirut* (October 22, 2012), https://en.wikipedia.org/wiki/Wissam_al-Hassan#cite_note-samia2212-19.

50. Alessandra Bajec, "Lebanon's Political Crisis Drags on as Politicians Agree to Extend their Mandate a Third Time." *Al-Araby News* (June 20, 2017), https://www.alaraby.co.uk/english/indepth/2017/6/20/lebanons-political-crisis-dragson-with-third-term-extension.

51. Paul Salem, "The Future of Lebanon." *Foreign Affairs* 85 (2006): 13.

52. Asher Kaufman, "Understanding the Shebaa Farms Dispute: Roots of the Anomaly and Prospects of Resolution." *Palestine-Israel Journal of Politics, Economics, and Culture* 11, no. 1 (2004): 37.

53. "Lebanon: Reveal Fate of Disappeared Syrians: Military Intelligence Detains Six Calling for Democratic Change in their Country." *Human Rights Watch* (March 9, 2011), https://www.hrw.org/news/2011/03/09/lebanon-reveal-fatedisappeared-syrians.

54. "Lebanon: Reveal Fate of Disappeared Syrians."

55. "Amnesty International Annual Report 2015/2016." *Relief Web*, http://reliefweb.int/report/lebanon/amnestyinternational-regrets-lebanon-s-decision-overturn-its-open-border-policy.

56. Maja Janmyr, "No Country of Asylum: 'Legitimizing' Lebanon's Rejection of the 1951 Refugee Convention." *International Journal of Refugee Law* 29, no. 3 (2017): 438–65.

57. "U.S. Welcomes Lebanon Plan for Syrian Refugees." *The Daily Star* (January 4, 2013), http://www.dailystar.com.lb/News/Politics/2013/Jan-04/200934-us-welcomes-lebanon-plan-for-syrian-refugees.

58. Janmyr, "Precarity in Exile," 58–78.

59. Karim El Mufti, "Official Response to the Syrian Refugee Crisis in Lebanon: The Disastrous Policy of No-Policy." *Civil Society Knowledge Center, Lebanon Support* (January 10, 2014), http://civilsociety-centre.org/paper/officialresponse-syrian-refugee-crisis-lebanon-disastrous-policy-no-policy.

60. Kholoud Mansour, "UN Humanitarian Coordination in Lebanon the Consequences of Excluding Syrian Actors International." *Chatham House the Royal Institute of International Affairs* (March 2017).

61. "Too Close for Comfort: Syrians in Lebanon." *The International Crisis Group (ICG) Middle East Report* (2013), 9.

62. Hezbollah—A Shiaa-based Lebanese paramilitary organization—offered unconditional support to the Assad Baath regime amid a regional Sunni–Shiaa antagonism within the whole Arab region. For them, a U.S.–Saudi initiative to topple the Assad regime only means a weakening of the Shiite Iranian Hezbollah influence

within the region. This led to a lot of tension and resentment from the Lebanese Sunni public who are anti-Assad regime and supporters of the Syrian resistance. They believe that the 90 percent of the Syrian population—Sunnis—should have a say in their country's politics and not let the current regime—8 percent Allawite pro-Shiia—control them. They heavily criticized and questioned Hezbollah's existence for it had no legal justification as a "Lebanese resistance" fighting other countries' wars.

63. Torie Rose DeGhett, "Is Syria About to Become Iran's New Vietnam?" *Vice News* (October 7, 2015), https://news.vice.com/article/is-syria-about-to-become-irans-vietnam.

64. Mirella Hodeib, "Hezbollah Fighters Find Nusra's Tactics in Qusair 'Irritatingly Familiar,'" *Daily Star Lebanon* (May 31, 2013), http://www.dailystar.com.lb/News/Local-News/2013/May31/218984-hezbollah-fighters-find-nusrastactics-in-qusair-irritatingly-familiar.ashx.

65. "Uncharted Waters: Thinking Through Syria's Dynamics, Middle East Briefing No. 31." *International Crisis Group Damascus/Brussels* (November 24, 2011).

66. "Syria's Civil War Explained from the Beginning." *AlJazeera* (2016), http://www.aljazeera.com/news/2016/05/syria-civil-war-explained-160505084119966.html.

67. Haytham Mahmoud, "Syrian Refugees Change the Lebanese Labor Scene." *Al-Arabiya* (July 8, 2016), http://english.alarabiya.net/en/business/economy/2016/07/08/Syrian-refugees-change-the-Lebanese-labor-scene.html.

68. Janmyr, "Precarity in Exile," 58–78.

69. Reuters, "Lebanese Parliament Extends Own Term Till 2017 Amid Protests." (November 5, 2014), http://www.reuters.com/article/2014/11/05/us-lebanonparliament-idUSKBN0IP18T20141105.

70. Imad K. Harb, "The Hezbollah-Iran Pivot: The Controlling Agencies Behind Lebanon's Sectarian Politics." Center for Security Studies, *SAGE International Australia* (2016), 1.

71. David Schenker, "Lebanon Unstable and Insecure." *The Washington Institute* (June 12, 2014), https://www.washingtoninstitute.org/policy-analysis/view/lebanon-unstable-and-insecure.

72. Lamia Estatie, "Lebanon Detains Men Behind Assault on Syrian Refugee." *BBC News* (July 19, 2017), http://www.bbc.com/news/blogs-trending-40653714.

73. "Syrian President Bashar Al-Assad Wins Third Term." *BBC NEWS, World, Middle East* (June 5, 2014), http://www.bbc.com/news/world-middle-east-27706471.

74. Ruth Sherlock Yarzeh, "Expat Syrians Join the Crush to Support Assad in Parody Election." *Telegraph UK* (May 28, 2014).

75. Angela Stent, "Putin's Power Play in Syria: How to Respond to Russia's Intervention." *Foreign Affairs* 95 (2016): 106.

76. "World Report 2014 Events of 2013 2014." *Human Rights Watch*, https://www.hrw.org/sites/default/files/wr2014_web_0.pdf.

77. "'Unprecedented' 65 Million People Displaced by War and Persecution in 2015." *UN News Centre*, http://www.un.org/apps/news/story.asp?NewsID=54269#.WahMY8h96bg.

78. "Trapped in Lebanon: The Alarming Human Rights and Human Security Situation of Syrian Refugees in Lebanon." *ALEF* (May 2016), https://aleffliban.org/wp-content/uploads/2016/11/Trapped-In-Lebanon-_ALEF_PAX _May2016.pdf.

79. "Struggling to Survive: Slavery and Exploitation of Syrian Refugees in Lebanon." *Freedom Fund* (April 12, 2016), http://freedomfund.org/wp-content/uploads/Lebanon-Report-FINAL-8April16.pdf.

80. Arwa Ibrahim, "Syria: 'Absentees Law' Could See Millions of Refugees Lose Lands." *Al-Jazeera News* (April 7, 2018), www.aljazeera.com/news/2018/04/syria-absentees-law-millions-refugees-lose-lands180407073139495.html.

81. "The Future of Syria: How A Victorious Bashar Al-Assad Is Changing Syria." *The Economist* (June 28, 2018), https://www.economist.com/middle-east-and-africa/2018/06/28/how-a-victorious-bashar-al-assad-is-changing-syria.

82. Filippo Dionigi, "Rethinking Borders: The Dynamics of Syrian Displacement to Lebanon." *Middle East Law and Governance* 9, no. 3 (2017): 232–48.

83. "Patriarch al-Ra'i: "Syrian Refugees Threaten Lebanon Security." *Orient News* (December 26, 2016): https://www.orient-news.net/en/news_show/129448/0/Patriarch-al-Rai-"Syrian-refugees-threaten-Lebanon-security.

84. Ellen Francis, "Hostility Grows Towards Syrian Refugees in Lebanon." *Reuters* (August 28, 2017), https://www.reuters.com/article/us-lebanon-refugees-tension-idUSKCN1B8128.

85. Marta Agosti, "The Nationality Law in Light of the Refugee Crisis in Lebanon: Old Battles, New Consequences." *Contemporary Levant* 1, no. 2 (2016): 148–51.

86. "UNHCR Country Operation Profile: Lebanon." *UNHCR* (2013), http://www.al-monitor.com/pulse/ar/contents/articles/originals/2013/06/iraq-kurdistan-syrian-refugees-aid.html#.

87. Romola Sanyal, "A No-Camp Policy: Interrogating Informal Settlements in Lebanon." *Geoforum* 84 (2017): 117–25.

88. Boed Roman, "The State of the Right of Asylum in International Law." *Duke Journal of Comparative & International Law* 5 (1994): 1.

89. "Pushed To The Edge: Syrian Refugees Face Increased Restrictions in Lebanon." *Amnesty International* (June 2015), https://www.amnesty.org/en/documents/mde24/1785/2015/en/.

90. Maja Janmyr, "No Country of Asylum," 438–65.

91. Noll Gregor, "Securitizing Sovereignty? States, Refugees, and the Regionalization of International Law." *Refugees and Forced Displacement* (2003): 277–305.

92. The 1951 Convention Relating to the Status of Refugees and Its 1967 Protocol, http://www.refugeelegalaidinformation.org/1951-convention.

93. MoSA Expert interview with author (June 12, 2017).

94. Janmyr, "Precarity in Exile," 58–78.

95. Ibid., 58–78.

96. Scott Abramson, "Lebanese Armenians: A Distinctive Community in the Armenian Diaspora and in Lebanese Society." *The Levantine Review* 2, no. 2 (2013): 188–216.

97. Abramson, "Lebanese Armenians," 188–216.

98. Simon Haddad, "The Origins of Popular Opposition to Palestinian Resettlement in Lebanon." *International Migration Review* 38, no.2 (2004), 484.

99. Bruce Riedel and Bilal Y. Saab, "Lessons for Lebanon from Nahr El-Bared." *Op-Ed, Brookings* (October 4, 2007).

100. Farid El Khazen, "Permanent Settlement of Palestinians in Lebanon: A Recipe for Conflict." *Journal of Refugee Studies* 10, no. 3 (1997): 275–93.

101. El Khazen, "Permanent Settlement of Palestinians in Lebanon," 275–93.

102. Agosti, "The Nationality Law in Light of the Refugee Crisis in Lebanon," 148–51.

103. Ibid., 148–51.

104. Salah Dabbagh, George Deeb, Farid El-Khazen, and Maroun Kisirwani, "The Lebanese Constitution." *Arab Law Quarterly* 12, no. 2 (1997): 224–61.

105. "Did the PLO Die in Lebanon?" *Al Jazeera* (July 28, 2009), https://www.aljazeera.com/programmes/plohistoryofrevolution/2009/07/200972855032594820.html.

106. Franklin Lamb, "Will Hezbollah Support Right to Work for Palestinian Refugees?" *The Palestine Chronicle Beirut* (May 10, 2010), http://www.palestinechronicle.com/will-hezbollah-support-right-to-work-for-palestinianrefugees/.

107. Lamb, "Will Hezbollah Support Right to Work for Palestinian Refugees?"

108. Sari Hanafi and Taylor Long, "Governance, Governmentalities, and the State of Exception in the Palestinian Refugee Camps of Lebanon." *Journal of Refugee Studies* 23, no. 2 (2010): 134–59.

109. Hanafi and Long, "Governance, Governmentalities, and the State of Exception in the Palestinian Refugee Camps of Lebanon," 134–59.

110. Sarah Kenyon Lischer, *Dangerous Sanctuaries: Refugee Camps, Civil War, and the Dilemmas of Humanitarian Aid* (Ithaca, NY: Cornell University Press, 2015), 26.

111. Hanafi and Long, "Governance, Governmentalities, and the State of Exception in the Palestinian Refugee Camps of Lebanon," 134–59.

112. Ibid., 134–59.

113. UNHCR, "Country Operations Plan" (2004), http://www.unhcr.org/3fd9c6a14.pdf.

114. Maja Janmyr, "UNHCR and the Syrian Refugee Response: Negotiating Status and Registration in Lebanon." *The International Journal of Human Rights* 22, no. 3 (2018): 393–419.

115. Ghida Frangieh, "Relations Between UNHCR and Arab Governments: Memoranda of Understanding in Lebanon and Jordan." *Middle East Centre Blog* (2016).

116. Frangieh, "Relations Between UNHCR and Arab Governments."

117. Ibid.

118. Janmyr, "No Country of Asylum," 438–65.

119. UNHCR Regional Office in Lebanon, Country Operations Plan 1 (2004), http://www.unhcr.org/3fd9c6a14.pd

120. Frangieh, "Relations Between UNHCR and Arab Governments."

121. Janmyr, "UNHCR and the Syrian Refugee Response," 393–419.

122. "Country Operations Plan." *UNHCR Regional Office in Lebanon* (2004), http://www.unhcr.org/3fd9c6a14.pd

123. MoSa Expert Interview with author (June 12, 2017).

124. The UNHCR notes that although numbers of people from Syria applying for asylum in European countries is rising, that figure accounts for only 10 percent of all refugees from Syria, http://data.unhcr.org/syrianrefugees/regional.php.

125. Maja Janmyr, "Precarity in Exile: The Legal Status of Syrian Refugees in Lebanon." *Refugee Survey Quarterly* 35, no. 4 (2016): 58–9.

126. Janmyr, "Precarity in Exile," 58–9.

127. Benedetta Berti, "The Syrian Refugee Crisis: Regional and Human Security Implications." *Strategic Assessment* 17, no. 4 (2015): 41–53.

128. Richard Hall, "Lebanon Doesn't Want Syrian Refugees Getting Too Comfortable, Even in Winter." *Agence FrancePresse* (February 15, 2016), https://www.pri.org/stories/2016-02-15/lebanon-doesnt-want-syrian-refugees-getting-toocomfortable-even-winter.

129. Hall, "Lebanon Doesn't Want Syrian Refugees Getting Too Comfortable, Even in Winter."

130. Daniel Meier, "La Strategie Du Regime Assad Au Liban Entre 1970 Et2013. Du Pouvoir Symbolique A La Coercion." *Revue EurOrient*, no. 41(2013): 171–88. ebanon: The Refugee Issue and the Threat of a Sectarian Confrontation.

131. Meier, "La Strategie Du Regime Assad Au Liban Entre 1970 Et2013."

132. Francis, "Hostility Grows Towards Syrian Refugees in Lebanon."

133. Hassan Krayem, "The Lebanese Civil War and the Taif Agreement," in *Conflict Resolution in the Arab World: Selected Essays*, ed. Paul Salem (Beirut, Lebanon: American University of Beirut, 1997), 411–36.

134. "Lebanon's President Aoun Calls for National Unity, Liberating Palestinian Territories." *Albawaba* (November 1), http://www. albawaba.com/news/lebanon's-president-aoun-calls-national-unity-liberating-palestinian-territories899220.

135. Tom Perry, "Lebanon Near 'Breaking Point' Over Syrian Refugee Crisis: PM Hariri." *Reuters* (March 31, 2017), http://www.reuters.com/article/us-mideast-crisis-syria-lebanon-idUSKBN1722JM.

136. Carole Alsharabati and Jihad Nammour, "Survey on Perceptions of Syrian Refugees in Lebanon." *Institut De Science Politiques* (March 2015), http://rdpp-me.org/RDPP/files/survey_1499127955.pdf.

137. Are John Knudsen, "Syria's Refugees in Lebanon: Brothers, Burden, and Bone of Contention," in *Lebanon Facing the Arab Uprisings* (London: Palgrave Pivot, 2017), 135–54.

138. Janmyr, "UNHCR and the Syrian Refugee Response," 393–419.

139. Yazan Al-Saadi, "The Diversion Strategy: Lebanese Racism, Classism, and the Refugees." *Al-Akhbar* (June 10, 2014), https://english.al-akhbar.com/node/20121.

140. "Amnesty International Regrets Lebanon's Decision to Overturn its Open Border Policy Towards Refugees and Refusal to Address Discrimination against Women and Migrants." *Amnesty International* (March 16, 2016), http://reliefweb.int/report/lebanon/amnesty-international-regrets-lebanon-s-decision-overturn-its-open-border-policy.

141. "Amnesty International Regrets Lebanon's Decision to Overturn its Open Border Policy Towards Refugees and Refusal to Address Discrimination against Women and Migrants."

142. Monika Borgmann and Lokman Slim, "Lebanon 2017/2018: Fewer Refugees More Refugeeism." *UMAM D&R Documentation and Research* (2018), https://umam-dr.org/en/home/projects/14/advance-contents/188/fewer-refugeesmore-refugeeism.

143. Morgan Meaker, "When Aid Funds a Country—Not Its Refugees." *Devex News* (March 10, 2017), https://www.devex.com/news/when-aid-funds-a-country-not-its-refugees-89744.

144. Meaker, "When Aid Funds a Country—Not Its Refugees."

145. Are John Knudsen, "Syria's Refugees in Lebanon: Brothers, Burden, and Bone of Contention," in *Lebanon Facing the Arab Uprisings* (London: Palgrave Pivot, 2017), 135–54.

146. Janmyr, "Precarity in Exile," 58–9.

147. Sami Atallah and Dima Mahdi, "Law and Politics of 'Safe Zones' and Forced Returns to Syria: Refugee Politics in Lebanon." *The Lebanese Center for Policy Studies* 39 (2017): 36.

148. Filippo Dionigi, "The Syrian Refugee Crisis in Lebanon: State Fragility and Social Resilience." *LSE Middle East Centre Paper Series, 15* (London, UK, 2016).

149. "Trapped in Lebanon: The Alarming Human Rights and Human Security Situation of Syrian Refugees in Lebanon." *ALEF*, 18 (May, 2016), https://alefliban.org/wp-content/uploads/2016/11/Trapped-In-Lebanon ALEF_PA X _ May2016.pdf.

150. "A Convoy of 300 Syrian Displaced Returned from the Town of Arsal to the Syrian Town Isal al Ward." *AnNahar* (July 12, 2017), https://www.annahar.com/article/617319F.

151. MoSa Expert Interview with author (June 12, 2017).

152. Martin Armstrong, "Lebanon Resists Granting Work Permits to Syrian Refugees." *Middle East Eye* (February 4, 2016), http://www.middleeasteye.net/news/lebanon-syria-refugees-jobs-554259285.

153. Armstrong, "Lebanon Resists Granting Work Permits to Syrian Refugees."

154. *Annahar News* (October 21, 2018), https://newspaper.annahar.com/article/181890.

155. "I Want a Safe Space: Refugee Women from Syria Uprooted and Unprotected in Lebanon." *Amnesty International* (February, 2016), https://www.alnap.org/system/files/content/resource/files/main/i-want-a-safe-place.pdf.

156. "Lebanon: 250,000 Syrian Children Out of School." *Human Rights Watch, UNHCR* (July 19, 2016), https://www.refworld.org/docid/578e2d8a4.html#_ftn231.

157. General Directorate of General Security in Lebanon, http://www.general-security.gov.lb/en/posts/3.

158. "Lebanon Cabinet Votes to Stop Accepting Syrian Refugees." *Daily Star* (October 23, 2014), www.dailystar.com.lb/News/Lebanon-News/2014/Oct-23/275075-refugee-crisis-tops-lebanoncabinetagenda.ashx.

159. Robert Rabil, *The Syrian Refugee Crisis in Lebanon: The Double Tragedy of Refugees and Impacted Host Communities* (Lexington Books, 2016), 20.

160. Lebanon News, "UNHCR to Cross 5,500 Syrian Refugees: Derbas." *The Daily Star* (August 29, 2015), https://www.dailystar.com.lb/News/LebanonNews /2015/Apr-29/296164-unhcr-to-cross-off-5500-syrianrefugeesderbas.ashx.

161. Rola Yasmine and Catherine Moughalian, "Systemic Violence Against Syrian Refugee Women and the Myth of Effective Intrapersonal Interventions." *Reproductive Health Matters* (2016).

162. A 2015 Assessment by the Lebanese Institute for Democracy and Human Rights (LIFE).

163. Frangieh Ghida, "Lebanon Places Discriminatory Entry Restrictions on Syrians." *Legal Agenda* 22 (2015).

164. Dina Mansour-Ille and Maegan Hendow, "From Exclusion to Resistance: Migrant Domestic Workers and the Evolution of Agency in Lebanon." *Journal of Immigrant & Refugee Studies* (2018): 1–21.

165. "Reform of the KAFALA (Sponsorship) System." *Migrant Forum in Asia, Policy Brief No. 2* (July 3, 2013), http://www.ilo.org/dyn/migpractice/docs/132/P B2.pdf.

166. Ray Jureidini, "An Exploratory Study of Psychoanalytic and Social Factors in the Abuse of Migrant Domestic Workers by Female Employers in Lebanon." *KAFA (Enough) Violence & Exploitation* (2011).

167. "Lebanon Immigration Detention Profile." *Global Detention Project* (February 2018), https://www.global detentionproject.org/countries/middle-east/lebanon.

168. Katharine Jones, "Syrian Refugees in Lebanon Are Falling into Slavery and Exploitation." *The Conversation* (April 13, 2016), https://theconversation.com/sy rian-refugees-in-lebanon-are-falling-into-slavery-and-exploitation-57521.

169. OXFAM, Discussion Paper, "Lebanon: Looking Ahead in Times of Crisis" (December 2015), https://www.oxfam.org/sites/www.oxfam.org/files/file_attachm ents/dp-lebanon-looking-ahead-time-crisis-141215en_0.pdf.

170. "The Syrian Refugee Crisis: Labour Market Implications in Jordan and Lebanon." *European Economy Discussion Paper*, European Union (2016), https://ec.euro pa.eu/info/sites/info/files/dp029_en.pdf.

171. Tine Gade, "Lebanon on the Brink." *Norwegian Institute of International Affairs, Policy Brief* 23 (2016), https://core.ac.uk/download/pdf/154676181.pdf.

172. "Syrians Who Obtain Work Permits in Lebanon Risk Losing Refugee Aid." *Lebanon News, The Daily Star* (March 6, 2017), http://www.dailystar.com.lb/Ne ws/Lebanon-News/2017/Mar-06/396311-syrians-who-obtain-work-permits-inlebano n-risk-losing-refugee-status.ashx.

173. "Pushed to the Edge."

174. Ibid.

175. "I Just Wanted to be Treated like a Person: How Lebanon's Residency Rules Facilitate Abuse of Syrian Refugees." *Human Rights Watch* (January 12, 2016), https ://www.hrw.org/report/2016/01/12/i-just-wanted-be-treated-person/howlebanons-res idency-rules-facilitate-abuse.

176. James Haines-Young, "Lebanon's Bassil Meets UNHCR to Defuse Refugee Row." *The National* (June 17, 2018), https://www.thenational.ae/world/mena/le banon-s-bassil-meets-unhcr-to-defuse-refugee-row-1.741039.

177. "I Just Wanted to be Treated like a Person."

178. "Protection Sector, Monthly Dashboard." *UN Inter-Agency Coordination Lebanon* (July 2015), http://data.unhcr.org/ syrianrefugees/download.php?id=9508.

179. "I Just Wanted to be Treated like a Person."

180. "Q&A For Syrians Seeking Registration." *United Nations* (July 15, 2017), https://www.refugeeslebanon.org/en/news/88/qa-for-syrians-seeking-registration.

181. Tim Schultz, "Combating Statelessness in the Wake of the Syrian Conflict: A Right Without a Remedy." *Notre Dame Journal of International & Comparative Law* 8, no. 2 (2018): 147.

182. Schultz, "Combating Statelessness in the Wake of the Syrian Conflict," 132.

183. John Davison, "Redrawing the Middle East: A Generation of Syrian Children Who Don't Count." *Thompson Reuters* (May 3, 2016), http://www.reuters.com/in vestigates/special-report/syria-refugeesstateless/.

184. "Trapped in Lebanon: The Alarming Human Rights and Human Security Situation of Syrian Refugees in Lebanon." *ALEF* (May 2016), 18, https://alefliban.or g/wp-content/uploads/2016/11/Trapped-In-Lebanon-_ALEF_ PAX_ May2016.pdf.

185. "Lebanon: New Entry Requirements for Syrians Likely to Block Would-Be Refugees." *Amnesty International* (January 6, 2015), www.amnesty.org/en/docume nts/document/?indexNumber=mde24%2F002%2F2015&language=en.

186. Maja Janmyr and Lama Mourad, "Modes of Ordering: Labelling, Classification and Categorization in Lebanon's Refugee Response." *Journal of Refugee Studies* (2017).

187. Richard Hall, "Lebanon Doesn't Want Syrian Refugees Getting Too Comfortable, Even in Winter."

188. "Ensuring Birth Registration for the Prevention of Statelessness." *UNHCR.* Ending Statelessness Within 10 Years (2017), https://www.unhcr.org/ke/wp-content /uploads/sites/2/2017/11/Good-Practices-Paper-on-Ensuring-Birth Registration -for-the-Prevention-of-Statelessness.pdf.

189. Dawn Chatty, "Bedouin in Lebanon: The Transformation of a Way of Life or an Attitude?" *International Journal of Migration, Health and Social Care* 6, no. 3 (2011): 21–30.

190. Dawn Chatty, Nisrine Mansour, and Nasser Yassin, "Statelessness and Tribal Identity on Lebanon's Eastern Borders." *Mediterranean Politics* 18, no. 3 (2013): 411–26.

191. "VASyR 2017: Vulnerability Assessment of Syrian Refugees in Lebanon." World Food Program, United Nations Children's Fund (UNICEF), and UNHCR (2016), http://documents.wfp.org/stellent/groups/public/documents/ena/ wfp289533.pdf.

192. Sanyal, "A No-Camp Policy," 117–25.

193. Ibid., 117–25.

194. Faten Kikano, M. Fayazi, and G. Lizarralde, "Understanding Forms of Sheltering by (and for) Syrian Refugees in Lebanon," in *7th iRec Conference 2015: Reconstruction and Recovery in Urban Contexts*, London. 2015.

195. Kikano, Fayazi, and Lizarralde, "Understanding Forms of Sheltering by (and for) Syrian Refugees in Lebanon."

196. Ibid.

197. Mona Fawaz, "Planning and the Refugee Crisis: Informality as a Framework of Analysis and Reflection." *Planning Theory* 16, no. 1 (2017): 99–115.

198. "Lebanon Security and Justice Sector Wide Assessment." *UNDP* (March 2016), file:///C:/Users/Jessy/Downloads/SecurityandJusticeSectorWideAssessment.pdf.

199. "Lebanon Security and Justice Sector Wide Assessment."

200. Lizzie Porter and Kareem Chehayeb, "EXCLUSIVE: Lebanese Army Accused of Torturing Syrian Refugees." *Middle East Eye* (July 17, 2017), http://www.middleeasteye.net/news/exclusive-syrian-refugees-tortured-death-lebanese-army481522780.

201. Hassan Krayem, "The Lebanese Civil War and the Taif Agreement." *Conflict Resolution in the Arab World: Selected Essays* (1997): 411–36.

202. "Lebanon Security and Justice Sector Wide Assessment."

203. Ibid.

204. Lama Mourad, "Inaction as Policy-Making: Understanding Lebanon's Early Response to the Refugee Influx." *POMEPS Studies* no. 25 (March, 2017): 49–55.

205. "Lebanon: At Least 45 Local Curfews Imposed on Syrian Refugees." *Human Rights Watch* (October 3, 2014), https://www.hrw.org/news/2014/10/03/lebanon-least-45-local-curfews-imposed-syrian-refugees.

206. Yasmine Rola and Moughalian Catherine, "Systemic Violence Against Syrian Refugee Women and the Myth of Effective Intrapersonal Interventions." *Reproductive Health Matters* (2016).

207. "VASyR 2017: Vulnerability Assessment of Syrian Refugees in Lebanon." UNHCR, World Food Program, and United Nations Children's Fund (UNICEF) (December, 2017), 4, https://data2.unhcr.org/fr/documents/download /61312.

208. Amnesty International Interviews with Refugee Women from Syria and with NGOs Working with Refugees (June and October 2015), Lebanon.

209. "I Want A Safe Space: Refugee Women from Syria Uprooted and Unprotected in Lebanon." *Amnesty International* (February, 2016), https://www.alnap.org/system/files/content/resource/files/main/i-want-a-safe-place.pdf.

210. "Third Periodic Report of Lebanon, UN Doc." *CEDAW* (July 2006), 14–16, http://tbinternet.ohchr.org/_layouts/treatybodyexternal/Download.aspx?symbolno=CEDAW%2fC%2fLBN% 2f3&Lang=en.

211. Bassma Atassi, "Syria's War Widows Fight For Survival." *Al Jazzera News* (July 2014), https://www.aljazeera.com/humanrights/2014/07/syrian-women-struggle-as-sole-providers-201478122435631439.html.

212. Marguerite Helou, "Women's Political Participation in Lebanon: Gaps in Research and Approaches." *Al-Raida Journal* (2014): 74–84.

213. Helou, "Women's Political Participation in Lebanon," 74–84.

214. Marguerite Helou, "Lebanese Women and Politics: A Comparison Between Two Field Studies." *Al-Raida Journal* (2001), 33–40.

215. "Lebanon Elects Six Women To Parliament." *The Daily Star* (May 09, 2018), http://www.dailystar.com.lb/News/Lebanon-Elections/2018/May-09/448633-lebanon-elects-six-women-to-parliament.ashx.

216. Helou, "Lebanese Women and Politics," 33–40.

217. "Lebanon First Ever Womens Affairs Minister Man Jean Ogasapian Rights Equal." *Independent* (December 19, 2016), https://www.independent.co.uk/news/world/middle-east/lebanon-first-ever-womens-affairs-minister-man-jeanogasapian-rights-equal-a7484221.html.

218. Maya Mansour and Sarah Abou-Aad, "Women's Citizenship Rights in Lebanon." *Research and Policy-Making in the Arab World* (2012).

219. Mansour and Abou-Aad, "Women's Citizenship Rights in Lebanon."

220. Georgi Azar, "Lebanese President Draws Fire with Naturalization Decree." *Annahar News* (June 1, 2018), https://en.annahar.com/article/812753-lebanese-president-draws-fire-with-naturalization-decree.

221. "Ensuring Birth Registration for the Prevention of Statelessness." *UNHCR.* Ending Statelessness within 10 Years (2017), https://www.unhcr.org/ke/wp-content/uploads/sites/2/2017/11/Good-Practices-Paper-on-Ensuring-BirthRegistration-for-the-Prevention-of-Statelessness.pdf.

222. Ibid.

223. "Concluding Observations on the Combined Fourth and Fifth Periodic Reports of Lebanon." *CEDAW.* UN Doc. CEDAW/C/LBN/4-5 (November 3, 2015), http://docstore.ohchr.org/SelfServices/FilesHandler.ashx?

224. Amnesty International Interviews with Refugee Women from Syria and with NGOs Working with Refugees (June and October 2015), Lebanon.

225. "I Want A Safe Space: Refugee Women from Syria Uprooted and Unprotected in Lebanon." *Amnesty International* (February, 2016), https://www.alnap.org/system/files/content/resource/files/main/i-want-a-safe-place.pdf.

226. William Avis, "Gender Equality and Women's Empowerment in Lebanon." *Helpdesk Report.* University of Birmingham (August 16, 2017), https://www.alnap.org/system/files/content/resource/files/main/175-gender-equalityand-womens-empowerment-in-lebanon.pdf.

227. Elizabeth Thompson, "Public and Private in Middle Eastern Women's History." *Journal of Women's History* 15, no. 1 (2003): 52–69.

228. "Roula Yaacoub's Husband Found Not Guilty after Beating Her to Death." *Beirut* (Novemeber 1, 2018), https://www.beirut.com/l/56670.

229. "Without Protection: Women's Rights under Lebanese Personal Status Laws." *Human Rights Watch* (January, 2015).

230. "Human Rights Watch Submission to the CEDAW Committee of Lebanon's Periodic Report 62nd Session." *Human Rights Watch* (February, 2015), https://tbinternet.ohchr.org/Treaties/CEDAW/Shared%20Documents/ LBN/INT_ CEDAW_NGO_LBN_19385_E.pdf.

231. Claire Harvey, Rosa Garwood, and Roula El-Masri, "Shifting Sands: Changing Gender Roles among Refugees in Lebanon." *Oxfam International* (2013), https://oxfam.qc.ca/sites/oxfam.qc.ca/files/rr-shifting-sands-lebanonsyriarefugees-gender-030913-en_0.pdf; Ghida Anani, "Syria Crisis—Dimensions of Gender-Based Violence Against Syrian Refugees in Lebanon." *Forced Migration Review*, no. 44 (2013), http://www.fmreview.org/en/detention/anani.pdf.

232. Lene Hansen, "The Little Mermaid's Silent Security Dilemma and the Absence of Gender in the Copenhagen School." *Millennium* 29, no. 2 (2000): 285–306.

233. Marguerite, Helou, "Lebanese Women and Politics: A Comparison between Two Field Studies." *Al-Raida Journal* (2001), 33–40.

234. "Extremist Ain El Hilweh Group Threatens Escalation." *The Daily Star* (May 8, 2017), http://www.dailystar.com.lb/News/Lebanon-News/2017/May-08/404971-extremist-ain-al-hilweh-groupthreatensescalation.ashx.

235. "Extremist Ain El Hilweh Group Threatens Escalation."

236. "Syrian Refugees in Lebanon." *Syrian Civic Platform* (September 29, 2017), http://www.scplatform.net/en/syrianrefugees-in-lebanon/.

237. "A Convoy of 300 Syrian Displaced Returned from the Town of Arsal to the Syrian Town Isal Al-Ward." *AnNahar* (July 12, 2017), https://www.annahar.com/article/617319F.

238. Hansen, "The Little Mermaid's Silent Security Dilemma and the Absence of Gender in the Copenhagen School," 285–306.

239. Lene Hansen, "Theorizing the Image for Security Studies: Visual Securitization and the Muhammad Cartoon Crisis." *European Journal of International Relations* 17, no. 1 (2011): 51–74.

Chapter 3

(En)Gendering Lebanon Crisis Response Plan(s)

REFUGEE PROTECTION REGIME

Since the modern system of nation states inhabits an evolving international humanitarian regime, the study of refugee protection policy construction and management practice is essential to understanding the contextual tension and resistance dynamics that go into formulating refugee crisis response plans. Within the realm of refugee assistance, the UNHCR is commonly the most authoritative agency.[1] Till this date, the 1951 Convention Relating to the Status of Refugees and its 1967 Protocol, through UNHCR, remain the sole legal instruments that determine the policy of refugee protection and assistance.[2] Even with official declarations in favor of refugee protection, most refugee security rhetoric portrays refugees as faceless people who need saving and, at the same time, pose a burden on the already prevailing social, political, economic, and environmental troubles within the host state's communities.

By labeling refugees as victims, the assumption is that they are helpless and passively dependent on those whose mission is to save, protect, and modernize them.[3] One of the problematic issues with emergency relief is that it is designed based on the assumption that humanitarian agents have the moral capacity and duty to save refugees and do for them, rather than empower them as active and resilient survivors in their own right.[4] These lofty humanitarian goals tend to mask the power dynamics of social relations, reinforcing structural and individual gender hierarchies between the different micro-groups that form the refugee populations. This neoliberal portrayal of a refugee community that is passive, innocent, and vulnerable seems to narrowly focus on the utility perspective of gender in garnering international and host states' support and funds.[5] The expectations of the refugee protection agencies intersect with their aid workers' class, nationality, and background privileges, constructing a false refugee identity in the humanitarian quest to protect asylum seekers.[6] Consequently, neoliberal humanitarian practices vacillate between the tendencies of developing and modernizing the perceived "backward" refugee society and the need to respect harmful cultural relativist state practices that challenge basic women's rights. False gender identities are thus hierarchically constructed around the benevolent, altruistic humanitarian aid workers and the backward, oppressed victims, whom host governments should neither criminalize nor manage on their own.[7] The result is that relief efforts often undermine the potential for refugees' own resilience and coping strategies, whether positive or negative, through the way in which humanitarian *selves* and refugee *others* are constructed.[8]

In the case of refugees in Lebanon, most Syrians were racialized, victimized, and even feminized by humanitarian agencies through the visual construction of a fabricated refugee identity, in which female refugees are portrayed as innocent victims with no agency. These same visuals also excluded men, denying them their personal status as fathers, husbands, and sons.[9] Various groups of refugees became heavily dependent on the framing of different aid agencies, incapable of capitalizing on their own skills as self-help mechanisms. The refugee protection policies that emanated from such perceptions ended up silencing the diversity within the residing Syrian population legally, socially, and economically for the sake of continuing humanitarian missions.[10] Notably, governing processes for the management of refugee gender equality construction, interpretation, and application are promoted either on "the basis of their usefulness" or as a means to different ends, limiting refugee gender empowerment and social change.[89] Gender equality in global refugee governance is thus "rarely treated as a goal in its own right."[11] Bureaucratic organizations, such as the UNHCR, struggle to adapt their internationally recognized norms within a sovereign domestic polity, privileging feminizing standard operating procedures.[12,13]

Managing actors, such as sovereign states and humanitarian agencies, are too self-interested and, at the same time, too constrained to apply these international norms without compromising sustainable long-term development programs to short-term host community priorities and concerned donor funds with distinct securitized goals—*realpolitik*.[14] UNHCR operations rely on and compete almost entirely for voluntary contributions from member states, international and regional organizations, as well as some pooled funding mechanisms that include the private and politically affiliated sectors. Donor states became the UNHCR's main patrons, with up to 98 percent of funds provided by sovereign states, thus limiting the organization's commitments to refugees.[15] These donor states voluntarily choose who, what, where, and when to fund.[16] Accordingly, the universally recognized human rights regime translates into a plethora of competing humanitarian agencies whose specializations depend on the number of funds they get from different interest groups, while also supporting the host government in procuring technical administrative state support in managing registered refugees.[17]

For the sake of success, UNHCR programs meticulously count, calculate, and code refugees, contradicting their main goal of gendered refugee protection.[18] Ultimately, they reinforce existing rhetoric that depoliticizes women and children refugees as passive victims heavily dependent on aid assistance.[19] When collaborating with host states in refugee management policy creation and implementation, the neutrality and independence of humanitarian agencies such as the UNHCR is undermined and becomes more politicized.[20] Most refugee protection policies are shared with host government authorities, humanitarian NGOs, and other UN agencies, among many other interest groups. This means that the UNHCR's multilateral involvement in refugee protection can never be objectively altruistic, as states, interest groups, and multilateral governing institutions intersubjectively prioritize their interests in securitizing the refugee threat through different processes, such as institutional funding or labeling a situation as a "humanitarian crisis." Humanitarian agencies, such as the UNHCR, are therefore not only biased but also codependent on a state-based system. They tend to work closely with host states that would ultimately influence over whom to feminize as a refugee victim and whom to label as a hypermasculine foreign threat. After all, constructing and (re)shaping host states' "strategic partnership" with concerned humanitarian agencies is an important step in the creation of refugee crisis policy plans.

Interorganizational collaborative dynamics, usually exhibited through "artifacts" such as shared policy language, organizational structures, practices, and technologies, often hold central guiding principles for invested practitioners operating in a given bureaucratic culture at a particular point in time.[21] However, organizational cultures are neither monolithic nor constant. Endogenous and exogenous interdependent factors that are deeply embedded in organizational cultures shape and are shaped by the different bodies who bring their own set of perspectives, values, and assumptions when adopting a joint mission.[22] Unsurprisingly, global organizational cultures and norms in refugee governance get distorted when translated domestically through various sights of constructions, (re)definitions, and contestations by engaged, often competing, interest groups that are trying to translate their shared vision into actual transnational activities and contextual policy practices.[23] In that respect, contested global refugee norms do not linearly diffuse in the local context. A translation process occurs depending on engaged translation work through norms entrepreneurs and social advances. Therefore, it is essential to establish an adequate framework that better explores the explicit and latent power dynamics between collaborating organizations that guide refugee protection regime construction and goals, where (en)gendered refugee insecurity is often a matter of local context.[24]

The Lebanon Crisis Response Plan (LCRP), a joint strategic plan co-created by the Lebanese government, the UNHCR, and a growing collective effort of different interest groups at the sectoral level, provides an example of how refugee protection norms are translated and managed in a local context. The power dynamics between the UNHCR and Lebanese government institutions, which have distinct understandings of refugee (in)security and goals, influence the crisis response plan's agenda and policy tools.[25] Combining transnational feminist theory with a longitudinal examination of organizational cultural change provides a useful analytical framework for tracing policy plan fluctuations and offers significant insight into the Syrian crisis management strategy in Lebanon. By exposing the rationalities and power relations of managing refugees, this approach challenges the universalist assumptions of a human rights approach diffusing into gender-sensitive local refugee practices.

In that respect, this chapter explores the Lebanese government and UNHCR's level of cooperation in assessing and mediating the translation of Syrian refugee (in)security norms within the country. The chapter first looks at the general background of the creation and evolution of the Syrian crisis response plans. Secondly, the chapter provides a longitudinal qualitative analysis of the cultural themes and patterns of two LCRP documents, highlighting the various sites of norm constructions, (re)definitions, and contestations. Finally, the chapter evaluates the themes found within both LCRPs, analyzing how the documents neglect to capture the discriminations and depoliticization that refugee women faced as *women*, and demonstrating the centrality of power politics and cultural influence in the (re)shaping of crisis response plans.

LCRP BACKGROUND

As elaborated in Chapter 2, 2014 saw a critical shift in the Lebanese paradigm, in which an extreme form of politicization of what became the Syrian refugee crisis enabled the Lebanese government to prioritize security policies over refugee protection norms. Meanwhile, the UNHCR advocated the benefit of keeping their internationally recognized humanitarian "savior" approach in place. In the name of national security and refugee protection, cooperative organizational plans emerged, setting a direction for Syrian refugee crisis management in Lebanon. By devising shared objectives and responsibilities, a comprehensive crisis response plan was first published on December 19, 2014, in a collaboration between Lebanon and the UNHCR, providing a guidebook on how the crisis management groups planned to respond to the Syrian influx in Lebanon.

It is crucial to note that this LCRP constituted Lebanon's chapter in a greater 2015 Regional Refugee & Resilience Plan, better known as the "3RP"—a coherent regional strategy developed with support from the UN and NGOs with the aim to provide an effective and coordinated response to the Syrian refugee crisis in the region. The 3RP process produced an overarching plan to coordinate, monitor, and evaluate immediate refugee vulnerabilities and mechanisms facilitating humanitarian aid, protection, and assistance throughout the MENA region. It focused primarily on Syria's neighboring host countries affected by the increasing refugee influx, such as Lebanon, Turkey, Jordan, Iraq, and Egypt.

The Lebanese chapter of the 3RP grounded Lebanon's relation to the international refugee regime. It determined, under the leadership of the national government, all aspects of humanitarian assistance provided to the most vulnerable groups (in)directly affected by the Syrian crisis in Lebanon. Moreover, it set out to develop more sustainable long-term strategies to alleviate human suffering and improve the overall quality of life of the plan's "beneficiaries."[26] Numerous cooperation agreements complement the LCRP, such as the UN Strategic Framework, the World Bank Country Partnership, and the EU–Lebanon Partnership. The LCRP was also aligned with the Lebanese government's stance that it is "neither a country of asylum nor a final destination for refugees, let alone a country of resettlement."[27] At the same time, the LCRP seemed to be compliant with the United Nations Strategic Framework (UNSF), which guided the overall vision of the UN's engagement within Lebanese territories.[28]

Due to the temporal and spatial expansion of the Syrian crisis, rapid changes within the national and international context pushed for a revised plan that aimed to adapt to the new local realities. Lessons learned from the implementation of the first LCRP laid the groundwork for a more elaborate second version in 2017. This updated LCRP reflected the cultural changes that had occurred since the first strategic plan was implemented in 2015. Both LCRP versions delineate the limbo between state-centric policy interests and international humanitarian values and principles. The interplay between organizations' divergent interests is best illustrated by looking into the LCRP vocabulary. On the one hand, the UN referred to forced migrants from Syria as "refugees" eligible to benefit from international protective measures.[29] On the other hand, the Lebanese government identified all Syrian citizens who entered Lebanon after March 2011 as temporarily "displaced" individuals subject to Lebanese sovereign laws and jurisdiction. As a result, the LCRP reflected a compromise between the two groups by identifying all people who fled Syria and were unable to return as either "displaced Syrians,"

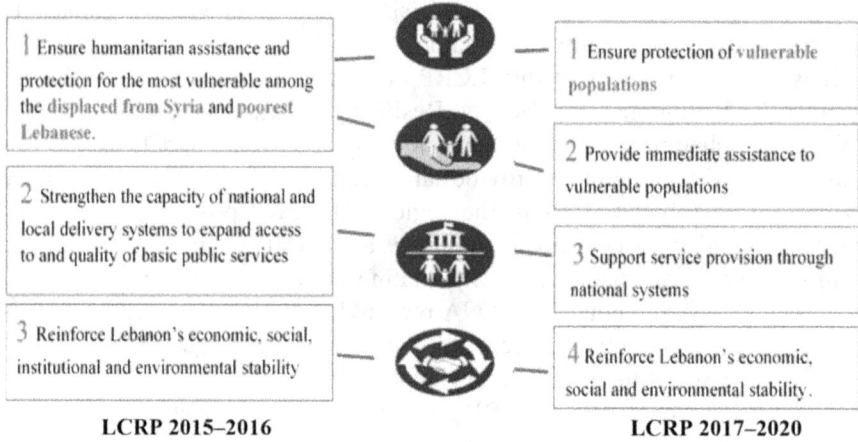

| LCRP 2015–2016 | LCRP 2017–2020 |

1 Ensure humanitarian assistance and protection for the most vulnerable among the displaced from Syria and poorest Lebanese.

2 Strengthen the capacity of national and local delivery systems to expand access to and quality of basic public services

3 Reinforce Lebanon's economic, social, institutional and environmental stability

1 Ensure protection of vulnerable populations

2 Provide immediate assistance to vulnerable populations

3 Support service provision through national systems

4 Reinforce Lebanon's economic, social and environmental stability.

Figure 3.1   Comparative Figure of Both LCRPs' Response Strategies. *Source:* Photo by Author.

"persons displaced from Syria," or "persons registered as de facto refugees by UNHCR."[30]

The fact that the LCRP does not recognize these masses as refugees with universally acknowledged rights exposes the gendered power struggle between the national government and the UNHCR in a clash of interests when deciding on legal status terminologies. Lebanese authorities discriminatorily labeled Syrians as "displaced" in an attempt to shield Lebanon from any potential obligations and responsibilities toward Syrian refugee communities. In contrast, the UNHCR, with limited authority over domestic decisions, kept the categorical label of a "person registered as a refugee" in order to fit its humanitarian programs.

Figure 3.1 depicts the major response areas of the 2015 LCRP mandate, comparing it with the updated 2017 version. The 2015–16 LCRP focused on three main objectives: to "ensure humanitarian assistance and protection" for displaced Syrians and vulnerable Lebanese constituents; to "strengthen the capacities of national and local delivering systems"; and to reinforce national socioeconomic and institutional stability.[31] The focus in 2015 was to expand the targeted vulnerable population in a 50–50 approach to burden sharing between the Lebanese government and the UNHCR by including both 1.5 million "vulnerable Lebanese" and 1.5 million "displaced Syrians."[32]

By the end of 2016, the decline in refugee livelihood and the increase of indebtedness exacerbated local negative coping mechanisms, calling for the 2017 LCRP proposal to expand refugee security measures into four strategic objectives. The updated partnership of UN and NGO partners thus grew from 77 in 2015 to 104 in 2017.[33] The updated plan's first goal was to ensure, through laws and regulations, the protection of vulnerable populations. Second, the LCRP 2017–2020 prioritized immediate aid assistance to *all* vulnerable populations living in substandard dwellings. Third, it aimed to support national systems in the provision of adequate water, hygiene, health care, energy, and child education, among many other sectors.[34] Fourth, it planned for the reinforcement of Lebanon's economic, social, and environmental stability that would expand livelihood opportunities and local resilience.

However, as highlighted in figure 3.1, Lebanese decision-making authorities imposed organizational changes to the LCRP in 2017, including a wider range of "vulnerable populations" that would encompass Iraqis, Somalis, and most importantly, the inaccurate government estimate of 300,000 preexisting Palestine refugees residing in Lebanon.[35] In reality, a "National Population and Housing Census of Palestinian Camps and Gatherings in Lebanon 2017" estimated that the actual number of Palestinian refugees in Lebanon was less than half of what the Lebanese authorities claimed.[36] The vagueness of policy language regarding "vulnerable populations" created room for opportunistic interest groups to engage in personal agendas unrelated to the Syrian refugee crisis, taking advantage of humanitarian aid. These changes, even if subtle, illustrate some of the complex dynamics between different agentic norm entrepreneurs who elaborated a short-term plan with a relatively limited role into a broader version with a focus on sustainable development.

LONGITUDINAL ANALYSIS OF THE 2015 AND 2017 LCRPS

The following visual representation of the major themes within the 2015 and 2017 LCRPs illustrates the thematic connections between the different initiatives, referred to in the LCRP as "targeted populations" and "targeting programs," for managing the Syrian refugee crisis in Lebanon.[37] Developed through textual interpretation and systemic coding, this form of *Code Mapping* provides an overall image of thematic labels, or "In Vivo" themes, that emerged from within both LCRP documents. It highlights the specific cultural themes of the evolving crisis through recurrent words that have a strategic impact on guiding future crisis response practices, making them dynamic forces of culturally accepted behavior.[38] The visual description in figure 3.1 also documents how a list of elected themes categorized and intersected with each other throughout both LCRP documents, comprising a complex web of interconnected networks.

The central nodes, each of which represents a significant theme in the LCRPs, such as "Humanitarian Assistance" and "Protection of Vulnerable Populations," reflect the proposed response strategies to the refugee crisis in Lebanon. The marked nodes at the top left, which include "Women" and "Elderly," among others, represent the targeted groups that the crisis response plans mainly focused on when providing protection, aid, and assistance. The marked nodes on the top right, which include "Community Engagement" and "Conflict Sensitivity Do No Harm," among others, represent the approaches that both plans concentrated the response efforts on. The arrows connecting one node to another are co-constitutive, visually representing the two-way thematic connections between targeted populations and strategies in the LCRPs. As one example, the "Crisis Response Plan" node interconnects with humanitarian assistance, which aims, for one, to provide education for the youth population. The density of arrows in certain areas illustrates the degree of attention targeted groups and approaches received as a means to reach the various crisis response goals.

While figure 3.2 provides an interesting visual representation of the major themes within both documents, and how they interconnect with each other, it does not help us analyze the changes that occurred from one LCRP version to the other. Therefore, it is imperative to trace the changes longitudinally

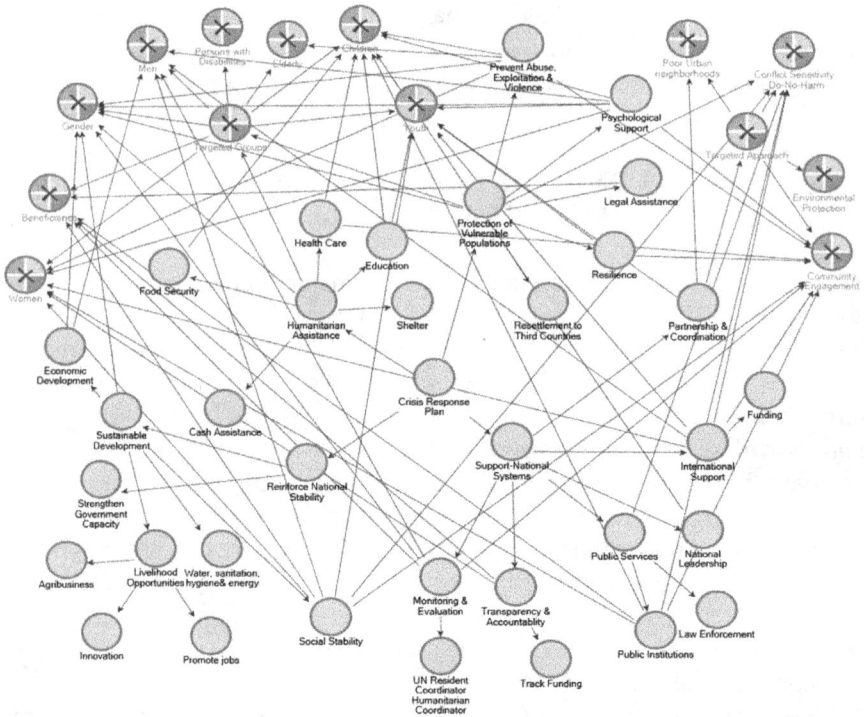

Figure 3.2   2015, 2017 Crisis Response Plans Thematical Project Map. *Source:* Photo by Author.

across the two LCRPs. A longitudinal cultural theme analysis provides an empirical example of how norm construction is affected by the dynamics of refugee (in)security management. It yields further insights into how strategic plans emerge and change across time from their original intentions, thus reflecting contextual variances.[39] And given that both LCRP plans deal with a "crisis," the comparatively short timeframe between the two versions is justified by the highly dynamic changes of interest when coping with the volatile realities of Lebanon's insecurities. To that end, the goal of this longitudinal cultural theme analysis is to comparatively analyze the two versions of the LCRP: the first two-year plan (2015–2016) and its revised four-year version (2017–2020).

A Visual Analysis of the LCRP Covers

The covers of both LCRP documents focused on a humanitarian view of assisting and protecting vulnerable populations. We find a sense of hope, comfort, and resilience being portrayed with images of women and children in positive environments. Such images posed a lesser threat than those of working men, who are absent from the LCRP covers, perceived as threatening and less likely to entice humanitarian funds. Interestingly, these visual techniques do not portray the "imagined figure" of refugees as powerless victims, desperately poor and in need of humanitarian aid, that refugee regimes typically rely on to mobilize public support and gather funds.[40]

Though these visuals took a more positive turn in the refugee story from "pictures [that] convey messages of conflict, of poverty and of suffering [. . .] the starving, fly-ridden child accompanied by a request for 'a dollar a day to save this child's life,'"[41] they are not objective. Published images are political acts, dependent on their authors' politicized frame to entice emotional reaction.[42] Images have agency by actively producing their own biased "truths," conveniently framing different groups of refugees aesthetically to entice empathy and compassion. As such, the impact of visuals prints a strong impression on readers' minds, provoking an immediate and complex emotional reaction. Politicized images can be somewhat helpful in that they reinforce the humanitarian perception of refugees as innocent and dependent, which garners empathy and compassion from audiences willing to fund humanitarian endeavors. However, such images are also problematic in that they visually engender depoliticized and non-threatening women and children, which misconstrues and silences the intersectional diversity within the Syrian refugee population in Lebanon.

In reality, the Syrian situation in Lebanon is far from this view of a helpless child requesting a hug, or one optimistic woman medically treating another in a safe indoor setting. These images are not representative of the Syrian refugee crisis and can lead to audiences misunderstanding the gravity of this crisis that the LCRPs aimed to manage. The million and some Syrians residing in Lebanon challenged this imagined depiction in that, in reality, 58 percent of displaced Syrian children were not attending school.[43] In addition, registered de facto Syrian women refugees were legally prohibited from any employment, let alone professional medicine. These visual constructions on the LCRP covers contributed to a mythical refugee identity, in which female refugees and children were portrayed amicably, and the absence of adult men resulted in the loss of their identity as productive members of the Lebanese community.

Thematic Analysis

Figure 3.3 outlines the continuation, diminishment, transformation, and change of the major themes deducted from both LCRP documents. As most of the themes collected fell within the first three categories in the table, the 2017 LCRP seemed to be continuing with the original crisis response mission, further operationalizing and elaborating the 2015 plan. It offered greater detail in the implementation schemes of mostly leadership, coordination, transparency, and accountability. In that respect, the 2017 LCRP (re)affirmed that the highest national authority in responding to the refugee crisis is the Lebanese government, with which all (inter)national partners need to coordinate when operating inside Lebanese territory.[44] One of the major operationalized themes was the "Promotion of National Leadership," which presented an opportunity to strengthen aid coordination and harmonization.

The Lebanese government made a slight but major change between both plans that would tremendously diminish its commitment to international refugee law: boosting its sovereign right to regulate the Syrian presence within the country according to its domestic laws. The qualitative comparison showed that in the 2015 LCRP, Lebanon "considers that it is being subject to a situation of mass influx and reserves the right to take measures aligning with international law and practice in such situations."[45] As for the updated 2017 LCRP version, the document bore no mention of any alignment with international law nor its practice. Instead, Lebanon reinforced its sovereign right to (en)gender the legal status of Syrians residing within the country by considering that "individuals who fled from Syria into its territory after March 2011 [were] temporarily displaced individuals and [Lebanon] reserves its sovereign right to determine their status according to Lebanese laws and regulations."[46] This small but impactful claim increased the Lebanese government's upper hand and impunity in managing the refugee crisis within the country, making room for unreceptive ad hoc Lebanese practices of controlling the magnified (il)legal Syrian presence.[47] As mentioned in the previous

Operational Themes: *Structures and personnel required for proper functioning of Plan*	
National Leadership: *Supporting national leadership and ownership of the response*	
Partnership & Coordination: *Mechanisms to coordinate and help systematize assessment processes and harmonize data collection and visualization tools. between different humanitarian partners*	
Transparency and Accountability: *Promote transparency and accountability*	
Monitoring & Evaluation: *Reinforced and objective monitoring and evaluation (M&E) is critical to improving effectiveness and accountability*	
Track Funding: *Improve the tracking of funds*	
Energy: *Increasing the level and quality of electricity supply*	
Continuous Themes: *Clearly and consistently articulated*	
International Support & Financing the LCRP: *Initiatives funded by the wider international community & donors*	
Refugee (In)securities: *Deteriorating environmental, socio-economic, health, water, sanitation, and electric capacities*	
Negative Coping Strategies: *Resorting to unsustainable and damaging coping mechanisms*	
Public Services: *Equitable access to and quality of sustainable public services*	
Elaborated Themes: *Detailed and specific with similar words and meanings*	
Protection: *Aims to strengthen protection services and interventions*	
Vulnerable Communities: *The most vulnerable and deprived parts of the country*	
Livelihood Opportunities: *Improve living conditions through job creation, increase market-based skills training and employability, apprenticeships, income-generation opportunities*	
Agribusiness: *Promote sustainable farming and animal management practices*	
Food Insecurity: *Malnutrition due to inadequate diets and unsanitary conditions*	
Targeted Assistance: *Persons with disabilities, youth, gender*	
Child Marriage, Labor & Trafficking: *Human rights violations*	
Violence Against Women and Children: *Human rights violations*	
Education: *Expanding formal and non-formal education*	
Shelter: *Promote affordable shelter and support for rental-related tenure security*	
Legal Status: *Regularize residency in Lebanon and access to civil registration processes*	
UN Resident Coordinator/Humanitarian Coordinator: *RC/HC*	
Resilience: *Resources and capacities that are needed to absorb, adapt and transform in the face of risks*	
Transforming Themes: *Contemporary words and phrases with similar meanings*	
Poor Urban Neighborhoods: *Urban cadasters in concentrated poverty*	
Resettlement to Third Countries: *Provide persons displaced from Syria humanitarian access to third countries*	
Diminishing Themes: *De-emphasized or absent*	
Institutional Stability: *Strengthening government, municipal, civic and community capacities to promote dialogue*	
Cash Assistance: *Aid program targeting the poorest with cash transfers*	
Beneficiaries: *Persons who gain or benefit in some way from something*	
Terrorist Threat & LAF: Militancy menace spreading from Syria provoking LAF and security personnel working to address multiple challenges	
Law Enforcement: *Enhancing the capacity of Lebanese law enforcement and justice systems*	
New Themes: *Outside of the original themes, meanings, and intentions*	
Elderly: *The accepted minimum chronological age of 65 years*	
Persons with disabilities: *Any person who has a physical or mental impairment that substantially limits one or more major life activities*	

Figure 3.3   Longitudinal Analysis of Major Cultural Themes from the LCRP2015–2016 to the LCRP 2017–2020. *Source:* Photo by Author.

chapter, legal status was of the utmost importance to Syrians residing in Lebanon. Subsequently, Lebanon's uncooperative claim further complicated the UNHCR's mandate to adequately protect and assist what they saw as an obvious case of de facto Syrian refugees. Most Syrian refugees, minority or not, were stuck in a legal limbo with limited mobility, potential deportation, and inability to access basic safety and emergency resources, among many

other problems. Having an ambiguous status could only lead to the detri-
ment of refugee assistance and protection in accessing essential services. The
UNHCR response techniques ended up downplaying their Global Refugee
Policy practices, which would have theoretically guaranteed the asylum seekers local integration and assimilation, for the sake of funding and practical
opportunities.

Another operational theme was "Partnership and Coordination." The 2017
LCRP proposed better planning and coordination with its international partners to "increase the focus on aid coordination with and through government
and non-government structures including UN agencies, NGOs, the private
sector, and academic institutions to promote transparency and enhanced
coordination."[48] This broadly defined term of "coordination" was politicized
by different partners with perceivably different interests. Several times, tension arose between involved parties, in which the Lebanese government
condemned the UNHCR for concealing the actual number of unofficially
registered Syrians with the UNHCR post-2015.[49] While Lebanon ordered the
cessation of Syrian registrations, the goals toward the management of Syrian residents were not shared by both agencies. In contestation, the UNHCR
practice of informally registering Syrians continued without official Lebanese
oversight over the updated number of residing refugees.[50] These day-to-day
response arrangements exposed a lack of strategic refugee crisis policy coordination between the Lebanese government and the UNHCR.

In addition, reports showed a lack of "Transparency and Accountability"
in sharing information about the different agencies' projects, funding, and
timing.[51] The 2015 LCRP's original idea of information-sharing and tracking through an online program named ActivityInfo increasingly developed
in the 2017 version in order to "provide a multi-year framework for mea-
suring progress in implementation, ensuring transparency, and facilitating
strategic and programmatic adjustments" (LCRP 2017). Theoretically, then,
the appealing partners were supposed to file full reports on funding and
other resources received through agreed upon systematic and transparent
reporting mechanisms. In practice, however, financial self-reporting was not
compulsory in that it "all depends on the extent to which organizations are
committed."[52] Therefore, measures for transparency and accountability were
not as prioritized by agencies in practice as much as they were proposed in
the LCRP documents, for there were no enforcement mechanisms in place to
encourage aid agencies' timely information disclosures.

Initially, a seemingly shared goal of transparency and accountability
between the international community and Lebanese government was evi-
denced by the use of common appropriation of agenda initiatives and goals.
However, upon closer inspection, a more complex gendered story of both
harmony and tension becomes apparent. While both parties genuinely aimed

for socioeconomic stability and an increase in government services and aid, the specific monitoring mechanisms regarding full disclosure, transparency, and accountability between partner agencies failed to deliver. As such, the fates of funding and other resources received were left at the discretion of the appealing partners. The partners' unwillingness to fully disclose information about received funds made it more difficult for LCRP steering committees to monitor individual agencies' activities and to hold them accountable for any discrepancies. Many political bodies are likely to allocate their funding directly to their constituents without documenting transactions in the ActivityInfo tracking system, leading to a poor exchange of sensitive information.

The politicization of the Syrian crisis in Lebanon created space for non-traditional donors, such as the Gulf Cooperation Council (GCC) and faith-based organizations, to play a central role in refugee management. An increasing number of non-traditional donors reportedly made up 12 percent of official humanitarian funding sources.[53] Sharing neither the same values nor the same goals as the international community, politically and ideologically motivated agencies consequently undermined need-driven aid policies. This led to a politicization of specific interests that excluded vulnerable groups who did not share the same religious, political, or cultural affiliations from accessing the non-traditional donors' funds. Additionally, given women's dire legal status in most Arab countries, gender stereotyping was exacerbated with the increase in non-traditional Arab states' funding assistance. Ultimately, these donors (en)gendered asymmetrical humanitarian aid systems, in which unchecked funding prioritized local patriarchal charities.[54] Consequently, the most vulnerable groups of refugees were (in)directly marginalized and silenced, undervaluing women-specific needs for the sake of non-traditional funding donors' gendered agendas. It became difficult for LCRP steering committees to oversee the non-traditional donors' work, let alone draw a clear picture of the type of funds, assistance, and aid distributions, and which groups those resources were targeting.

Beyond the operational themes discussed earlier, the interrelated diminishing themes of "Law Enforcement," "Lebanese Armed Forces," and "Terrorist Threats" were less visible in the 2017 LCRP. This can be attributed to the drastic weakening of the Islamic State of Iraq and the Levant (ISIL) in the region and the consequent decrease in terrorist threats affecting Lebanon's stability. In fact, we find that due to the surge of ISIL in 2014, the 2015 LCRP emphasized support for the LAF in thwarting terrorist threats (Lebanon witnessed around thirty terrorist attacks between 2013 and 2016, with thousands of Lebanese citizens deliberately targeted and hundreds killed).[55] That number tremendously decreased to almost no successful terrorist attacks claimed by ISIL in 2017, diminishing the need for the later LCRP to focus on those issues.[56]

New themes arose in the 2017 LCRP with terminologies such as "Elderly" and "Persons with Disabilities." The increased collaboration between the Lebanese government and humanitarian aid partners for the 2017 crisis response plan led to greater inclusion of previously marginalized groups, whose (in)securities were mostly silenced in the earlier LCRP document. This seemingly positive move for the 2017 LCRP to be more inclusive of a long list of previously marginalized vulnerable groups was, in reality, aimed at garnering greater funds from new potential donors for the non-prioritized sectors of "Shelter," "Water," "Health," and "Energy."[57] In practice, despite the efforts to use more inclusive terminology in the newer LCRP version, the translation of the plan into concrete domestic policies that would encourage inclusivity toward minority groups fell short, outpaced resource and capacity wise. Most of the funding received for the 2017 LCRP focused on themes such as "Basic Assistance," "Food Security," and "Education," which mentioned neither the "Elderly" nor "Persons with Disabilities."[58]

It is important to note that both LCRPs were mainly addressed to international donors, as stated in their "Needs Overview" sections, in requests for "International Support and Financing" from the international community. In fact, the 2017 version "reaffirms the international community's commitment to support and reinforce the response capacity of national/local institutions and humanitarian actors [. . .] through the development of a four-year plan that asks for an investment in Lebanon and supports to the population that Lebanon hosts."[59] These repeated calls for funding stemmed from the shortfall of pledged resources which donor countries had yet to provide.[60] With only 45 percent of the 2017 interagency appeals having been met, the immediate humanitarian needs of the "targeted vulnerable groups" of Syrian refugees were barely met.[61]

Both plans called for innovative responses that could address the deteriorating refugee crisis within the country."[62] In theory, the 2015 LCRP was a transitional plan to the 2017 LCRP, which expanded on stabilization and development by calling for a transition from immediate emergency relief efforts to long-term sustainable plans for empowering local vulnerable bodies, sustaining their livelihood and resilience efforts. Still, as a UNHCR expert interviewee stated, "it's very early to speak of development."[63] As such, the 2017 strategic plan aimed at strengthening the ideals of the 2015 plan, highlighting the challenges faced by refugees more holistically by creating new divisions such as the "Livelihoods Sector Steering Committee," which was a step toward more coordinated engagement in restoring and expanding economic opportunities for refugees.

But, as the Syrian crisis worsened, the repercussions in Lebanon became more profound. According to the World Bank's 2013 estimate, the Syrian war would go on to cost Lebanon's economy $7.5 billion USD annually with a significant decline in trade and tourism.[64] The four-year plan that was put in place in 2017 furthered its request for burden sharing, mostly through investment and local support, to strengthen government capacity and to protect and assist an elaborated group of vulnerable populations residing within the country. While warning of "increasing negative coping strategies" and "dependence on external aid," the 2017 LCRP document appealed for further aid and collaboration in easing the chronic problems without recognizing the targeted vulnerable people's potential of being strategic partners in finding the right solutions. Even when an average of $1.5 billion in aid funds was allocated every year to Lebanon, those resources mainly targeted unsustainable short-term humanitarian projects.[65] Counterintuitively, a considerable ratio of those funds neither supported Syrian refugees' livelihood and resilience efforts nor the host state's stability and social solidarity in the areas where displaced Syrians were living. Instead, reports, as illustrated in figure 3.3, show that the severity of Syrian refugee living conditions worsened to the point that most funds were limited to direct aid such as food, cash assistance, education, and basic health services.[66] Important sectors geared toward long-term sustainable development, such as social stability and livelihood, were the most underfunded.[67] As such, newspapers, such as *Annahar*, reported that the dire consequences of Syrian poor living conditions were fast increasing, becoming more visible with the rise of chronic disease, suicide, use of violence, and hard labor cases.[68]

It is important to note here that Lebanese integration rhetoric religiously nationalized citizenship by privileging those who are perceived to belong to specific sects (such as Christians) for not threatening the overall sectarian balance that keeps Lebanon (dis)functional.[69] Accordingly, Lebanon's outcries toward the global community's lack of participation in refugee burden sharing were coupled with a demand for the prioritization of Lebanon's own infrastructure and vulnerable communities over the residing Syrians' welfare.

The only favored solution that was further elaborated in the 2017 LCRP document was "Resettlement to Third Countries." The 2017 plan changed the approach from stating that resettlement is a preferred solution to advocating for an actual mechanism to be put in place to provide "persons displaced from Syria humanitarian access to third countries."[70] Still, with less than one percent of the global refugee population resettled as of 2016, no third-party country had shown any interest in accommodating enough Syrian refugees to make a viable contribution to this plan.[71] Therefore, stressing the need to resettle Syrians in third countries furthered unrealistic expectations about the degree to which resettlement measures could reach enough Syrian refugees in Lebanon, constituting a major setback for any durable solution proposed.

A Gender Analysis

Table 3.1 displays the figures, per sector, of appealing partners, financial requirements, target population, and, most importantly, the gender markers prioritized in each LCRP document. As the UNHCR's expert interviewee stated, "Each sector has a gender marker. So, any code that is attributed to the sector is based on the international gender marker scoring that indicated to which level the sector was integrating gender analysis and responses that were gender oriented in the plan." That said, a pool of gender experts that were part of the Gender-Based Violence (GBV) task force were tasked with reviewing and rating each sector during the planning process.[72] According to these experts, the alterations of gender markers between the two LCRP documents reflect the material interpretation, cultural expression, and written evidence of change in guiding future crisis response plans. With a gender marker included in both plans, it is crucial to note that this critical tool did not only score humanitarian projects on whether they provide enough aid and support to different groups of men, women, girls, and boys with sustainable outcomes.[73] It also tracks the level of funding these groups were allocated, and whether the plans themselves actually promoted greater reflection on gender issues and projects.

Generally, during any project design, gender specialists from the Inter-Agency Standing Committee (IASC) support each sector's team in coding their cluster's projects.[74] The IASC would then "explore and gain an appreci-ation of how to integrate gender issues well in their projects."[75] Theoretically, this technique would therefore benefit policy planners, as the given feedback can be used to improve each sector's operational plan, implementation, and monitoring system. Typically, the IASC provides one of three markers as a way to strengthen gender-sensitive humanitarian assistance.[76] However, according to the UNHCR's SGBV coordinator:

> We do not have, like in Jordan, a gender expert in Lebanon but we have [an] SGBV task force which is acting for this role [. . .] What we currently have is partially related to gender but more focusing on the GBV. So, Lebanon is one of the countries that is [. . . .] not fully in terms of gender equality yet, but it covers one aspect of this [gender-based violence].[77]

As seen in table 3.1, gender mainstreaming efforts beyond Sexual Gender Based Violence (SGBV) were not a priority in any of the ten LCRP response sectors of the humanitarian crisis management mission in Lebanon. There seems to be a tendency to dismiss or deprioritize gender discrimination and inequality as secondary issues when moving forward with plans that do not tackle, beyond GBV, gender issues. In the LCRPs, most gender mainstream-ing initiatives took a back seat under the banner of long-term development or social-empowerment sustainable projects.

Table 3.1 Major Comparisons between the 2015–2016 and 2017–2020 Lebanon Crisis Response Plans

LCRP		Protection	Social Stability	Livelihood	Health	Basic Assistance	Water	Energy	Education	Food Security	Shelter	Total
LCRP15-16	Partners	33	27	27	24	29	33		28	13	23	77
	Requirements (millions US$)	$183.00	$157.30	$175.90	$249.20	$288.60	$391.20		$26.60	$447.00	$147.20	$2,480.20
	Target	2185000	242	242536	204000	889500	2862291		377000	1236976	1368255	2.9 million
	Gender Marker	2a	1	2a	1	1	1		1	1	2a	
LCRP17-20	Partners	61	51	47	43	42	37	13	32	30	28	104
	Requirements (millions US$)	$163.80	$123.80	$195.70	$308.00	$571.50	$280.00	$99.20	$376.60	$507.20	$128.70	$2,750.50
	Target	1887502	2236299	65557	1535297	1276000	1959428	1119171	543616	961388	536002	2.8 million
	Gender Marker	2a	2a	2a	2a	2a	2a	2a	1	2a	0	

Photo by Author.

Still, a detailed account of how gender markers came to be established within each LCRP sector helps us understand how and why each marker shown in table 3.1 was given. In that respect, what was coded in the 2015 LCRP as the gender marker "1," coding the "Education" sector, meant that only one of the three essential gender components (needs assessment, sector responses or performance indicators) were included in the plan, making a limited contribution to gender equality. Meanwhile, the "2a" gender marker, coding most of the sectors of the 2017 LCRP, signified that a significant step forward was made in including gender analysis in the project's design and some of its activities, creating one or more gender mainstreamed outcomes. However, the third gender marker, "2b," was still absent from both plans' evaluations, as concluded by the relevant authorities' examination, which meant that neither LCRP advanced gender equality nor built gender-specific services that would reach the level of gender inclusivity were required for their successful implementation. As for marking a sector "0," it meant that the sector response plan did not reflect any gender component, risking the (un)intentional deepening of existing gender inequalities.[78] Looking closely, the 2015 LCRP document had the "Shelter" sector rated at "2a," while in the 2017 plan, the gender marker dropped to "0." This sharp drop should cause serious alarm for an external reviewer who is contemplating on funding the crisis response plan in general, and the shelter sector specifically. The only reasonable justification that could be given here is that the collaborating agencies did not properly assess the "shelter" sector, or that it wasn't a priority goal to be sought anymore.

Gender equality policies remained narrowly articulated and limited by the goal of simply adding "women" to existing policies and operations. On that note, when looking at the evolution of the LCRP plan from 2015 to 2017, from the first read, it is noticeable that both LCRP documents barely mentioned "women," homogenizing them as part of a growing list of vulnerable groups. And, when mentioned, women were loosely associated with vulnerable groups in general, and no clear plans addressed their specific gendered (in)securities. Although they formed the majority of registered refugees, Syrian "women" were mostly dispersed in both plans among the different "targeted groups," such as "women, girls, boys and men, including pregnant and lactating women, youth, persons with disabilities, elderly, survivors of gender-based violence, persons living with HIV/AIDS, persons facing gender-based discrimination and other vulnerable groups."[79] Even though increased attention was paid to the various targeted vulnerable groups, whose troubles were deemed necessary to include in the later LCRP, these vulnerable populations' needs were barely assessed. The constant marginalization of women as mere victims of abuse and violence is particularly seen in the case of unemployment noted in LCRP documents, furthering Syrian women refugees' daily (in)securities. Gender-specific policies for women are practically nonexistent outside of "eliminating sexual exploitation and sexual and gender-based violence."[80] Consequently, both LCRPs marginalized the "78 percent of Syrians registered as refugees with UNHCR [that] are women and children,"[81] stripping them of any productive agency by conflating their specific needs and policies under one targeted group.

Even when there were female leaders in Lebanese ministries, knowledgeable in gender-inclusive urban planning or other related fields, the level of commitment to enhancing gender-inclusive response plans could not overcome the preexisting system of oppression established within Lebanon's confessional system. As mentioned in the previous chapter, women in Lebanon were expected to have a lesser status than their male counterparts. These women were objectified and heavily marginalized due to intersectional structural inequalities and a discriminatory legal system. That is why genuine gender mainstreaming efforts took a back seat, depoliticized as administrative long-term development goals that were not a priority.

After all, gender equality initiatives were mostly used as lip service in a "Needs Overview" section with no power or concrete measures included to address the gendered asymmetries in Syrian refugee situations, (re)producing global hierarchies. As the Abaad expert stated, the LCRP documents were at the end of a funding appeal. Their main targets were donors. The Lebanese state directed its attention toward its own stability while attempting to tolerate the problematic "temporary displaced individuals," granting them securitized conditional asylum. Due to the unprecedented strain on the country's economy, infrastructure, and public services, the state's security was deemed more important than properly aligning incoming funds to restore and expand adequate initiatives for economic and livelihood opportunities for refugees. Meanwhile, the UNHCR and appealing partners reinforced a false gender identity in both LCRPs' "Needs Overview" sections, depicting a conflated and feminized de facto refugee population of oppressed victims with no agency, in "need of rescue, protection, assistance, activation, and reform."[82] Counterintuitively, the humanitarian protection, assistance, and aid advertised within both plans mostly aimed at acquiring more funds, rather than considering these individuals' complex dilemmas as serious issues that needed to be tackled instantly.

While the LCRP commends the amelioration of the policy initiatives within its sustainable development programs, this enhancement is valued but still considered insufficient, not prioritizing the need to address gender inequality with clear-cut synergies. While a reasonable goal was to protect most Syrians residing in Lebanon, women and girls were still disproportionately burdened by restrictions on their access to adequate and affordable services. In many instances, the LCRP mechanisms that sought to promote de facto Syrian refugees' livelihood goals seemed to undermine the gendered barriers to women's employment within the legally approved fields of construction, agribusiness, and sanitation. Consequently, using such approach without tackling the system's gender hierarchies within Lebanese polities ended up (in)directly denying Syrian women refugees the fundamental right to find a decent job to procure food, water, and most importantly, safety. Given the Lebanese context, the cultural and legal discrimination against women working in public spaces, far from any form of palpable security, impeded their safety from any type of local violence, such as sexual abuse, harassment, and exploitation.

In the meantime, the UNHCR practices seemed stuck between the tendencies of developing and modernizing the perceived "backward" refugee society by calling for more livelihood initiatives, while, at the same time, no tangible initiative was implemented on their part to redress the harmful state laws and practices that challenged Syrian women's fundamental rights to live free from harm and free from want.[83] The portrayal of a vulnerable de facto refugee community narrowly focused on the utility perspective of gender mainstreaming in garnering international support and funds.[84] This analysis shows that the LCRP efforts to empower Syrian women and eradicate gender-based violence were complicated by the tradition of the feminized long-term development of women's issues with no tangible solutions. Without an all-encompassing gender-sensitive livelihood approach, Syrian women were silenced through piecemeal remedies to aid "temporary displaced individuals" within the patriarchal Lebanese culture that isolates gender violence from other feminized "women's issues."[85]

For instance, one case highlighting the reality of GBV was the unprecedented scandal in Lebanon in April 2016, in which the media exposed major prostitution and human trafficking rings operating in the country.[86] In fact, one of these rings was found to have enslaved hundreds of Syrian women for periods of months, and even years, since the onset of the refugee crisis in 2011.[87] What initially seemed to be a single prostitution ring turned out to be multiple rings, involving hundreds of helpless female victims that had been lured, captured, and held against their will at several touristic locations.[88] Within weeks, several arrests took place, and the traffickers and brothel owners, such as Maurice Geagea, were placed in custody, only to be discharged a few months later.[89] Despite allegations to the contrary, these human trafficking and prostitution rings benefited from protection from corrupt politicians and security officers, which allowed them to escape the extreme punitive measures they deserved under the rule of law. When Chez Maurice nightclub was raided, the owner Maurice Haddad already had criminal charges for trafficking women into forced prostitution. The police knew of his criminal background, but he remained free.[90] Investigations and media coverage stopped after the arrest of significant ring operators, failing to address the structural, legal, and cultural factors that had permitted the continuation of such crimes in the first place.

Several observations are highly relevant in this context. First, all the female victims enslaved and exploited by these rings were Syrian girls and women, with a considerable number of them being under the age of eighteen when they were first subjected to this systemic exploitation.[91] Second, these women were ensnared in human trafficking and prostitution rings in the context of an armed conflict in their country, but the humanitarian regime failed to protect them adequately. They were, in fact, tarnished as probable prostitutes in a neighboring country where they were supposed to have at least a minimal degree of protection in accordance with international and domestic laws. Third, even though the mechanisms that protect women against these atrocities were widely publicized, state agents and humanitarian agencies (un)willingly failed to prevent the sex trafficking and exploitation of several hundred of Syrian women.[92]

According to *The Guardian* interview with Rama, a twenty-four-year-old Syrian woman who escaped sex trafficking with other captives from a local Lebanese brothel where they were held hostage, the deficiencies in Lebanon's human trafficking law coexist with an already discriminatory prostitution law in the penal code, which treats female victims in prostitution rings as equivalent to their traffickers. Rama, a Syrian woman and a survivor of GBV, initially lost faith in her country when she crossed over to Lebanon. Once in the host country, she then claimed to have lost faith in everyone, as she was forced to "have sex on average ten times a day and [was] imprisoned in a decrepit house without even a glimpse of sunlight."[93] The case of Rama is a good example of how resilient Syrian women survivors were pushed to seek protection under informal networks as they had to go to paramilitary political organizations' local offices, such as Hezbollah's, rather than reaching out to the Lebanese Internal Security Forces or a renowned humanitarian agency.[94]

Still, the shocking exposure of the prostitution rings did not significantly result to alleviating the gender-based insecurities that the majority of Syrian women residing in Lebanon face daily. On the contrary, official and non-official statements in the mainstream media and social media mainly focused on condemning the criminal acts, while sometimes even faulting the victims for being in that position. At the beginning, various statements highlighted the fact that Lebanon, as a state and as a nation, was treating Syrian refugees in accordance with international standards despite the great burden of hosting a massive population of Syrian refugees.[95] Within weeks after exposing the prostitution rings, the entire issue of women's refugee rights and suffering was almost forgotten. In the meantime, the UNHCR condemned such actions, stating that the LCRP plans provided mechanisms for Syrian women survivors to seek post-trauma emergency and life-saving services, without being able to tackle the broader economic, institutional, and policy constraints that hinder women from accessing and receiving the type of care they need.

All in all, even with the few improvements that were made in the later LCRP, this chapter has shown that a gender-based analysis was not a priority in determining the needs of the different vulnerable groups that the 2017 LCRP document sought to identify. Both LCRPs fell short when prescribing adequate solutions, where most Syrian refugees, minority or not, lost their legal status in the country with limited mobility. Recognizing the diversity among the vulnerable populations was imperative and needed further exploration. However, it seems that the plans' primary crisis response was still discriminatory, for neither LCRP seemed to focus on advancing gender equality, or targeting women, girls, boys, and men according to their specific needs. Still, one should not disregard the sporadic moments in the LCRPs when gender differences were clearly acknowledged and targeted groups were clearly described, such as in the case of the protection sector, which gained more attention than the shelter sector. Not surprisingly, the leading figure of both sectors at that time in the government's MoSA was Dr. Aimee Karam, whose doctorate in criminal justice adds to her working experience in UNICEF Beirut as a Child Protection Specialist would naturally lead her to focus more on protection.[96]

SYNTHESIZING THE REFUGEE
CRISIS RESPONSE PLANS

This chapter showed how the Lebanese crisis response plans were social constructions tied to both the international community and local polities, highlighting the dynamics between the main contributors: the Lebanese government and the UNHCR. The analysis underscored the organizational theme changes from 2015 to 2017, broadly connecting them to the complex dynamics of norm translation practices that engage with their fluid environment. On the one hand, many nodes and themes diminished from one plan to the other, such as "terrorist threats," "Lebanese armed forces," and security. This indicates that security problems related to those themes were either successfully controlled or ceased to be a major problem in the public eye. On the other hand, only two new themes—elderly and disabled persons—emerged in the 2017 plan, which can be considered a reflection of the host society's adoption of elaborated strategies for sustainable development such as the expansion of targeted groups and protection techniques. Meanwhile, important themes identified in the 2015 LCRP—such as funding, livelihood, education, and public services—continued, recurring in the 2017 LCRP through mundane bureaucratic practices and refugee management efforts that reinforced the ad hoc securitization technique of an (en)gendered conditional hospitality.[97] Most challenges facing Syrian refugees in Lebanon addressed in 2015 were still mentioned in the 2017 plan, reflecting the host society's feeling of unease toward a feminized Syrian population residing within the country.

Still, the discussed changes between the two LCRPs created room for hope in the refugee crisis management approach, with the setbacks from the first version instigating innovative responses that could empower both Lebanese citizens and Syrian refugees. The second LCRP version seemed more focused and inclusive to previously invisible and new realities—"energy," persons with specific needs such as "elderly" and "persons with disabilities," and "youth." It built on the 2015 LCRP version to generate various programming activities, seemingly eliminating issues such as gender-based violence. However, in practice the second plan's development project for social stability did not match up to the continuing insecurities on the ground. The refugee crisis was still on emergency mode, not controlled yet, such that Lebanese national interest measures justified exceptional mechanisms of refugee deterrence and exclusion. In all the interviews that were conducted, the interviewees stated that the main weakness of the 2017 LCRP program was the lack of funding and disproportionate deterioration of the refugee crisis situation. Even though the expert interviewees raised many continuing serious issues, such as limited refugee participation, lack of transparency, and legal discriminations, funding seemed to be the main theme of their complaints and not the root cause of the unsustainable structural system of interrelating privileges, power, and status quo.

Although this analysis showed some improvement in addressing the challenges facing refugees in a sustainable contextual manner, still the stereotyped perception of Syrian refugees as both dependent and problematic, which both Lebanon and the international community bought into, mostly remained. Despite official declarations in favor of refugee protection in general, both states and international organizations did not accurately address Syrian women's insecurities, and in turn, their human rights, livelihoods, and resilience were often objectified and not prioritized. Other than momentarily mentioning women in specific refugees' protection measures, such as those combating sexual and gender-based violence or targeting psychological support and monitoring systems, within both crisis response plans, women were absent from major response approaches with no gender-specific empowerment measures.[98] Subsequently, limited refugee emergency relief offered neither refugees gender-comprehensive aid protection nor real prospects in the long term, especially in the context of a protracted crisis.[99] This latter was highlighted in the gender marker change within both documents, where (en)gendered security concerns were still often prioritized, commonly leading to a gap between stated gender empowerment intentions and the local refugee management practices that objectified the majority of Syrian refugee women's insecurities. According to both LCRP documents, Syrian women were still viewed as lacking both the legal status and local support within their patriarchal environment to have their concerns prioritized, including those that were directly linked to their personal security and survival.

While Syrian women residing in Lebanon were forced to engage the public sphere to secure their livelihoods, this study shows that neither LCRP provided them with the necessary tools to successfully navigate the public sphere as productive members. In effect, one of the most problematic issues with the LCRPs' design is that they were based on the assumption that the top crisis response managers had the moral responsibility and exclusive role to save the de facto refugees and vulnerable Lebanese communities by *doing for them* rather than *working with them* to empower their self-reliance efforts.[100] As much as the initiatives pushed for refugee security, there was a disjuncture between international norms promoted by state representatives, international agencies, and bureaucrats, and the reality on the ground. Looking at the covers of both refugee crisis response plans, the images of depoliticized women and children were displayed to incite empathy.[101] These images were strategic in the construction of political (non)agency, further objectifying vulnerable groups in hopes of mobilizing public support and gathering more funds to address the refugees and their insecurities.[102] These images were justified as being necessary for the LCRPs' mission and survival in theory and practice, for these were the tools that would generate enough money to keep their relief programs and jobs up and running within the host communities.

On another note, this chapter showed that most of the alterations made between the two LCRPs did not seem to ease the Syrian presence in Lebanon. Dealing with such a critical humanitarian situation with an increasing collection of competing nongovernmental partners (104 appealing UN and NGO organizations) brings up many challenges and criticisms from all parties. This created room for misperception, where numbers have become essential to monitoring and evaluating the feminized Syrian population as a burden: backward and dependent on aid assistance. The inaccurate statistics and numbers became necessary to convey as much human misery as possible and mobilize sufficient donor funds for one of the competing sustainable solutions offered within the crisis response plans. Standard operating procedures, regarding who gets what, when, and how, were spread among thousands of interested NGOs that did not necessarily partner with the LCRP plans and whose accountability was poorly managed by both the Lebanese government and UNHCR.[103] Accordingly, resilience intervention programs through these agencies hardly empowered refugees' livelihoods without the government's blessing, counterintuitively discriminating against the same refugees they were attempting to protect.

In that respect, using a longitudinal organizational cultural theme analysis, this chapter was able to shed light on the dynamics of refugee management, aid assistance, and prevention of violence in an already fragile country. This study fills an empirical void on exploring the gendered power relations between a developing host country like Lebanon, which has a long history with the population seeking asylum, and a seasoned international humanitarian agency like the UNHCR. These institutions had to adapt to the case of a protracted Syrian refugee crisis and cooperate in refugee management practices, showing elements of resistance, compromise, and (re)construction of gendered crisis response plans for the sake of refugee protection and national stability. As such, the altruistic-intentioned crisis response plans assumed that the providers and administrators of relief possessed a mandate to save those who were oppressed and in need. These discourses emphasized the politicization of the refugee crisis while, at the same time, depoliticizing the Syrian refugees, excluding them from the crisis response strategy formulation and practice. Simultaneously, the vulnerable otherness that the Syrian refugees represented was contested within Lebanese public discourse, which capitalized on the assumption that Syrian refugees were opportunistic, "needy, helpless, and dependent on those who will help, save and modernize them."[104] Consequently, these strategies objectified the refugees' insecurities, reinforcing and (re)producing the unsustainability of the Syrian refugee crisis in Lebanon.

NOTES

1. Jennifer Hyndman, "Managing Difference: Gender and Culture in Humanitarian Emergencies." *Gender, Place and Culture: A Journal of Feminist Geography* 5, no. 3 (1998): 241–60.

2. Anne Hammerstad, *The Rise and Decline of a Global Security Actor: UNHCR, Refugee Protection, and Security* (Oxford University Press, 2014), 2.

3. Hammerstad, *The Rise and Decline of a Global Security Actor,* 2.

4. Ibid., 2.

5. R. Charli Carpenter, "Women, Children, and Other Vulnerable Groups: Gender, Strategic Frames, and the Protection of Civilians as a Transnational Issue." *International Studies Quarterly* 49, no. 2 (June 2005): 295–355.

6. Carpenter, "Women, Children, and Other Vulnerable Groups," 295–355.

7. Emma Haddad, *The Refugee in International Society: Between Sovereigns,* Vol. 106 (Cambridge University Press, 2008), 35.

8. Elisabeth Olivius, "Constructing Humanitarian Selves and Refugee Others: Gender Equality and the Global Governance of Refugees." *International Feminist Journal of Politics* 18, no. 2 (2016): 270–90.

9. Heather L. Johnson, "Click To Donate: Visual Images, Constructing Victims and Imagining the Female Refugee." *Third World Quarterly* 32, no. 6 (2011): 1015–37.

10. Johnson, "Click To Donate," 1015–37.

11. Ibid., 1015–37.

12. Alison Gerard and Sharon Pickering, "Gender, Securitization and Transit: Refugee Women and the Journey to the EU." *Journal of Refugee Studies* 27, no. 3 (2014): 338–59.

13. Jane Freedman, "Mainstreaming Gender in Refugee Protection." *Cambridge Review of International Affairs* 23, no. 4 (2010): 589–607.

14. James Milner, "Introduction: Understanding Global Refugee Policy." *Journal of Refugee Studies* 27, no. 4 (2014): 477–94.

15. Freedman, "Mainstreaming Gender in Refugee Protection," 596.

16. Skran Claudena, "UNHCR's Gender Policy for Refugees and Returnees in Sierra Leone." *African and Asian Studies* 14, no. 1–2 (2015): 108–33.

17. "Country Operations Plan." *UNHCR,* 2004, http://www.unhcr.org/3fd9c6a14.pdf

18. Alice Szczepanikova, "Performing Refugeeness in the Czech Republic: Gendered Depoliticisation through NGO Assistance." *Gender, Place & Culture* 17, no. 4 (2010): 461–77.

19. Johnson, "Click to Donate," 1015–37.

20. Michael Barnett, "Humanitarianism Transformed." *Perspectives on Politics* 3, no. 4 (2005): 723–40.

21. Edgar H. Schein, "Defining Organizational Culture." *Classics of Organization Theory* 3, no. 1 (1985): 490–502.

22. Franke Ulrich, "Inter-organizational Relations: Five Theoretical Approaches," *Oxford Research Encyclopedia of International Studies* (Oxford University Press, 2017).

23. Susanne Zwingel, *Translating International Women's Rights: The CEDAW Convention in Context* (Palgrave Macmillan, 2016).

24. Kerstin Rosenow-Williams and Katharina Behmer, "Gendered Environmental Security in IDP and Refugee Camps." *Peace Review* 27, no. 2 (2015): 188–95.

25. Anne Schneider and Helen Ingram, "Social Construction of Target Populations: Implications for Politics and Policy." *American Political Science Review* 87, no. 2 (1993): 334–47.

26. Government of Lebanon and UNHCR, *Lebanon Crisis Response Plan 2015–2016* (2015), 14.

27. Government of Lebanon and the United Nations, *Lebanon Crisis Response Plan 2015–2016* (2015), 4.

28. Government of Lebanon and the United Nations, *Lebanon Crisis Response Plan 2017–2020* (2017), 20.

29. Ibid., 20.

30. Ibid., 4.

31. Ibid., 4.

32. Government of Lebanon and UNHCR, *Lebanon Crisis Response Plan 2015–2016* (2015), 14.

33. Government of Lebanon and UNHCR, *Lebanon Crisis Response Plan 2017–2020* (2017), 15.

34. Ibid., 15.

35. Ibid., 11, 48.

36. Monika Borgmann and Lokman Slim, "Fewer Refugees More Refugeeism." *UMAM D&R Documentation and Research* (2018), https://umam-dr.org/en/home/projects/14/advance-contents/188/fewer-refugees-more-refugeeism

37. Government of Lebanon and UNHCR, *Lebanon Crisis Response Plan 2015–2016* (2015), 7.

38. Dennis Wiedman and Iveris L. Martinez, "Organizational Culture Theme Theory and Analysis of Strategic Planning for a New Medical School." *Human Organization* 76, no. 3 (2017): 265.

39. Wiedman and Martinez, "Organizational Culture Theme Theory and Analysis of Strategic Planning for a New Medical School," 266.

40. Johnson, "Click to Donate," 1015–37.

41. Ibid., 1015–37.

42. Ibid., 1015–37.

43. LCRP 2017 P.

44. LCRP 2017.

45. Government of Lebanon and UNHCR, *Lebanon Crisis Response Plan 2015–2016* (2015), x.

46. Government of Lebanon and UNHCR, *Lebanon Crisis Response Plan 2017–2021* (2017), 4.

47. Nabih Bulos, "In Lebanon, a Rape and Murder Galvanize Anti-Syrian Fervor." *Los Angeles Times* (October 13, 2017), http://www.latimes.com/world/middleeast/la-fg-lebanon-syria-slaying-2017-story.html.

48. LCRP 2017.

49. "Lebanon Freezes UNHCR Staff Residency Applications In Row Over Syrian Refugees," *Reuters* (June 8, 2018).

50. Dionigi Filippo, "The Syrian Refugee Crisis in Lebanon: State Fragility and Social Resilience." *LSE, Middle East Centre paper series, 15.* UK (2016), 25.

51. "Following the Money Lack of Transparency in Donor Funding for Syrian Refugee Education." *Human Rights Watch* (September 14, 2017), https://www.hrw.org/report/2017/09/14/following-money/lack-transparency-donorfunding-syrian-refugee-education.

52. Abadd expert

53. Dalya Mitri, "Challenges of Aid Coordination in a Complex Crisis: An Overview of Funding Policies and Conditions Regarding Aid Provision to Syrian Refugees in Lebanon." *Civil Society Knowledge Center* (2014): 15.

54. Batl Sadliwal. "Including Women, Excluding Migrants, and Reimagining National Belonging in the GCC." *World Peace Foundation* (March 12, 2018), https://sites.tufts.edu/reinventingpeace/2018/03/12/including-women-excludingmigrants-and-reimagining- national-belonging-in-the-gcc/.

55. Cherri Zeinab, Pedro Arcos González, and Rafael Castro Delgado, "The Lebanese–Syrian Crisis: Impact of Influx of Syrian Refugees to an Already Weak State." *Risk Management and Healthcare Policy* 9 (2016): 165.

56. Global Terrorism Database, https://www.start.umd.edu/gtd/search/Results. aspx?expanded=no&search=Lebanon&ob=GTDID&od=desc&page=1&count=100 #results-table.

57. Government of Lebanon and UNHCR, *Lebanon Crisis Response Plan 2017–2020* (2017), 68, 93,142, 166.

58. Ibid., 10.

59. Ibid., 22.

60. "Lebanon Between the Largest Displacement and the Least Aid." *Emirates News Agency* (June 6, 2017), https://www.zawya.com/mena/en/story/ Some_60000_Syrian_refugees_in_Lebanon__   Jordan_could_lose_assistance_ warns_UNHCR-WAM20170606192048379.

61. "Lebanon Between the Largest Displacement and the Least Aid."

62. Government of Lebanon and UNHCR, *Lebanon Crisis Response Plan 2017–2020* (2017), 5.

63. UNHCR Expert Interview.

64. Dominic Evans, "Syria War, Refugees to Cost Lebanon $7.5 Billion: World Bank." *Reuters* (September 19, 2013), https://www.reuters.com/article/us-syria-cris is-lebanon-idUSBRE98I0T320130919.

65. Jad Chaaban, "Should Lebanon Get More Funds for Hosting Refugees?" *Al Jazeera* (April 5, 2017), https://www.aljazeera.com/indepth/features/2017/04/leba non-funds-hosting-refugees-170405082414586.html.

66. UNHCR, "LCRP Steering Committee Meeting Report." July 3, 2018, https:// data2.unhcr.org/en/documents/ download /64971.

67. UNHCR Expert Interview with Author (May 18, 2017).

68. Rita Sfeir, "Migration Is Increasing and the 'Specter' of Bosnia and Rwanda Present Any Repercussions of Russian Military Intervention on Asylum?"*Annahar News* (September 20, 2015), https://newspaper.annahar.com/article/276860

69. Meier Daniel, "Lebanon: The Refugee Issue and the Threat of a Sectarian Confrontation." *Oriente Moderno* 94, no. 2 (2014): 382–401.

70. Government of Lebanon and the United Nations, *Lebanon Crisis Response Plan: 2017–2020* (2017), 19.

71. "Global Trends: Forced Displacement in 2015" *UNHCR* (2016), https:// www.unhcr.org/576408cd7.

72. UNHCR Expert Interview with Author (May 18, 2017).

73. Check Appendix A.

74. Check Appendix A.

75. Ibid.

76. Ibid. See also Government of Lebanon and the United Nations, *Lebanon Crisis Response Plan 2017–2020* (2017).

77. UNHCR Expert Interview with Author (May 18, 2017).

78. Siobhán Foran, Aisling Swaine, and Kate Burns, "Improving the Effective-ness of Humanitarian Action: Progress in Implementing the Inter-Agency Standing

Committee (IASC) Gender Marker." *Gender & Development* 20, no. 2 (2012): 233–47.

79. Government of Lebanon and the United Nations, *Lebanon Crisis Response Plan: 2017–2020* (2017), 93.

80. Ibid., 24.

81. "VASyR 2017: Vulnerability Assessment of Syrian Refugees in Lebanon." *World Food Program, United Nations Children's Fund (UNICEF), and UNHCR* (2016), http://documents.wfp.org/stellent/ groups/public/documents/ ena/ wfp289533.pdf.

82. Olivius, "Constructing Humanitarian Selves and Refugee Others," 270–90.

83. Rola Yasmine and Catherine Moughalian, "Systemic Violence Against Syrian Refugee Women and the Myth of Effective Intrapersonal Interventions." *Reproductive Health Matters* 24, no. 47 (2016): 27–35.

84. Carpenter, "Women, Children, and Other Vulnerable Groups," 295–355.

85. Joy L. Chia, "Piercing the Confucian Veil: Lenagan's Implications for East Asia and Human Rights." *American University Journal of Gender, Social Policy & the Law* 21 (2012): 402.

86. Kareem Shaheen, "Lebanon Sex Trafficking: Syrian Woman Describes Nine-Month Ordeal." *The Guardian* (August 1, 2016), https://www.theguardian.com/wo rld/2016/aug/01/lebanon-sex-trafficking-syrian-woman-describes-ninemonth-ordeal.

87. Shaheen, "Lebanon Sex Trafficking."

88. Ashley Gallagher, "Syrian Refugees are Turning to Prostitution at Super Nightclubs." *Vice News* (June 11, 2014), https://news.vice.com/article/syrian-ref ugees-are-turning-to-prostitution-at-super-nightclubs.

89. "Lebanon: Syrian Women at Risk of Sex Trafficking." *Human Rights Watch* (July 28, 2016), https://www.hrw.org/news/2016/07/28/lebanon-syrian-women-ris k-sex-trafficking.

90. "Lebanon: Syrian Women at Risk of Sex Trafficking."

91. "Syrian Refugee Women Tell Stories About Sexual Exploitation in Lebanon." *Naharnet Newsdesk* (August 2014), http://www.naharnet.com/stories/ar/ 141494.

92. The Lebanese Internal Security Forces launched A National Awareness Campaign in 2014 and 2015 to Inform Women About the Availability of Hotline and the mechanisms through which women could seek Protection from Domestic Violence and other Violations.

93. Shaheen, "Lebanon Sex Trafficking."

94. Ibid.

95. "The 2015–16 Lebanon Crisis Response Plan." *UNHCR* (December 15, 2014), http://www.alnap.org/resource/20702.

96. LinkedIn Profile Page, https://lb.linkedin.com/in/aimee-karam-ph-d-9 6760a29.

97. Didier Bigo, "Security and Immigration: Toward a Critique of the Governmentality of Unease." *Alternatives* 27, no. 1 suppl (2002): 63–92.

98. Gerard and Pickering, "Gender, Securitization and Transit," 338–59.

99. Sue Lautze and John Hammock, "Saving Lives and Livelihoods: The Fundamentals of a Livelihood Strategy." *Feinstein International Famine Center*, Tufts University (1997).

100. Olivius, "Constructing Humanitarian Selves and Refugee Others," 270–90.

101. Haddad Emma, *"The Refugee in International Society: Between Sovereigns."* Vol. 106 (Cambridge University Press, 2008), 35.

102. Johnson, "Click To Donate," 1015–37.

103. Volker Turk and Elizabeth Eyster, "Strengthening Accountability in UNHCR." *International Journal of Refugee Law* 22, no. 2 (2010): 159–72.

104. Olivius, "Constructing Humanitarian Selves and Refugee Others," 270–90.

Chapter 4

Alternative Refugee Insecurity Narratives

IMPACT TRANSLATION AND RESILIENCE EFFORTS

Top-down norm diffusion is biased and inaccurate.[1] The process of translating refugee protection norms from a global discourse into securitized local understandings of social justice faces varying reactions in a domestic context. Geographical and sociopolitical elements impact the practical translation of refugee protection norms. As such, residing Syrians and host communities are not passive recipients of refugee (in)security norms.[2] Instead, they appropriate, negotiate, reject, and modify established rules as norm entrepreneurs for personal use, further complicating the translation effects of refugee humanitarian interventions.

Refugee realities are complex, with room for both opportunities and misfortunes when adapting to new adversities through resilience efforts.[3] The concept of identity, with all its ramifications, is particularly relevant in exploring a silenced body such as the Syrian refugees. A refugee's identity construction influences their agency when experiencing multidimensional and (dis)continuous (in)securities in the case of Lebanon. History and context significantly influence the appropriation, translation, and remaking of transnational discourses into local practices of resilience.[4] Resilience, in this context, may be defined as a dynamic social process by which groups and communities can "bounce back" by engaging in everyday life activities and creating a form of normalcy in the lives of asylum-seeking groups facing adversity.[5] After all, the story of every refugee is a story of resilience. This resilience is present not only at the individual level; but it is apparent in the micro-, meso-, and macro-supportive environments, empowering individuals in ways that are relevant to their culture.[6]

Abstract macro-level policies do not deterministically inform localized practices and resilience efforts. They generally discount the dimensions of normalcy, resilience, and livelihood that silenced refugees strive so hard to achieve.[7] This concept of *norm internalization*—"the phase where the norm is implemented in domestic settings, e.g., in state bureaucracies"[8]—sheds light on how transnational actors, such as Syrian refugees, appropriate, negotiate, modify, and contest imposed gender-blind policies, (re)producing (in)securities within their host communities. Consequently, various refugee resilience practices internalize and externalize different localized norms for personal goals, further complicating issues of agency and ownership.

The complex nature of resilience is influenced by biological, socioeconomic, cultural, and legal factors that intersect with one another, determining how one responds to stressful experiences. Through resilience practices, refugees (re)construct their gendered insecurities by "shifting, changing, building, learning and moving on."[9] When disturbances happen, resilience occurs through various adapting practices. "It is the day-to-day pathways through which resilience outcomes are achieved."[10] Refugee resilience is multilayered in nature, and should not be stereotyped into a binary of existing or not.[11] Different individuals witnessing the same disturbances might practice resilience differently at different times, making resilience a very subjective concept. "More attention should be paid to daily pathways through which refugee

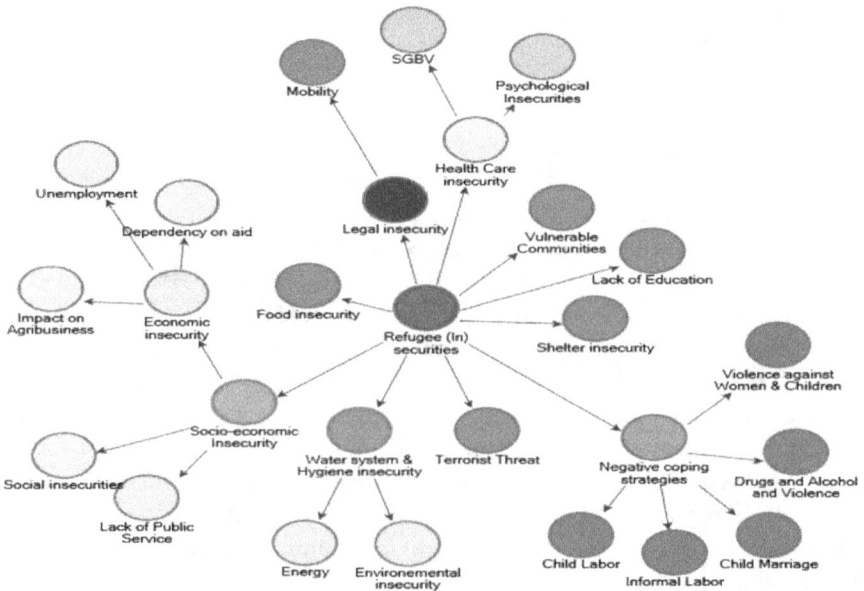

Figure 4.1 Refugee Insecurities Thematic Project Map. *Source:* Photo by Author.

resilience practices are achieved" in order to move beyond these simplistic binaries of whether resilience is present or absent.[12] Refugee resilience can be interpreted in many ways by different interested bodies; it can range from adapting to new realities and maintaining the securitized refugee system to contesting unfavorable practices and creating disturbances within the status quo.[13] Accordingly, without inclusive support, resilience as a contestation can become counterproductive to all the involved bodies. As a result, this type of resilience reinforces a vicious cycle of insecurities within host states, such as Lebanon, (re)affecting the refugees and the international system as a whole. In turn, as the frequency of securitized refugee management practices increases, the retaliatory grievances against their (in)direct environment taken by refugees intensify accordingly, aggravating the host state's security. This gendered phenomenon is central to the impact translation of Syrian refugees' (in)securities and multifaced experiences.

Figure 4.1 depicts the Syrian refugee insecurities that both LCRP documents highlighted in order to solicit support. Based on both crisis response plans, the nodes in the map visualize a network diagram of the projected refugee insecurities experienced in Lebanon. The network mapping provides a complex image of co-constructing local experiences that Syrian forced migration exacerbated in the Lebanese context. As in practice, the different nodes are interconnected and (re)affect each other in an interplay of self-reinforcing and codependent insecurities that all underprivileged but resilient people in Lebanon braved, mostly through negative coping strategies.

As such, this chapter explores how gender (in)security norms are applied on the ground with local repercussions. An adapted version of Wang and Burris's participatory method called Photovoice guided this research. Through visual and auditory reflections given by local Lebanese volunteers, the goal of this project was to increase the visibility of Syrian refugee insecurities beyond those highlighted in both LCRP documents. The study opted to conduct research through Lebanese volunteers as coresearchers in observing, reading, listening, and learning more about refugee (in)security on multiple levels of analysis, rather than interacting with Syrian women directly. This chapter, first, discusses the benefits of using this Participatory Action-oriented Research method (PAR) by describing its novel approach and contributions to understanding the (en)gendering of Syrian refugee insecurities. It, then, highlights the views of local Lebanese volunteers when addressing the issue of Syrian refugee insecurity in the case of Lebanon. The chapter incorporates three major themes: Extreme Impoverishment and Devastating Living Conditions; Identity and Security; and Labor and Gender Roles. Thirdly, this chapter explores the research findings and implications of using the Photovoice method. Finally, the chapter evaluates the (en)gendered local implications and discusses the deterioration of the Syrian refugee crisis in Lebanon.

THE BENEFITS OF USING PHOTOVOICE

The main purpose of PAR was to formulate alternative knowledge produced by individuals closest to the problem that is under investigation.[14] The visual and auditory representation of Syrian refugees in Lebanon was a key component in exploring how refugee policies—such as the LCRP—actually impact local contexts. Even though the elected Lebanese research participants were not living in the refugee informal settlements and experiencing the daily (in)securities that Syrians faced, they were still affected by those security practices. After all, the Syrian refugees' agency and responses did affect the local Lebanese communities (in)directly. And, due to the geographical and cultural proximity with the Syrian refugees, local volunteers were well positioned to address the local practices and challenges of refugee security policies. The local volunteers became the subjects of the study, showcasing the impact of specific policies on the (re)production of refugees' (in)securities within their communities. In effect, as the main participants, the Lebanese volunteers became coresearchers by collecting pictures, analyzing data, discussing, elaborating, and sharing their findings, while, at the same time, recognizing their own anxieties as Lebanese citizens toward the Syrian refugee presence within their communities. Through an inductive bottom-up approach, the trained participants took photographs, voiced their concerns, and conversed about the significance of their respective and each other's photographs. This grounded approach enriched the contextual analysis of gendered impact translation by highlighting the intersectionality of Syrian refugees' insecurities and resilience efforts, while at the same time generating a group discussion between the Lebanese coresearchers.

Since, this participatory action-oriented methodology lacks a definitive structure for designing, practicing, or implementing Photovoice research, there was room for certain flexibility within the methodological framework of the study.[15] Accordingly, having access to local networks and government officials, I was able to identify nonpartisan Lebanese individuals and groups that worked or volunteered with Syrian refugees. Guitta Hourani, the Director of the Lebanese Emigration Research Center (LERC), played a crucial role in the successful completion of the IRB procedure and recruitment efforts. She provided institutional support and academic referrals of potential participants to partake in the field research safely and ethically. Meeting virtually and in person with several volunteers and college students referred by local networks, organizations, and Notre Dame University's faculty and friends, I introduced myself and informed the potential participants about the project's aim and method, inviting them to an introductory training session. Five Lebanese research participants collaborated throughout the entire research project, welcoming the idea of becoming co-researchers and taking on the role of photographers:

Maria S. worked as a senior outreach and psychosocial support (PSS) worker under two UNICEF projects with the Makhzoumi Foundation: Child Protection and Gender Based Violence. Her task was to provide psychosocial support for Syrian refugee women and children. She was referred to the project by common acquaintances from the Lebanese Red Cross. Her work experience motivated her to voice the real conditions that Syrian refugees endure in different parts of Lebanon.

Diana H. is a design practitioner by trade and a volunteer at the Kayany Foundation. The latter organization was founded in response to the growing needs of Syrian refugee children in Lebanon. Diana spent three months providing basic aid to some of the most vulnerable youth living in ITSs scattered throughout her hometown of Kefraya, Bekaa.

Bechara B. is an undergraduate engineering student at the American University of Beirut (AUB). His interest in social work started with the AUB Neighborhood Initiative promoting the neighborhood's livability and diversity through innovative outreach activities such as the "Civic Engagement and Community Service" (CCECS), teaching English to vulnerable Lebanese locals and Syrian refugees in Hamra, Beirut.

Mazen J. worked as the head of the Statistics department at a non-disclosed research company. Mazen showed much interest in the project. He later volunteered, wanting to voice the refugee insecurities within his hometown village in Bekka, Mansoura. This town is strategically located by one of the most important rivers in the area, the Litani river, hosting one of the biggest informal Syrian camps in Lebanon: Ghaze.

Hanan A. was referred to the project by her close friend Mazen. She joined the team, showing much interest in the Photovoice methodology, and wanted to partake in the fieldwork to highlight the fact that Syrian women and children were begging for money in the streets of Beirut. She also wanted to shed light on the reasons behind this phenomenon that, in her view, dehumanizes this vulnerable population.

The preliminary session explained all the fieldwork responsibilities, such as capturing photographic evidence, setting research goals, data collection, and data analysis. As it was necessary to protect all parties—the Lebanese research participants, Syrian refugees, and the research as a whole—participants were to refrain from photographing any illegal activities. Instead, they were to suspend all photographic activities, warn of any unexpected situation, and retreat when there were risks. Participants needed to also refrain from entering dangerous spaces or situations to complete the project. Having prior knowledge of the areas and different contexts helped evade dangerous positions. If they were ever put in any emergency or health situation that would inhibit the participants from continuing the project, they were expected to communicate it to the principal investigator.

The participants needed to protect the communities they were research-
ing by abstaining from taking pictures that could harm people's reputation,
safety, or individual liberty.[16] Consequently, no pictures were taken in private
settings or without the subject's consent. All photos included partial facial
and body parts that do not identify a specific person or an illicit activity. As
for the issue of false light, the participants were previously warned that it
was necessary to make sure that the situations in the refugee communities
were reflected accurately. Necessary steps were introduced in the first session
to portray the community accurately and to avoid taking photographs and
images that could be out of context.

The participants used personal smartphones to take meaningful pictures.
After training the participants on how to take pictures safely and ethically, I
outlined the suggestive vision for the project and welcomed their comments,
recommendations, and concerns. All participants agreed on the logistics and
the four-week time frame. Some even suggested the idea of having group field
trips during the weekend, where, each Saturday, one of the participants would
try to get permission, through institutional or personal connections, to visit
some of the informal camps or locations deemed interesting and accessible.

The established field project was short-term, spanning for four weeks.
Adapting to the volunteers' availability and accommodating everyone's time,
the study encouraged the participants to take photographs on their own whenever they encountered, worked, and/or volunteered with Syrian refugees.
Two participants managed to get permissions for the entire group to conduct
simultaneous field research on two different occasions inside a couple of
informal Syrian settlements.

On both occasions, I visited the Syrian refugee informal camps with the
group, under the role of the research group supervisor. While the participants were busy taking photographs and engaging the refugee community,
I was conducting participant observations and informal face-to-face discussions with Syrian refugees, mostly women voicing complaints and personal
requests. It seemed that they, initially, confused the research group with
practitioners or activists coming on behalf of either the government, the
United Nations High Commissioner for Refugees (UNHCR), or other nongovernmental organizations (NGOs). When the refugees found out about
the study project, they were eager to let the participants wander around and
take photographs of the public spaces, wanting to share with the principal
researcher their destitute and troubled stories of neglect and despair. The
fieldwork ended with the distribution of donations acquired before each visit
to thank the local Syrian communities for hosting the participants.

After the fieldwork was finished, the participants agreed on a specific date
to meet for a follow-up session to discuss the photographs. Meanwhile, they
needed to share individual photographs with respective narratives, before

initiating a critical group discussion in the final session.[17] The interpretation of the photographs was critical to the success of the project, for the visual narratives were the ultimate objects of group reflection. All coresearchers agreed to create a shared google drive and upload their captioned photographs with annotated narratives answering the following five questions using the original Wang's and Burris technique termed as "SHOWeD":[18]

1. What do you See here?
2. What is Happening here?
3. How does this relate to Our Lives?
4. Why does this situation, concern or strength exist?
5. What can we Do about it?

These questions engaged group discussions and generated new findings of different experiences and reflections, creating new forward-thinking knowledge. Consequently, the participants became agents of change, shifting their role from being a silent group of local actors to a powerful complementary voice with unique perspectives on Syrian refugee (in)securities. This method also acted as a conduit to look deeper into the Lebanese participants' positions on the Syrian refugee crisis. By collaborating in the visual analysis during the photo-elicitation session, the photo-narratives depicting the Syrian refugee crisis helped the coresearchers understand their own positionalities, reflecting their subjective "beliefs, feelings, and cultural experiences" held at a certain point in time.[19] By voicing their own insecurities, the Lebanese participants (re)examined how refugees were situated and received within Lebanese communities. Accordingly, the participants (in)directly discussed the (in)visible Syrian refugees' agency, as well as the complex (in)securities they (re)produced within their host communities.

At the end of the process, the participants chose the top-ten elected themes deduced from the group discussions. The corresponding photo-narratives found most relevant to this study were selected and coded. As coresearchers, all the participants signed a release form for their pictures and narratives to be handed to me, while still having access to the google drive document in case anyone would like to review, edit, add, or update any information within. The session ended with a unanimous recommendation for a follow-up meeting session once the research was done to plan future opportunities for the project.

The group discussions and photo-analysis brought out a deeper understanding of the complex intersectional realities that Syrian refugees, especially women, endured "solely by virtue of belonging to a particular gender, a certain age group, or social status."[20] By sharing individual and group intake of all the photos collected, this method challenged the narrow assumptions of a universal refugee's experience. A collaborative work in discussing each visual and sharing narratives within a safe space brought to light significant considerations of what types of Syrian refugee insecurities exist, while still exhibiting the local participants' anxieties, hopes, and fears. As such, the participatory nature of the Photovoice methodology made the implicit explicit. It educated everyone who participated, including the principal investigator, on the complexity of relevant refugee insecurities when explored within a bottom-up sociocultural gender approach.

There were various challenges in using this method. Using inductive research, I had little control over the participants' choice of subject matters for their analysis. Participants had the complete freedom to decide what to include or exclude in their photographs and respective narratives. These choices influenced the research findings and interpretations. Still, the aim of this study was not to provide a non-biased accurate representation of all the micro-dynamics of refugee (in)securities, nor did it present the principal researcher's sole perception. The goal of this research was to promote visual ethnography methods for exploring the local impact of refugee (in)security and practices. Moreover, the various findings, when triangulated, provided rich and complementing knowledge on the intersectional gendered Syrian refugee insecurities in the case of Lebanon.

The Lebanese participants' subjective thoughts on the visual narratives contributed to gaining an alternative understanding of co-constructed community discourses that (en)gender Syrian refugee (in)security. The participant-oriented analysis process—known as photo-elicitation—involved all participants sharing their findings, acknowledging that each image might generate different meanings and critiques. The main purpose of the photo-elicitation sessions was to record the Lebanese participants' interpretations of each picture. The coresearchers and I engaged in a group discussion and reflected on what was important to contextualize within the pictures based on the discussants' backgrounds, professional knowledge, and field experiences. Together, we selected the pictures to be focused on in the project, created captions for the selected images, and reflected on our different inferences regarding each image.[21] This process encouraged both individual storytelling and group dialogue for each picture, such that the Lebanese volunteers positioned their arguments within the greater refugee (in)security context. Participants ended up personalizing each picture, attributing to the images their knowledge, social, and personal values when explaining their respective views. Reflecting on their individual interactions with different Syrian refugee groups allowed the Lebanese participants to provide field knowledge of refugee (in)security practices and local repercussions. Even when a group consensus was lacking, the multiple inputs provided on each photograph in the photo-elicitation process enriched our understanding of the Syrian refugee impact norm translation and the subsequent insecurities felt by the Lebanese host population.

THEMATIC ANALYSIS

The photo-elicitation process involved the co-identification of major themes among participants with ongoing, deliberative discussions about the meaning behind each photograph. The general themes extracted during this project exposed the lack of attention toward Syrian refugees' basic needs that (re)produced (in)securities and harmful policy practices within the informal camps and their surrounding areas. Accordingly, this study showcases how negotiated refugee (in)security norms and practices resonated in different contexts, (re)producing sites of Syrian refugee (re)constructions, (re)definitions, and contestations. These themes also made the relationality between each Lebanese coresearcher involved in the refugee assistance efforts apparent. Based on their own individual experiences working with different Syrian refugee groups, the coresearchers highlighted various Syrian refugee agencies at play—such as child labor and working women—within Lebanese communities. The Lebanese participants thus elaborated on the background of certain insecurity aspects within the chosen photos that might not be obvious in an objective sense. As such, the three major themes extracted from the photo-elicitation sessions encompass an assortment of subthemes collectively captioned by the research participants. It is important to note that the captions, photos, and analysis provided below are based on the discussions that took place during the photo-elicitation process between the main researcher and the five coresearchers. The following thematic analysis is thus a product of the group's collective perceptions highlighted during the process.

Theme 1: Extreme Impoverishment and Devastating Living Conditions

Ten photos addressed the issues of extreme impoverishment and devastating living conditions that Syrian refugees in Lebanon endured in some of the approximately 2,000 informal settlements scattered in rural areas all over the country. These ten photos were divided into four subthemes with accompanying summaries of the Lebanese participants' major reflective contributions.

In figure 4.2, two young children are trying to fill large empty plastic containers with water from a dirty puddle near a rural highway. According to one Lebanese volunteer, the children were not playing in the mud. Instead, they were tasked with collecting water for their household(s), and the muddy water was probably the only available source of water near them. In the group

Figure 4.2   I am Thirsty! *Source:* Photo by Diana H.

reflections on the photo, all Lebanese coresearchers stated that this reality was a shocking contrast to modern ways of life, illustrating the unacceptable standards of living and degradation of human dignity that Syrian refugees endured. The coresearchers all agreed that this photo sums up the situation of hundreds of thousands of Syrian refugee children who were uprooted and forced to adapt to a neighboring country already suffering from weak infrastructure, limited resources, and dwindling support from the international community. For these forced migrant children, unsanitary water containing deadly bacteria and viruses was a normal source of sustenance.

The Lebanese coresearchers acknowledged that the lack of clean water had been a major issue in Lebanon long before the refugee crisis due to preexisting sociopolitical dynamics within the country. Though accredited programs, such as Water Sanitation and Hygiene (WASH), implemented specific projects to improve access to safe drinking water, only 65 percent of 150,000 Syrians living in ITSs received basic aid regarding water, sanitation, and infrastructure, which jeopardized local residents' safety from preventable diseases.[22] All Lebanese participants also agreed that the exponential population increase and the poor measures for water management made it more difficult to enhance hygiene practices. Several participants spoke negatively of short-term initiatives that introduced clean water, basic toilets, and good hygiene practices, claiming that such initiatives were either corrupt or insufficient. In the Lebanese volunteers' view, this problem could not be solved without a political arrangement—the ending of violence in Syria and Syrians' safe return to their home country, in the best-case scenario. The coresearchers surmised that until such a solution was reached, there was a need to develop Lebanon's infrastructure and ensure transparency of financial resources acquired from the international community to prevent corruption.

The Lebanese participants' reflections on figure 4.2 bring to light the agency of Syrian children, who apparently played a crucial part in residing refugees' household maintenance. The fact that Syrian children were the ones acquiring water from a dirty puddle demonstrates their increasing role within the domestic sphere. As made clear through the research group's analysis of this photo, residing Syrians were not passive recipients of the local humanitarian aid system. Instead, these Syrians adapted, negotiated, and modified their surroundings to survive their new realities. Therefore, the top-down humanitarian relief model implemented in the LCRPs failed to capture important dimensions of the resilience and normalcy efforts inherent in the refugee population.

In figure 4.3, Syrian children are seen drying up bread in the sun on a UNHCR-labeled recycled tent. At first, this practice may seem to be part of preparing a traditional food of sorts. In reality, this is a process by which Syrian refugees disinfected and preserved bread in the sun for later consumption, mainly because bread, food supplies, and donations reached refugee populations on an irregular basis. Hence, some Lebanese coresearchers claimed that Syrian refugee women were forced to take unusual measures to disinfect stale bread and secure food availability for their families whenever supplies did not arrive on time.

This subtheme was recurrent during the photo-elicitation discussion, illustrating the degradation of quality of life for many Syrian refugees to an extent incomparable to standard everyday life in Lebanon. Most of the coresearchers likened this scenery to the misery usually depicted in films and novels documenting destitute conditions in times of desperation. This image generated divisions in the research group into two main perceptions. One group justified such a scenario as a natural result of forceful displacement, while the other normalized this behavior of unsanitary diets frequently performed by rural families as part of the Syrian-Bedouin tribal customs and practices. This photo-elicitation highlighted the typical gendered case where Syrian women resiliently adapted new measures to curb hunger.[23] In that respect, the research participants' views seemed to complement the gendered cultural theme of women making sacrifices through harmful health practices such as reducing their own food intake so that their "children and men in the household can eat."[24] This was especially the case when the cash assistance and food vouchers given by aid workers were insufficient, such that Syrian women sold their vouchers at lower than face value to pay rent or other expenses. Some of the suggested solutions that the Lebanese participants

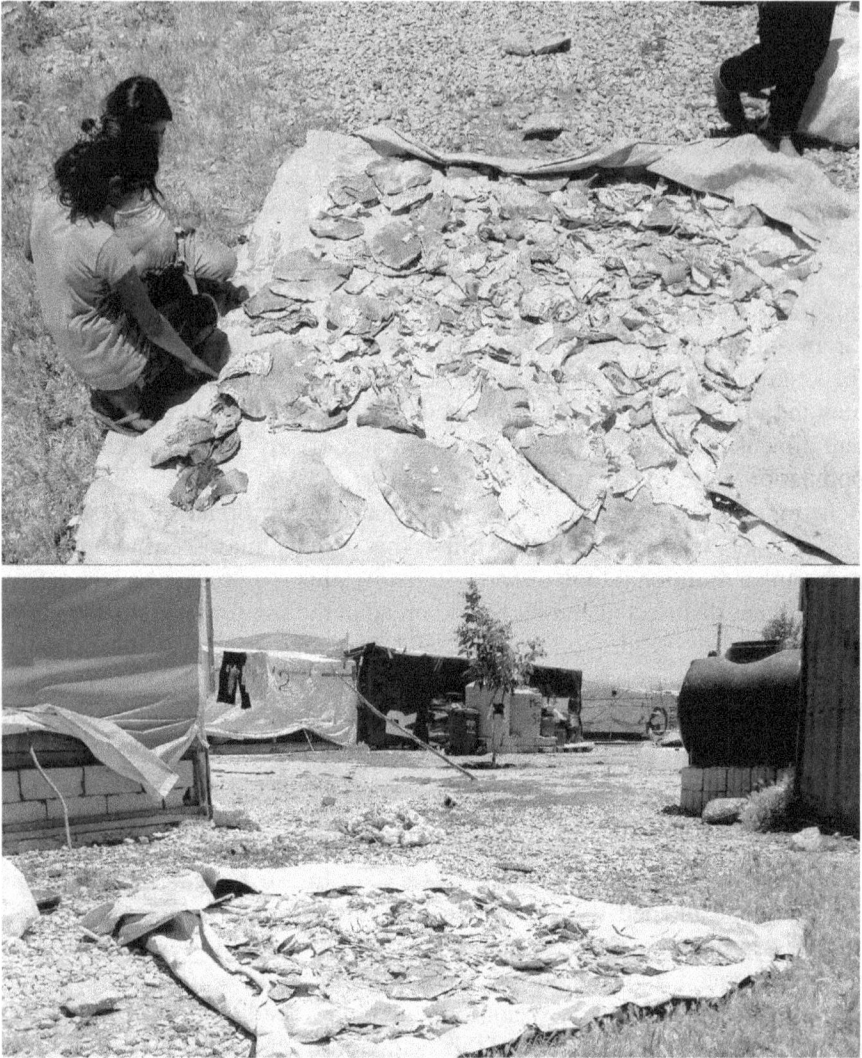

Figure 4.3   I Am Disinfecting Bread. *Source:* Photo by Hanan A.

elaborated included finding ways to ensure that food donations reached all targeted refugee populations immediately, rather than subcontracting them through large organizations, often too corrupted and slow to deliver on time. Another suggestion made by all of the coresearchers was to push the international community to be more involved in providing direct aid and awareness to refugees, not only by increasing support to the Lebanese government but also by improving the management, supervision, and efficiency of the one-on-one donation programs.

All of the Lebanese participants agreed that the humanitarian aid and refugee relief systems set in place were inadequate and suffered from under-funding, poor management, and corruption. Some participants discussed the available electronic food voucher (E-card system) that allowed registered Syrian refugees to purchase food from hundreds of the World Food Program (WFP) contracted shops. Still, most participants believed that the E-card system created a hierarchical space for opportunism and oppression, where privileged men, often more adequately knowledgeable in handling transac-tions, took advantage of the unified system for cash transfers and control over their extended family members' incomes. Accordingly, this photo-elicitation provided an illustration of the masculinized impact of refugee insecurity, where women were doubly discriminated: once by the availability of the aid and funds provided through the E-card system and again by the gendered aid mechanisms that limited women from avoiding unpleasant and undigni-fied shopping experiences at the scarce partner stores available in their area. On the one hand, Syrian households were generally controlled by male cash recipients, who decided how money should be spent. On the other hand, female-headed refugee households were, according to one study, excluded from receiving aid as cultural norms often prevented most Syrian women from being able to register and follow up with the UNHCR's partner agencies without a male chaperone.[25]

Figure 4.4 depicts the exteriors of makeshift tents and shelters that were typically seen in Syrian refugee camps across Lebanese territories. One of the photos shows a collection of materials, including tarps, cloth, cardboard, barrels, plastic containers, and metal sheets, among other accessible material, that were scavenged, outsourced, and even possibly stolen to build tent-like structures to shelter Syrian families. In the group photo-elicitation discus-sions, the coresearchers agreed that these photos perfectly depict the state of most informal Syrian settlements, which were commonly deprived of ade-quate resources for shelter. The participants explained that since most Syrian refugees lack legal status, access to housing became difficult. The increase of rent in most cities pushed the establishment of informal camps in agricultural areas. Consequently, ITSs, makeshift shelters, and substandard dwellings erupted, establishing temporary accommodation for the influx of Syrian refu-gees that provided neither privacy nor protection from intrusion or attacks. As such, residing Syrians were vulnerable to any type of harassment, assault, or abduction, where "homelessness, hunger, disease outbreaks, violence, abuse, and exploitation were few of the many consequences that arose."[26]

According to the Lebanese participants, the severe issue of inadequate shelter worsened, in part, due to the failure of the international commu-nity, especially the United Nations, to properly manage the refugee crisis in Lebanon. As a result, the participants argued that too much funding was

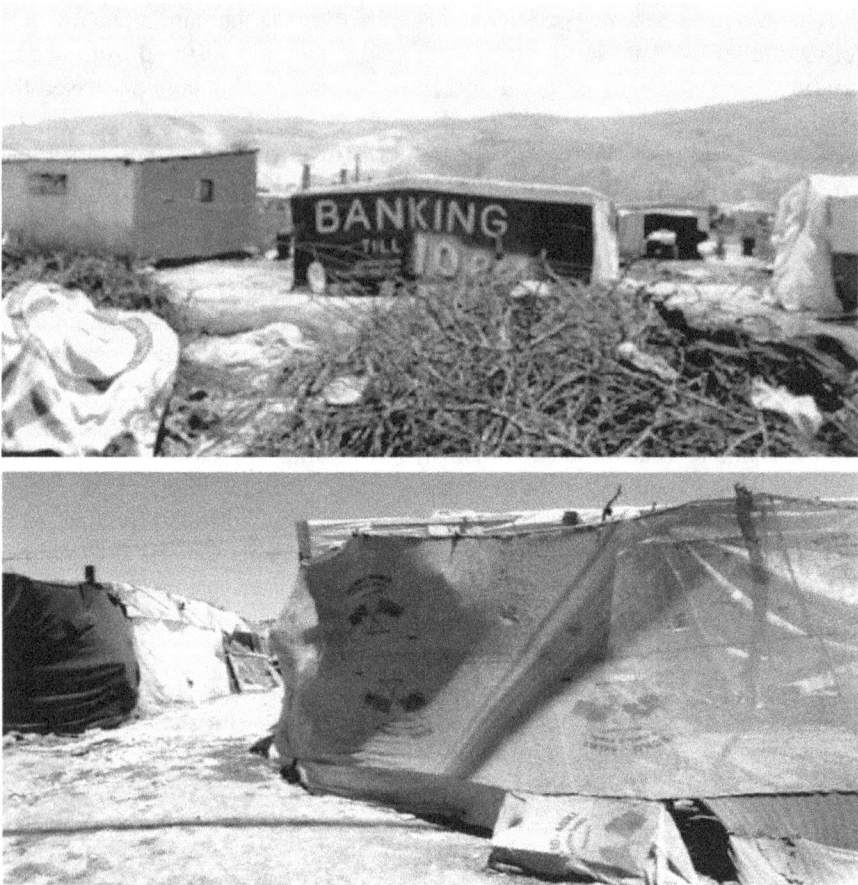

Figure 4.4   Scavengers. *Source:* Photo by Mazen J.

supposedly allocated to food aid, while very little went to shelter, which they considered to be the most pressing concern for most Syrian refugees given the extreme weather conditions in some areas of Lebanon. With no concrete plan to host the million and some Syrians, who, according to a couples of the coresearchers, "swarmed" into Lebanon between 2011 and 2015, illicit forms of resilience—what the participants captioned as "scavenging"—were adopted by the refugees. The Lebanese participants' derogatory use of the term "scavenger" during the photo-elicitation session provides an example of the host community's anxieties being projected onto Syrian agency and resilience efforts. Interestingly, the Lebanese coresearchers' perspective of Syrian refugees' identities and practices was very dyadic. While the coresearchers described women and children as the "weakest links," vulnerable to harassment and assault, they also denounced the "scavengers" in refugee camps in an abstract way, disregarding the fact that the majority of residing Syrians in ITSs were the same vulnerable women and children whose agency was just marginalized. This gendered image of Syrian refugee women and children as passive victims does not help us understand that this "scavenger" image represents one of the many ways refugee women brave through the worst humanitarian crisis by "shifting, changing, building"[27] their surrounding environment in order to adapt.

Despite this subconsciously negative attitude toward the Syrian presence, all of the Lebanese participants were keen to place the blame on the Lebanese government's refusal to accommodate Syrians and provide viable shelters. Most of the coresearchers further projected Lebanese anxieties by supporting the Lebanese government's decision to outlaw official refugee camps like the ones provided for the Palestinians, arguing that simply providing viable shelters would be a step in the right direction. This photo-elicitation session thus brought to light the participants' anxieties toward the idea of Syrians permanently settling. However, it is important to note that the participants justified their position, explaining that permanent settlement might lead to Syrians losing their identity and becoming another group of permanently displaced refugees, much like what happened with the Palestinians in Lebanon for over seventy years.

On another note, some of the Lebanese participants correlated the scavenging situation with the experiences of many Syrians residing on the outskirts of urban areas, criticizing specific humanitarian programs. For example, one participant mentioned that the UN-Habitat focused its efforts mostly on liaising with landlords to identify new shelter units and rehabilitate existing ones. In the coresearcher's view, the informality of a renting agreement between landlords and Syrian tenants further complicated the modality of "cash-per-task" basis programs, which had limited control over the state of the illicit relationships between both parties. Therefore, other than the main impediment of corruption, there was unanimity among the Lebanese coresearchers that most aid programs, such as "cash-per-task," failed to reach and support Syrians efficiently, not able to prioritize and implement adequate shelter rehabilitation activities.[28]

Many participants echoed Syrian women's outcries toward the low quality of shelter materials being provided, if provided at all. The 2017 LCRP document clearly stated in the "need assessment" section that only 40 percent of the targeted funds were allocated to the shelter assistance, where "only 27 percent of the sector targets outside informal settlements were disproportionately reached."[29] Accordingly, almost 30 percent of female-headed households, compared to 15 percent of male-headed households, were forced to live in "non-residential spaces, such as garages or workshops, or in temporary, makeshift shelters" that were below standard, structurally dangerous, not appropriate for living conditions, and "inadequate especially for women and girls."[30]

All the participants agreed that there were no immediate solutions to the shelter problem, except for the inconceivable political decisions of either authorizing formal refugee camps or guaranteeing the safe return of Syrian refugees to safe zones in Syria. Overall, the Lebanese participants' depiction of Syrians as scavengers illustrates the dynamic process of refugee resilience. In effect, as contextualized actors, Syrian refugees seem to have contested the imposed gendered policies and harmful securitization practices to bounce back, (re)producing refugee insecurities and creating disturbances within the status quo. The refugees' resilience efforts showcase the use of negative coping strategies as local mechanisms of retaliation against the oppressive environments within the informal camps.

Figure 4.5 shows the impact of the presence of informal settlements on the Litany Riverside. Many refugee camps were erected near rivers simply because of the proximity to water sources. The Lebanese participants chose to include these photos as illustrations of the exacerbated Lebanese infrastructure and waste management deterioration due to the Syrian influx on land already suffering from pollution. The first photo shows two young girls standing at the gate of a tin cottage watching a green patch nearby. In the photo-elicitation discussion of these images, the Lebanese coresearchers stated that the green patch was, in fact, a pond of algae that formed as garbage flowed down from the Litany River into the periphery of the refugee camp. The participants claimed that this phenomenon related to their own lives in several ways.

First, these images reminded them of the environmental catastrophe in Lebanon, which was present long before the Syrian crisis due to ineffective intervention measures on the part of the Lebanese government. On this, the participants highlighted the issue of ongoing corruption in Lebanese organizations, many of which conducted unlicensed and illegal activities along Lebanon's main rivers, such as the Litany. Some of the participants recapped the "You Stink" (*Tul3it Rihetkun*) movement, protesting the garbage crisis and lack of trash collection in most municipalities due to the scandals over public waste management that Lebanon was enduring.[31] According to the Lebanese participants, political demonstrations started when Lebanese communities were inundated with piled-up rubbish in the streets due to a shortage of garbage collection agencies and the expiration of a dubious contract between the Lebanese government and the exploitative company *Sukleen*, among many other issues. All the participants reiterated the social distrust in the inconsistent public services that subcontracted their managerial operations to monopolistic private businesses with crooked political connections and hiring personnel.

Secondly, these images show the severe nature of refugee life that is shocking from a humanitarian perspective, in which access to clean water

Figure 4.5 W.A.S.H. *Source:* Photo by Maria S.

was a luxury instead of a basic human right. According to the participants, the primary cause of this unsanitary foul-smelling water was the poor management and planning by the crisis response plan strategists—the Lebanese government, the UNHCR, and donors. According to the participants, these organizations were aware of, but mostly neglected, this long-standing water crisis, in which wastewater, human excrement, industrial chemical overflow, and residuals from quarries were left unattended. Figure 4.5 is thus a reminder of the serious issues that Lebanese residents blamed the Syrian crisis for, such as increased pollution and the spread of poverty-related problems.

At the same time, most of the Lebanese coresearchers agreed that the Syrian presence in certain areas further exacerbated the water pollution. Refugees often resorted to throwing their waste in the rivers instead of disposing of it in corresponding garbage collection bins. In addition, Syrians residing near rivers often installed pumps and pipes to carry water to their informal settlements, as displayed in figure 4.5. The problem with this, as the Lebanese coresearchers explained, is that the dirty river water was pumped directly to the informal settlements for consumption by Syrians, who ended up suffering from poor hygiene, sanitation issues, and various health problems. However, one coresearcher pointed out the unavailability of waste collection bins near the informal settlements, justifying these negative coping strategies that Syrian residents utilized to adapt to their (in)accessible environment.

During the photo-elicitation discussion, all Lebanese participants stated that most of the Syrians' health problems were related to a lack of clean water, proper sanitation, and hygiene. Accordingly, the last photo in this collection shows a man-made waterhole, intended to collect water for agricultural use, containing a pump and pipe, as well as wet clothes left to dry. Although this water was intended for agriculture use, the nearby Syrian refugee settlement accessed it for domestic use as well. This contaminated water was also used for cooking, bathing, washing, laundry, and other household practices. Some of the participants elaborated on Syrian women's agency, stating that even though women play a key role in managing food and water resources, these women had insufficient decision-making power within their household and community at large, meaning that it wasn't necessarily their choice to depend on the polluted water supply. Under those circumstances, Syrian women using this unhygienic water supply not only jeopardized the health of refugees living in the same camp but also threatened the well-being of nearby communities. Though the problems in acquiring access to safe and clean water differed slightly by shelter type, according to the Lebanese participants, this type of Syrian resilience prevented local health institutions from containing and preventing disease outbreaks.

In the Lebanese coresearchers' view, the neglected water resources set the country on a self-destructive path. The participants' suggested solutions were twofold. First, they recommended immediate relocation of refugee settlements away from the polluted rivers to areas where supplies of clean water were available. Second, the participants reiterated the need to hold the Lebanese government accountable for improving its public services and addressing the issue of river pollution as a sustainable long-term goal for the sake of its own citizens. Most of the participants advised water treatment and safe water-container maintenance for refugee households. In addition, the coresearchers deemed the creation of waste management initiatives through education, strict regulations, enforcement, and punishment as necessary tools to promote local awareness of caring for national water resources. Several of the Lebanese participants also highlighted the benefits of involving the international community in empowering Syrian refugees to be involved in the treatment of Lebanon's water supplies, which would foster a rapprochement between local communities when generating adequate sociocultural resilience for the residing Syrians facing protracted displacement.

Theme 2: Intersectionality of Refugee Insecurity

Nine photos were classified under the themes of identity and security. Both co-constituting themes were recurrent in the photo-elicitation process depicting the intersectional Syrian refugee (in)securities through visual narratives. The Lebanese participants believed that the daily insecurities faced by refugees were multileveled and not just the products of the failing refugee management regime in Lebanon. In fact, these daily insecurities (re)affected the power dynamics within ITSs, privileging some groups of Syrians over others, (re)impacting their relations with nearby Lebanese communities. Since the Lebanese volunteers were locally situated, they were knowledgeable about the unforeseen micro-variables that (en)gendered daily refugee anxieties within their respective communities. As such, each photograph critically assess the complicated and stereotypically simplistic views of Syrian refugees as either perpetrators or victims with no agency. At the same time, the coresearchers' own positionality as concerned Lebanese citizens in search of local stability is also highlighted in the captions and discussions of the following pictures, in which the participants (re)negotiated their individual perceptions toward the visible insecurities.

Figure 4.6 portrays rundown tents in one of the Syrian refugee settlements in Lebanon. Electricity cables can be seen hanging above some tents, with satellite dishes installed on top of others. According to the Lebanese coresearchers, the contrast in this picture depicts the resilience efforts and systemic privileges within the Syrian refugee communities. The rundown tents represent the well-known Syrian poverty, the hanging electricity cables depict some interesting signs of resilience efforts, and the satellite dishes characterize some form of overlooked luxury.

All coresearchers stated that most ITSs were built on privately owned lands, which Lebanese property owners were free to rent at any price to one designated residing Syrian (the *shawish*) who would manage other refugees living on the land. One coresearcher criticized the fact that the *shawish* was always a man who informally governed his camp as its sole representative, excluding other residing Syrians from most decision-making processes regarding their immediate setting. The fact that a *shawish* was oftentimes

Figure 4.6   I Want, But I Do Not Need. *Source:* Photo by Bechara B.

the only residing Syrian who negotiated the ITSs' rental with the Lebanese landlord, organized the structure of the camp, collected the rent from other residing Syrians, and coordinated humanitarian aid, protection, and assistance with the UNHCR and other agencies, gave him the decision-making privileges in the public sphere that other Syrians, especially women, did not enjoy. Several of the Lebanese participants questioned the UN humanitarian relief system's reliance on the *shawish* phenomenon as the interface between aid programs and refugees, privileging one (male) Syrian over others for the sake of facilitating their aid assistance. According to some of the Lebanese volunteers, the Lebanese government and NGOs depended on the *shawish* to keep other residing Syrians in check, and, at the same time, serve as informants to help with collecting data on who is doing what, when, and where. The *shawish* phenomenon thus created an uneven dynamic within ITSs, with room for manipulation and unequal opportunities such as the presence of satellite dishes and electricity on some tents and not others.

According to commentary made by the Century Foundation, Lebanon's treatment of Syrian refugees as a security problem (en)gendered a rise of "local Syrian strongmen known as the *shawishs* within Lebanese displacement camps," illustrating one of the many impacts of Lebanon's crisis response approach to the Syrian refugee crisis.[32] Consequently, the commentary states that "the *shawishs* are a perversion in a system that is reinforced by state security actors, ignored by the ministry of interior and local municipalities, convenient for landowners, and problematic for aid organizations and refugees."[33] Positioned as the middlemen, most *shawishs* controlled the Syrians' livelihood and aid opportunities, using their given power to (re)negotiate their status with the landowner and aid organizations and barely serving the interests of Syrian refugees living in the camps. As such, this elicitation session generated a clear understanding of the multilayered nature of refugee resilience. Resilience depends on a person's positionality within their environment, as exemplified by some Syrians adjusting to their new realities by becoming the informal settlements' de facto supervisors (*shawishs*). These *shawishs* mostly thrived by maintaining the securitized refugee management system that guaranteed them some power over controlling received aid and exploiting the relative vulnerability of other residing Syrian refugees.

On another note, most of the Lebanese participants believed that images like figure 4.6 were justified portrayals of the growing distrust between the Lebanese communities and Syrian refugees. As most Lebanese suffered from economic and social exhaustion, their views of Syrian refugees as privileged burdens and a source of insecurity rather than as people in need led to tension between the two communities. The various privileges, such as pilfered electricity, discussed in this photo-elicitation session reflected the broader problem in which Lebanon suffers from a chronic electricity problem, where most towns get less than eight or twelve hours of power daily.[34] As Lebanese citizens, the coresearchers could not escape their anxieties and weariness toward the informal refugee camps given that many Syrians, as illustrated in figure 4.6, abused and exploited electricity cables and dishes in a way that was seen as illegal. In their discussion, the coresearchers stated that ITSs tended to receive power and cable more regularly than Lebanese residents, at little-to-no cost. The Lebanese participants' position here can be interpreted as empathetic with the Lebanese complaints that some "Syrian refugees receive more benefits than they do."[35] As such, during the photo-elicitation, the participants justified several incidents of hostile attitudes toward Syrian refugees from local communities as a reaction to the illicit work committed by some refugees in urban and rural areas. According to the participants, this situation could have been attributed to the fact that many refugee camps were informal, pushing Syrians to use illicit means in order to thrive.

The pictures of satellite dishes and power lines on ITS tents triggered some criticism among the Lebanese participants, who wondered what other kinds of luxuries refugees "enjoyed" inside their tents. One participant highlighted the fact that the Lebanese uproar against Syrians abusing electricity was inappropriate given that Syria's steady supply of electricity to Lebanon remained intact despite the raging war it was witnessing.[36] This photo-elicitation also reinforced the participants' negative view of their government's ineptitude, as they believed Lebanese citizens should have been more concerned with the

corrupted and weak government causing severe electricity cuts due to domestic political turmoil and personal gains. Even though their proposed solutions
were limited, all of the participants blamed the Lebanese government, which
was expected to carefully manage these settlements and reduce them in scale
so that they would not threaten neighboring communities. Without such
solutions, the participants surmised that violence between Syrian refugees,
*shawish*es, and neighboring Lebanese communities was inevitable.

Figure 4.7 shows a store sign announcing that it is part of the food assistance program organized by the UNHCR. The Lebanese research participants
explained that the refugee aid system in Lebanon resulted in the monopoly
of a limited number of Lebanese stores over all debit E-cards issued by the
UNHCR for Syrian refugees to purchase food and supplies. The participants
explained that this UNHCR program was initiated as an attempt to fight corruption and ensure a feasible way to directly distribute food and other supplies to Syrian families, while also empowering local businesses. However,
the program seemed to have failed Syrians in this case, where one research
participant highlighted an interesting aspect of this photo—the fact that the
shop was closed. This detail triggered an interesting discussion among the
research participants, who speculated that the shop's closure could have been

Figure 4.7   Refugee Food Assistance Program. *Source:* Photo by Maria S.

due to either personal reasons, *Ramadan* (an important Muslim holy period), it ran out of supplies, or most E-cards ran out of debit. Having a closed shop during the daytime meant, to some of the Lebanese coresearchers, the failure of the food and aid program to deliver the required assistance to vulnerable Syrians, such that local store owners had the privilege to deny Syrians from accessing some of their daily needs. One participant also highlighted the severe impact of the Syrian refugee crisis on local Lebanese businesses. As a result of the crisis, many stores in remote areas were forced to close with the loss of their begrudged Lebanese clients and, thus, became dependent on desperate Syrian clienteles with irregular income. Overall, figure 4.7 relates to the devastating impact of the Syrian refugee crisis on local businesses where gendered power relations complexly impacted how aid assistance was translated in local context.

Under those circumstances, a local store's provision or denial of aid products (en)gendered local resilience efforts by both communities. Lebanese residents would boycott shops welcoming Syrians, and residing Syrians would adopt unhealthy food rationing strategies in order to survive. The Lebanese coresearchers claimed that many of the host communities initially welcomed Syrian refugees in their homes or on their properties. However, by 2014, the already economically embattled Lebanese citizens began to show definite signs of exhaustion and tension toward Syrian residents, especially with the terrorist attacks of 2014 that overtook Lebanese cities and the Lebanese Army. As a result, and according to the research participants, most Lebanese nationals blamed Syrian refugees for almost every economic or social problem, as well as any threat to security.

Based on the photo-elicitation discussions, the research participants persistently blamed the Lebanese government for failing to enforce local standards in regulating local businesses, which left both populations vulnerable to illicit opportunistic business activities. Some of the participants argued that the situation was as such because the Lebanese government was politically corrupt, giving business privileges to their devoted party members, while others pointed out the inconsistencies in foreign support and the failed outsourcing of humanitarian aid programs. One of the solutions suggested by the research group was to attract more local businesses to participate in the UNHCR food assistance program, and to push for more direct aid and customized support for Syrian refugees. The participants believed that increasing competition between more businesses would end the economic monopoly of the few while reducing local pressure and corruption. Another suggested solution was to organize and regulate the presence of Syrian refugees in Lebanon, at least as far as the informal settlements were concerned, for they represented the primary source of economic instability and security threats. The only solution unanimously agreed upon was to find ways to help the Syrian refugees safely return to their country given that, after seven years of refuge, Syrians' living standards in the ITSs had deteriorated tremendously.

Figure 4.8 shows a wallet vandalized and discarded on the sidewalk. The research group's interpretations were that it could have either fallen from someone, or it was stolen and then discarded. The coresearchers argued that the valuables inside a wallet included not only cash or credit cards but, more importantly, identity cards. In a country where identity politics prevail and where residing Syrians were classified and treated accordingly, one's self identity was often summed up in a plastic card issued by government officials. For a Lebanese citizen, losing their identity card would mean a real bureaucratic hassle and could lead to a colossal waste of time attempting to get a new one, if possible. For a Syrian refugee, losing their identity card meant the possibility of detention and deportation, with dim to no hope of living legitimately and humanely in Lebanon. In fact, the 2017 VASyR report jointly produced between the UNHCR, WFP, and UNICEF stated that more than 70 percent of Syrian refugees over the age of fifteen did not have any legal residency, and were at high risk of mistreatment, incarceration, and even deportation.[37] According to some of the research participants, this situation led Syrians to negatively adapt to their new realities using illegal measures to access socioeconomic gains, especially when relying on stolen identity cards to facilitate their mobility within the country.

All of the coresearchers agreed that Syrian women were the weaker link in this vicious cycle, since many of their identification cards were managed by either their spouses or, even worse, the informal settlements' *shawishs*, who ended up monopolizing most transactions within the public sphere. One participant echoed some Syrian women's lack of confidence in reporting

Figure 4.8 Lost Identity. *Source:* Photo by Diana H.

incidents of abuse, exploitation, and harassment to local authorities due to lack of trust in the Lebanese system taking appropriate action and, worse, the fear of reprisals by their abusers.[38]

Meanwhile, most of the Lebanese research participants approved of the suggested solution to develop more inclusive and stricter security measures. One example approved by some coresearchers was the possible implementation of an automated system for the UNHCR to issue temporary identification cards using biometrics that would be officially acknowledged by Lebanese authorities. This would help refugees to be legally visible to local authorities. However, a couple of participants were hesitant about using such intrusive measures that would end up surveilling the Syrian's daily activities and provide the potential to share their information with third-party interest groups, thus stripping away the residing Syrians' privacy. This commended recommendation of issuing legal identification cards to Syrian residents simultaneously came with some of the discriminatory fears of legalizing the permanent presence of Syrians within the participants' country. It seemed as though the Lebanese coresearchers' altruistic inclinations could not overpass the fears and enshrined vindications of Syrian (Sunni) hypermasculine domination over Lebanon. Still, we did find empathy from some of the participants, or perhaps it was more a self-projection of their own collective fear of an intrusive state that notoriously uses intelligence services (*Mukhabarat*) in order to track, terrorize, and eliminate individuals who pose a threat or are simply undesirable.

Figure 4.9 shows some of the published literature and large posters issued by the UNHCR and other humanitarian programs involved in aiding Syrian refugees in Lebanon. The posters are shown behind a pile of balls on the walls of a store and on boards installed in a remote area near refugee camps. These photos appear to reflect part of the failed efforts to create awareness among Syrian refugees and Lebanese citizens on important issues about the refugee crisis. Most of the photos reveal more technical problems rather than easy solutions to the refugee crisis. In the photo-elicitation session, one participant explained that the poster on the wall of the store could barely be seen, as it was (un)intentionally hidden by merchandise. Similarly, the pamphlets on the roads were difficult to recognize from a distance. This is not to mention that the posters were in remote locations, difficult to reach by pedestrians or by someone commuting on public transportation. Other participants reiterated that low literacy among many Syrians made these posters of limited use. In fact, the majority of the refugees in those informal settlements were children and young women from poor upbringings, mostly reserved in the private sphere, which, according to all participants, explains their lack of the necessary tools to successfully navigate the public sphere.

According to all participants, these posters existed because the UNHCR and governmental agencies found many difficulties in reaching out to Syrian

Figure 4.9   Raising Awareness Programs. *Source:* Photo by Maria S.

refugees and communicating with them on an individual basis. Even with printed banners with animation about the preferred processes on how to acquire security and support, many participants agreed that refugees distrusted the Lebanese government and international organizations, fearing that registration or submitting their personal information could cause trouble for them with the Lebanese law. Similarly, some participants added that neither the Lebanese government nor the relief agencies had the resources and capability to oversee all the informal settlements because of the chaotic way these camps were scattered. Given the lack of trust and the logistical obstacles regarding UNHCR raising awareness programs, the most effective solution suggested by the participants was to resort to social and mass media. Educational and informative programs on media, such as TV and radio, could always reach larger populations of Syrians, who got most of their information through these outlets. At the same time, all participants agreed that the UNHCR and other humanitarian organizations already used the WhatsApp application to reach Syrian refugees, sharing information and updates from respective agencies, which made the posters obsolete.

On the use of social media applications, some participants criticized the information gap as a significant barrier to most Syrians in accessing relevant news of the Syrian conflict, forging cross-boundary networks, and, most importantly, recognizing available aid programs. According to one participant, Syrian women were not the primary news bearers, vulnerable to inadequate, sporadic, and random misinformation. Most of these women did not have access to cellphones, impeded from accessing real-time information that would help them navigate safely within the public sphere. Most of the older Syrian women whom the volunteers worked with struggled to learn how to navigate the different types of communication devices, and the younger females often had their cellphones confiscated by their male counterparts. This information precarity was further exacerbated with the limited and costly

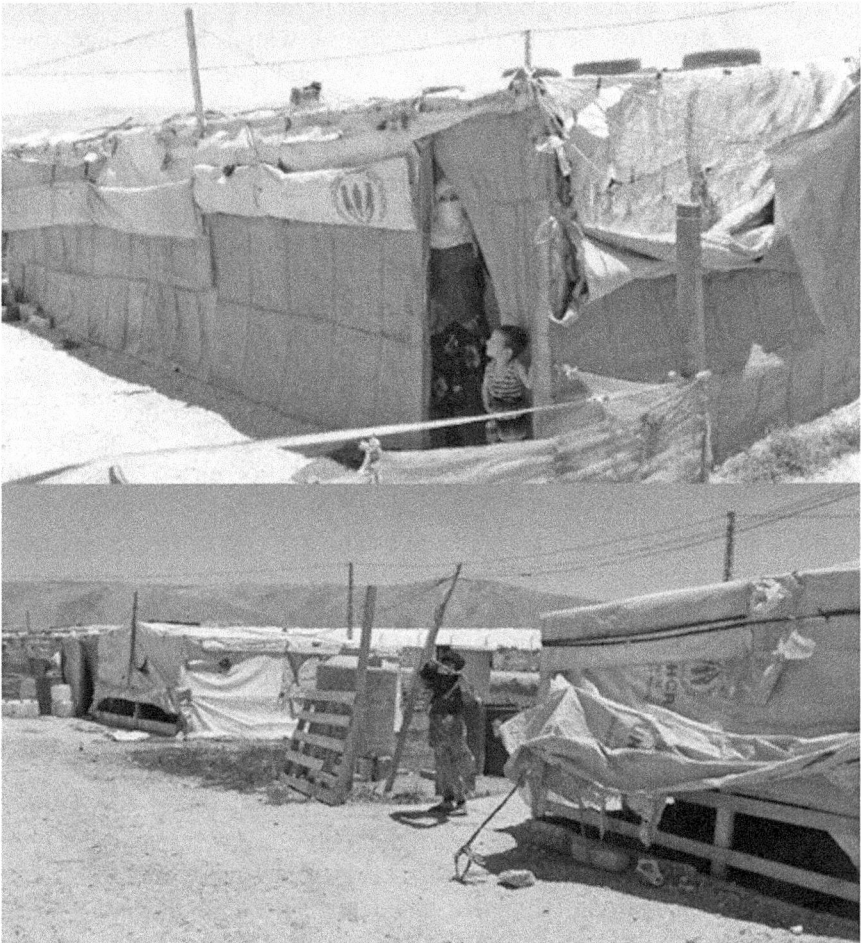

Figure 4.10   Fear of the Other. *Source:* Photo by Mazen J.

network coverage that isolated most Syrian women, who had little control over
the nuanced or inaccurate news circulated about them, becoming dependent on
versions of stories. According to one research participant, this situation created
a new dynamism of female-lead Syrian initiatives to rebuff those inaccuracies
by forging external alliances through media outlets. Online platforms, such
as the Facebook group "I am a Syrian in Lebanon," were utilized as viable
outlets to voice their realities, while at the same time crafting alternative Syrian stories and seeking adequate assistance and support from fellow Syrians.

This title included two photos of tents inside an informal Syrian settlement, showcasing Syrians' distrust of external visitors. The tents appear to
be vulnerable and exposed, and yet seem to aggressively hide whatever is
inside, with small entrances. The photos in figure 4.10 show the reality of life
inside informal refugee camps at the edge of towns, roadsides, near rivers, or
agricultural lands. Interestingly, on the exterior of the tents, the UNHCR logo
can be seen, depicting their ineffective presence within the occupied space
in providing refugees with some form of safety and protection from visiting
outsiders. The half-built open tents, the scavenged pallets, and the hazardous extended cables shown are nothing like what the UNHCR promoted for
refugee assistance and protection. One participant believed that the Syrian
adults and children living inside the tents could barely enjoy any security or
privacy, and were subject to voyeurism. Also, the participant highlighted that
most informal camps were isolated from nearby communities, by both physical and invisible cultural barriers. The Lebanese research volunteers chose
these photos to depict how most Syrian refugee women suffered from minimal privacy protection, especially those who lived in ITSs relatively far from
any town center, as they were vulnerable to harassment and attacks.[39] Street
vigilantes, local police, and soldiers raided the informal tents in the guise of
checking permits, only to harass the women residing there.[40] This dramati-
cally increased the exposure to GBV, as in the patriarchal social context, the
female body is a central subject of gazing, and Syrian women were perceived
as sexual beings, especially in the case of younger women not having developed sufficient experience in dealing with sexuality.[41]

On another note, all of the research participants agreed that most Syrian
inhabitants were apprehensive to intruders asking questions. Some participants recounted the many times that they themselves witnessed the same type
of unfriendliness during their visits to ITSs. Syrians residing in the camps,
especially women, were anxious and angry about being exploited by new-
comers whose sole purpose was to get a successful story out of their misery.
Some of the research participants stated that many Syrians were reluctant to
welcome journalists' visits, researchers, and agency representatives, since
most external visit purposes aimed to get interesting photographs while twist-
ing Syrian refugees' stories in order to gain public attention. Rightfully, this

could be described as "research fatigue"—a process through which various privileged individuals come up to refugees in order to rush questions without making any tangible positive change for the refugees.

The research participants also elaborated on the notion of special interest, where some agencies' goals and interests did not necessarily correspond to the messages that Syrians wanted to convey in interviews. The coresearchers' portrayal of Syrian distrust toward outsiders with external agendas resonated with this project's aim of exposing the tendencies of reports, policies, and studies to exploit an essentialist image of Syrian refugees—as either potential masculine threats that need to be controlled or feminized victims in dire need of protection—for personal benefit. Both of these narratives silenced the complex Syrian realities and forcibly stripped away their agency. According to one research participant, these ill-equipped intruders asked questions, took photographs, and, eventually, went back to the comfort of their homes, leaving the depicted Syrians in the same conundrum. Other participants mentioned that many refugees also seized the moment of foreigners coming to showcase their impoverishment and request further assistance. In fact, during both of the research group's visits to ITSs, the *shawish*, assisted by several women and a dozen children, gave us a tour around their informal camp, highlighting all sorts of problems that many Syrian residents faced. One example is when the *shawish* presented us with a couple of Syrian families and introduced them as illegal, having not acquired their UNHCR registration documents yet, not wanting to leave the camp out of fear of being apprehended. Others joined in and complained about their health problems, lack of medication, or even hospitalization, requesting aid to pay for these procedures. These examples illustrate the common theme of refugee agency and resilience in either wanting to voice their insecurities to outsiders or shutting down all communication efforts to prevent exploitation.

The research participants' suggested solution to this situation would be difficult and costly. One example was to provide an information outlet for these refugees to craft their own stories and be able to express their perceptions and feelings about their own realities publicly. At the same time, all of the coresearchers surmised that the ultimate solution required some political agreement and a strong will from the Lebanese government to allow refugees to access more secure housing until their safe return to their homeland. According to the coresearchers, the refugees' privacy and safety issues could only be solved with the latter solution, for most Syrians would continue to be exploited as long as there was news to "sell." In the meantime, all participants agreed that the terrible living conditions Syrians endured in Lebanon would not change, and if these types of news stories continued, neighboring Lebanese communities would feel more tension and apprehension about the weight and cost of the continued Syrian refugee presence within their neighborhoods.

Theme 3: (In)formal Labor and Shift of Gender Roles

Three subthemes were identified under this thematic category addressing the issues of labor among refugees, especially among children, as well as the research participants' perspective on the shifting and changing gender roles

Figure 4.11   Child Labor. *Source:* Photo by Hanan A.

that seemed to be imposed on many Syrian women as an impact of the Syrian Civil War.

One of the two photos in figure 4.11 shows a child filling a bottle with water from a muddy hole, while the other shows a young child watching a sibling work in a vegetable field next to a river filled with garbage. On the one hand, these photos speak of extreme poverty, unacceptable suffering, and despair combined with survival. On the other hand, they reflect issues of child labor as a result of the Syrian refugee crisis. The photos were taken during the holy month of Ramadan when most adults were fasting and sleeping during the day, while the children, who did not have to fast, worked. However, even during other months of the year, the research participants were used to seeing young children working, whereas mothers were more likely to stay inside the camps and fathers or adult males were barely seen. These photos tell the stories of refugee children striving to survive under inhumane conditions.

What made their suffering worse is the combination of cultural values and traditions that were not equipped for times of war. All of the Lebanese core-searchers agreed that due to the strong drive among refugees to beget more children for religious or cultural reasons, most of these children were born as refugees inside the informal settlements in the absence of adequate family planning. Either way, the research participants stated that the birth rates of Syrian refugees were growing exponentially, imposing a much more significant burden on the international community that was already unable to offer enough aid, and on the Lebanese government and society suffering mostly from over-population. In addition to the massive Syrian population residing in specific Lebanese communities, the limited capabilities of the Lebanese state, and the weak efforts of the UNHCR, the overpopulation problem was exacerbated by cultural factors. According to one research participant, many Syrians reiterated an ill-informed, birth-encouraging Arabic cultural saying when asked about the reasons for childbearing: "*Al walad rizkhou ya'ti ma3aho*—Child's livelihood comes with his birth." Many of the refugees believed that they must continue begetting children despite the crisis and lack of resources, partly for traditional reasons that had to do with the practice of raising children to help generate more possibilities of livelihood and expand family status, and therefore, strength.

It is important to note that there was also a lack of legal protection for refugee children that allowed their parents, *shawishs*, or others to exploit them in labor and other illicit trades, such as becoming beggars or even thieves on the streets, where they were subjected to all kinds of verbal, emotional, physical and sexual abuse. Interestingly, the Labor Code in Lebanon stated that no child under eight years old was allowed to work. Still, Lebanese laws did not extend to foreign residents, leaving Syrian children unchecked.[42] One Syrian child recounted, "It was very hostile—people used to call me the 'Syrian dog' and other things [. . .] I would get really hurt, sometimes I would just sit and cry. It was humiliating."[43]

All of the research participants believed that most refugee children born in Lebanon had no documents and were not registered, which raised many serious questions about their stateless future when they chose to stay, return home, or even sought asylum in third countries. According to one participant, the only recourse, which most impoverished Syrian families were unable to undertake given the need to prove family ties when legally crossing state borders, was a costly and complex legal process to register their children. Most participants agreed that roughly half a million Syrian children born in Lebanon lacked legal documentation. These children were, consequently, unable to enroll in public schools, for they were legally nonexistent and lacked proof of their age. The exploitation of child labor and lack of legal documentation thus threatened the healthy growth and development of children by restricting them from necessary educational programs.[44] Even with all the efforts made by LCRP initiatives to both ameliorate and expand the educational system, Lebanese schools barely accommodated 100,000 of the 300,000 Syrian children.[45] With not enough teachers qualified to cover this sudden increase in student registrations, "some schools [sent] Lebanese children home after half a day and then [taught] Syrians in the second half."[46]

Further exacerbating this issue was the fact that no Lebanese law entirely prohibited children of ten years or older from child labor, particularly in the agricultural sector. With less than 1 percent of Syrian refugees having working permits in Lebanon, Syrian parents could not afford to prioritize education over having their children bring income to support their family.[47] As a result, "93 percent of refugee families resort to child labor since adults are restricted from accessing the labor market."[48] In a Human Rights Watch interview with a Syrian refugee family, an interviewee stated, "We cannot afford to put them in school here. All my children were studying in Syria, but if I would put them in school here how would I live? We would have to buy them clothes and pay for transportation. Even if everything was free, the children could not go to school for they are the only ones that can work."[49]

The Lebanese research participants' ideal solutions on this theme were to educate, inform, and create awareness about family planning to motivate Syrian refugees to avoid giving birth on a large scale. However, some participants viewed this as extremely difficult when there were very few resources to provide Syrians their most basic needs, let alone finding enough resources for education and awareness about family planning. In addition to this, it was impossible to persuade Syrians not to carry on with their lives, avoid getting married, or to have children, when they had already spent seven years in Lebanon with no hope that the war in their country would come to an end any time soon. Thus, most participants acknowledged the presence of a few initiatives in certain hospitals and clinics to ease Syrian birth registration rules, providing birth certificates in hopes of reinstating some legal presence. All of the research participants agreed that the only viable solution left was to

Figure 4.12   Shift of Gender Roles. *Source:* Photo by Diana H.

create a low-cost legal mechanism to register the fraught Syrian children and allow them to access safety, education, and avoid informal labor at all costs.

Figure 4.12 showcase Syrian women's agency and what seemed to the Lebanese coresearchers to be a shift of gender roles among Syrian refugees in Lebanon. One photo shows a woman lifting a wooden plank. The second photo shows a young girl carrying a child. The most striking reality in these photos is the absence of men in all three situations. This did not come as a surprise to the coresearchers, however, since it was usual for few adult men

to be seen within the informal settlements. According to one research participant, most men were either away during the day or resting during Ramadan
season inside the tents. As a result, Syrian women and girls had to take on
their responsibilities in managing the camp by conducting their daily chores
within the open camp's public spaces without proper protection.

As Syrian women took on more responsibility and autonomy, for many
of them these opportunities and increasing responsibilities did not equate to
equality or security. While enabling women to work might be seen as a form
of emancipation, without proper care and governmental protection, working
women were further exposed to harassment and inadequate financial com-
pensation. All of the research participants agreed that the significant number
of females and children inside the refugee camps compared to adult men had
severe implications for both Syrian and Lebanese residents. Some of the coresearchers recounted that a sense of security was barely felt at the camps, and
even more so outside the camps, where women and children occasionally ventured to get supplies, get documents processed, or work informally to earn additional income. Many Syrian women, as young as fifteen years of age, witnessed
a dramatic increase in gender-based violence, as they were often seen as easy
and desperate targets for sexual assault, rape, and other forms of intimidation.
Additionally, early and forced marriages reportedly increased among Syrian
refugees in Lebanon during the crisis, creating a noticeable difference between
the girls and boys in the "children" group. In fact, girls in refugee camps were
at a higher risk of being subjected to "child marriage" because their parents
were unable to cater to their needs. One study showed that refugee parents tend
to marry daughters off immediately when they start menstruating as a coping
strategy to deter any abuse toward adolescent girls.[50] Due to the financial strains
from which Syrian households suffered during the refugee crisis, parents who
were struggling with poverty tended to think that their daughters would be in
a safer environment through this negative coping response of marrying their
daughters, hoping that they would be protected by their husband and in-laws,
limiting prospects of rape or kidnapping.[51] This culturally accepted practice of
child marriage can be attributed to the fact that, in patriarchal social contexts,
male providers feel that young daughters present a high liability that is not only
financial, which relates to "fewer mouths to feed," but also social and personal,
as marriage is the ultimate way of protecting women and their honor.[52]

One volunteer stated that young boys were not spared from additional
responsibilities, especially as many were sent to the streets by their designated *shawish* to work, beg, or even steal from the age of five.[53] According
to that research participant, a boy at the age of thirteen was a man and, thus,
eligible to be a breadwinner, which meant that he was under more pressure
to generate income with any means available, considering the possibility of
starting his own family within a few years.

The research participants further discussed several initiatives focused on training women facing adversity to develop enough skills to engage in a number of socioeconomically viable and productive activities. According to one research participant, the nonprofit organization that she worked with helped Syrian women develop ways to market and sell their products in the local economy. The organization hosted several funded projects to empower Syrian women by encouraging them to communicate, exchange experiences, share issues, and support each other at work, providing the women with adequate skills and training in the production of goods, marketing, distribution, and sales.[54] Some examples mentioned were vocational training, computer lessons, language courses, and instruction on gendered skills such as culinary activities, hair and make-up, and embroidery.

Despite the positive intentions behind such initiatives, most of the research participants agreed that they were insufficient, deeply affected by discriminatory personal laws that inhibited most of these women from thriving in the Lebanese context. According to some participants, most projects that focused on women's empowerment tended to be only somewhat encouraging, not really addressing the main problem of the patriarchal structures established within the Lebanese system. Although these programs did attempt to help Syrians in generating some safe income, one participant criticized them for stereotyping Syrian women into a division of labor that seemed to neither empower them as female refugees nor promote gender equality. The only viable solution suggested by the coresearchers was to remove the refugee and gender stigmas attached to Syrian women residing in Lebanon as part of a larger Syrian threat by calling for more gender-inclusive initiatives that would truly bridge the local anxieties toward their presence and empower the female communities.

The coresearchers' photo-elicitation of Syrian women's agency challenged the essentialist views of Syrian women refugees as a helpless and indistinguishable mass. Additionally, the participants' depiction of the disproportionate types of resilience activities—which most Syrian women had to adopt in order to survive within a discriminatory and gendering environment—resonated with the study's aims of exploring how the involved humanitarian agencies considered and addressed these inequalities within their refugee crisis response plans, and underscoring the intersectional gendered differences in the Syrian population in Lebanon.

The Lebanese coresearchers chose figure 4.13 to depict the overall tragedy of the Syrian crisis in Lebanon. In the photo, a woman is sitting on the floor of her bare tent, attending to her sick child, who is covered in laced cloth to protect her from flies and mosquitoes. On the one hand, all of the research participants claimed that these scenes were recurrent within most refugee camps. The participants elaborated that Syrian children living in unsanitary conditions were often at risk of terminal illness inside informal settlements,

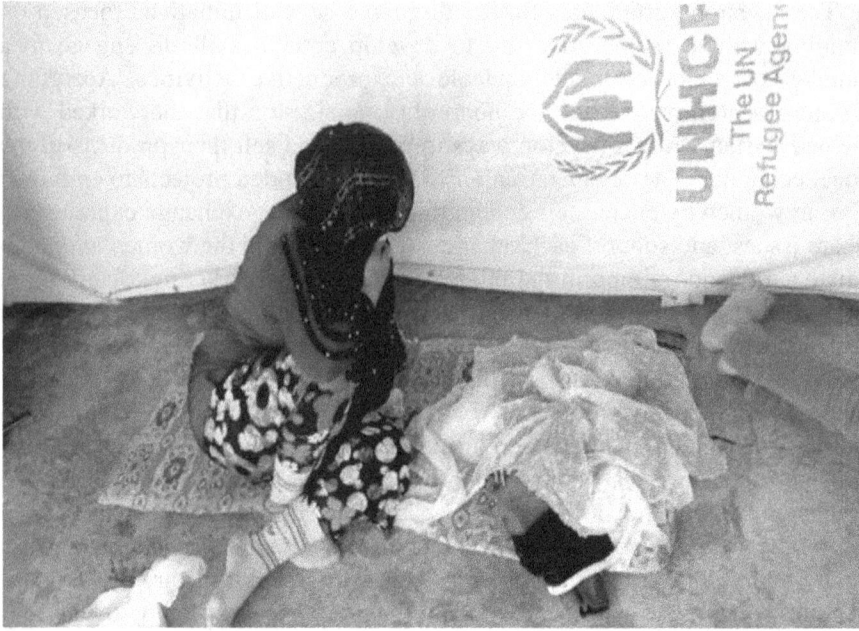

Figure 4.13   The Future. *Source:* Photo by Mazen J.

where access to appropriate health care was costly and difficult to reach. This was especially the case if the child or their parents lacked documentation, in which situation the participants believed that the process of acquiring adequate health care became almost impossible.

On the other hand, some of the participants pointed out that many photos like this were skewed in Lebanese media on a regular basis. At the beginning of the Syrian crisis, many media outlets published victimizing images of cases such as these in order to shock audiences and compel Lebanese officials and citizens to take immediate action to help refugees financially. However, the research participants stated that over the years, this warm support faded away with the increase of cases like these, and after witnessing much Syrian involvement in crimes and terrorist acts in Lebanon. One participant highlighted the fact that previous types of financial support dwindled, and many Syrian women complained to them that the aid provided by the UNHCR, whose logo appears in the photo on the back wall of the tent, became irregular and scarce. Today, photos such as the previous ones do not reach the media, since they are considered part of the normal experience of having so many refugees for so long in an overburdened developing host country. All of the research participants criticized the fact that official Lebanese rhetoric still blames Syrian refugees unsympathetically for many of the health problems within the country.[55] Some participants also claimed that the lack of legal protection, the absence of humanitarian assistance, and the sense of insecurity made women's and children's conditions much worse. All of the Lebanese coresearchers agreed that there should be an immediate effort to involve multiple parties to provide enough resources to ease the Syrian women's struggles and to provide safety, security, and resources to the majority of the vulnerable Syrian population, who, "despite being victims, became objects of blame and suspicion."[56]

A Gender Analysis

The majority of the themes extracted during the photo-elicitation process brought interesting criticism of the inefficiently gendered bureaucratic prioritization and stratification of crisis response management. All of the research participants agreed that Lebanon's refugee security strategies, networks, and discourses were ineffective in securing both the host and refugee populations from the burdens and threats they were facing daily as a result of the crisis. During the photo-elicitation discussions, the participants also agreed that those policies labeling Syrians as either "displaced" or "refugees" were especially failing at protecting the women precariously residing within Lebanon from all sorts of harm. We found cases where Syrian women registered through the UNHCR were not allowed to work legally, whereas those who chose to acquire a work visa under the *kafala* system were rarely qualified for at least two of the three work permits—sanitation work, construction, or agribusiness—as they were not culturally viable for Arab women who mostly work in feminized occupational trades such as secretarial work and school instruction. Consequently, to sustain their own and their families' livelihoods, Syrian women increasingly opted for informal work within the agribusiness, which came with a great deal of intimidation and manipulation from all parties, including fellow Syrian *shawishs*. Entering the (in)formal job market, made Syrian women an easy target for gender-based violence, as they were legally powerless, either dependent on their sponsors or the leniency of Lebanese GS officers, easily intimidated and coerced into providing sexual services to avoid harassment.[57]

As became apparent throughout the photo-elicitation discussions, most of the Lebanese coresearchers viewed their government's painful policies as mechanisms that (re)produced more insecurities within Lebanese communities. One of the many examples is the precarious legal situation of the Syrian children, such as the ones shown in figure 4.13. One Lebanese newspaper reported that, according to international organizations involved in the issue of Syrian refugees in Lebanon, of the 1.6 million refugees there were around 300,000 Syrian women who gave birth in 2017.[58] During an interview, a legal expert from Justice Without Borders stated that "there are maybe around 200,000 or more children who are not registered."[59] Other than such a procedure is costly, requiring a DNA exams and costly court fees, Syrian parents do not know that their children are stateless, uaware of the legal problems that they would have to face in the future, such as arrests without being able to return to their home country.

The expert provided an analysis of the legal implications associated with the birth rate of Syrians, stating that it carries additional negative consequences for both Syrian and Lebanese communities; however, the numbers were exaggerated, not reflective of the estimated data collected by the involved agencies. The Minister of State for Refugee Affairs, Mouin Merehbi, the UN refugee agency spokesman in Lebanon, Khaled Kabara, and Medical Coordinator for Doctors Without Borders, Mounia Amrani, quickly debunked this viral news, stating that such a number was impossible, fake news, and part of a xenophobic anti-Syrian refugee agenda in Lebanon.[60] Still, there was no doubt that an accurate number of Syrian births was impossible to provide. After all, the Syrian presence in Lebanon was not limited to those officially registered in the state records and with the UNHCR. Ultimately, even though the numbers were not as high as portrayed, the increasing annual rate of stateless births only posed a bigger demographic threat to both Lebanese institutions and Syrian refugees' livelihoods, justifying local and international anxieties over civil unrest between Lebanese and Syrians in many host communities.[61]

It is also crucial to note that there are severe gaps in general awareness on matters relating to reproductive and sexual health for both men and women who come from modest backgrounds with no literacy or sex education. These knowledge gaps have resulted in high birth rates and an increase in infant mortality and deformity percentages.[62] Most registered Syrian refugees received assistance from the UNHCR for payment of "basic" health services. However, Syrians still needed to cover the remaining 25 percent of "advanced" medical checkups and much needed health services that most pregnant women and nursing mothers undergo, which reflect conditions of gender discrimination.[63] Most efforts to include measures to control disease outbreaks, hunger, and childbirth were not prioritized as part of the health sector initiatives, even though these were the most endemic types of health hazards that the majority of Syrian refugees women and children endured.

Meanwhile, except primary health care and life-threatening emergencies, gender-specific medical services were almost absent, even when 80 percent of vulnerable targets such as women and children differed in health risks, conditions, and needs from those concerning men.[64] Syrian women would still need to cover the remaining 25 percent of "advanced" medical checkups and much needed health services that most pregnant women and nursing mothers undergo, reflecting conditions of gender discrimination.[65] Most efforts to include measures to control disease outbreaks, hunger, and childbirth were not prioritized as part of the health sector initiatives, even though these are the most endemic types of health hazards that the majority of Syrian refugee women endured. On the one hand, different structural hierarchies and social barriers hindered Syrian women and girls from seeking adequate health assistance due to "stigma, fear of mistreatment or discrimination, lack of awareness, fear of reporting violence, and difficulties obtaining legal status."[66] On the other hand, the availability and cost for seeking the already strained health services prevented most Syrian women and girls from accessing needed reproductive diagnoses and treatments, putting them at serious risk of avoidable mortality hazards.[67] While the humanitarian response-needs prioritized essential items such as food, protection, water, and shelter to fulfill the Syrian refugees' related needs, the study shows that their provision of services related to reproductive, maternal and child-health services were barely provided. One of the main reasons stated by health experts is the ill-equipped Lebanese healthcare system, already established before the crisis, that does not provide gender inclusively subsidized or discounted health services for women in Lebanon.[68]

This reality, along with the overall financial shortages and economic hardships, only resulted in a vicious spiral of poverty and desperation for both Lebanese and countless residing Syrians, where women-headed households were the most vulnerable groups. With the UN only receiving half of the funds it requested for its work in supporting refugees in Lebanon, the severe shortage of resources resulted in the reduction of monthly payment to Syrian refugees—from US$27.70 to US$13.50 per person per month.[69] As a consequence, the UN warned of an increase in Syrian refugees resorting to negative coping strategies such as a reduction of food intake and expenditure on education and health, coupled with an increase in debt, informal work and street begging.[70] Such actions resulted in various negative consequences on the already burdened Lebanese infrastructure.

Meanwhile, it is very tough for legal systems to separate child sex trafficking and early marriage. It is not unusual for early marriages to be a form of exploitation through disguised sex trafficking and prostitution in patriarchal contexts.[71] In fact, some Syrian families tend to pragmatically wed off a young daughter to the highest bidder, especially when there are times of financial and economic hardship and crisis.[72] Accordingly, early marriage cases in Lebanon may have been an indicator of forced prostitution and a precursor to GBV, where Syrian refugee girls in Lebanon were exploited by forcibly being married in exchange for legal support—getting a Lebanese residency when wedded to a Lebanese man—and economic support, which their low-income families sorely needed.[73] According to an expert from Justice Without Borders (a Lebanese NGO that promotes human rights), "when there are cases where they find the families sell their daughter to get some money from it, also it is legally not applicable to say that that is trafficking because, within the culture, they take money for their daughter."[74] This expert expanded the idea by stating that "when you talk about a penal issue, you consider the intention [. . .] if their [family] intention is to get money to live better knowing what future awaits their daughter, then [. . .] we cannot do many things."[75] This illustration adds to previous feminist critiques of supposed

refugee crisis management practices that actually perpetuate unequal relations and co-constitute systemic social, historical, and material forms of
oppression that are grounded and continually reformulated, elevating Syrian
women's insecurities and shifting their gendered roles, forced to adapt to
their new realities by providing sexual favors to bargain for food, shelter, and
other needs to secure themselves and their undocumented children.[76]

We find cases where, in some areas, the local population has doubled,
putting much pressure on the already dire Lebanese infrastructure, housing,
health services, and educational services. Overpopulation and waste management strategies were mismanaged, posing a threat to most female residents,
violating their right to access public health. As a result, trash could be seen
all over the ITSs, where dumping in public spaces became the norm, pollut-
ing the natural water reservoirs that female-headed Syrian refugee households
highly depended on to provide for their families. As a result, (un)aware Syrian refugee women resiliently adapted to their new environments, switching
gender roles in order to thwart the discriminative securitized practices that
silenced their gender insecurities.

SYNTHESIZING THE IMPACT TRANSLATION
OF REFUGEE INSECURITIES

Due to the reflexivity of the Photovoice process, the photo-elicitation sessions
conducted by the research group revealed the Lebanese participants' perceptions and criticisms of refugee policies' impact on residing Syrian insecurities.
The reflective analysis that resulted from these group discussions was thus
useful in the examination of the photos taken by the coresearchers, which
visually represent the complexity of local realities within refugee camps in
Lebanon. This exercise yielded more nuanced understandings of the impact
translation of Syrian refugee (in)securities in Lebanon. Mixed emotions were
elicited throughout the photo-analysis sessions, in which stimulating discussions bridged the participants' distinct views of each photo, facilitating more
open conversation about controversial issues within the Lebanese refugee management system. While the participants held multiple, and often competing,
perspectives on the definition of Syrian refugee (in)security, there was a strong
consensus about the systemic gendered violence and exploitation that Syrian
refugees endured, especially women. Some participants focused on blaming the
inadequate funding directed toward empowering Syrian women. Others complained that legal loopholes and corrupt Lebanese bureaucratic agencies naturally discriminated against all women in Lebanon, even when properly funded.

Interestingly, most participants' recommended solutions to these intersectional issues projected the politicized local fear of the continuing Syrian presence in the country, which revealed the duality of the coresearchers' roles as

both humanitarian actors and Lebanese nationals. On several occasions, the participants suggested that Syrian refugees were better off going back to Syria than remaining in a country that outlawed their assimilation, justifying this claim on humanitarian grounds. On the one foot, as humanitarian actors, these local volunteers had an interest in alleviating the (in)tangible human sufferings within their communities. On the other hand, in some of their commentary, the participants also projected the gendered values present in the Lebanese context, so that, unfortunately, their primordial humanitarian instincts were overridden by xenophobic Lebanese anxieties. Due to the daily discriminatory rhetoric that fueled their collective memory of fear toward the protracted Syrian presence within their country, some of the participants internalized the public paranoia regarding the possibility of Syrian integration into Lebanon, which was (and still is) on the brink of a socioeconomic, political, and sectarian collapse.

The Lebanese volunteers themselves seemed to recognize their own duality because of their experiences working with Syrian refugees. Most of the volunteers stated that they found satisfaction in being needed and doing meaningful work in their beloved home country, but, at the same time, they could not respect their government because it neither included them nor appreciated their presence. As a matter of fact, several of the participants reported that they either contemplated, tried to leave, or wished to migrate from Lebanon to any country that would appreciate their humanity, skills, and contributions, providing them with a real sense of security. Despite their criticisms of the Lebanese state, the volunteers' desire to do good, make a difference, and be part of an admirable contributing community prompted them to remain and assist their Syrian "guests," not wanting to leave them destitute.

The Photovoice exercise thus brought a fruitful dialogical reconstruction of the multiple gendered realities that the Syrian crisis (re)produced in Lebanon. All of the participants were aware that our work was framed by, and often unintentionally complicit with, the very power relations that we sought to dissect. After all, the participants knew that their views were subjective and nonrepresentative of the overall situation of Syrians within the Lebanese context. From the many photos assessed, the research participants chose the ones that would "sell" the themes of destitution that we all wanted to focus on. Even though all participants agreed that the photos they took of Syrians in the ITSs were by no means representative, they all believed that framing them in that context would better highlight the local insecurities. The participants were correct in that regard, for, according to the UN, around 85 percent of Syrian refugees did not reside in ITSs.[77] Most Syrian refugees were scattered in out-of-the-way urban and rural areas. An article posted by the New York Times described how Lebanon had "absorbed" most Syrians, in what the author labeled as "A Refugee Crisis in Lebanon Hides in Plain Sight."[78] While the bias of most of the Photovoice pictures was acknowledged, the coresearchers and I believed that the photo-elicitation sessions helped enhance our knowledge of the different legal, economic, social, and personal (in)securities that we deemed important to share.

Our analyses of the photos exposed several themes discussed in this chapter, such as lack of food, shelter, sanitation, and legal desperation. The research participants' differing interpretation of each photo reflected the diverging norms and values that each contributor held prior to the group sessions. Syrian refugees' agency was thus highlighted in the research group's reflections. As discussed throughout the chapter, the multifaceted population of Syrian refugees, legally labeled as displaced, (re)produced (in)direct (in)securities within their host communities. Some examples brought up by the research participants of Syrian agency fueling local insecurities included waste management, child labor, and development of informal economies.

This Photovoice experience encouraged a discussion over the precarity of residing Syrians' situation in Lebanon that was mostly marked with vulnerabilities and state disfunction. Both Photovoice and my own research findings confirm and add to these issues, bringing to light that top-bottom production of a stereotypical gendered image of "displaced" Syrians conveys counterintuitive results. It adds to feminist literature's critiques that overgeneralized refugee management policies end up ignoring the intersectionality of complex agencies within the refugee population. Thus, most of the research participants agreed that while the intent of photographic depictions of Syrian refugees may very well be to humanize their subjects and show their agency, the resulted photos could not capture the whole scenario of Syrian refugee insecurities in the Lebanese context. Still, the Lebanese coresearchers believed these pictures did a better job in capturing Syrian destitution and agency when compared to most media visual depictions, which often created distance between the privileged spectators and the object of their gaze: dehumanized Syrian refugees. Most Lebanese coresearchers criticized that news images tended to objectify Syrian women and children refugees as innocent victims, lacking protection and agency, and Syrian men as posing threats to Lebanon's security and identity. Also, the top-down physical marginalization of informal Syrian settlements pushed most Syrian women and their families to live in hazardous and unsanitary habitats. This exercise thus brought more information to the Syrians' situation than it may appear in public discourse.

The research participants highlighted that the geographic settings, the refugees' social background, and most importantly gender roles affected Syrians' position of power over others within different contexts. The degree of agency that Syrian women were legally allowed, due to their precarious legal status and due to their gender, affected their limited opportunities and expectations. Most participants agreed that the problematic generalization and misrepresentation of the Syrian refugees led to discriminatory policies and exclusionary practices that silenced the already marginalized voices of Syrian women, enticing societal acceptance of intersectional violence to occur toward the diverse groups of Syrian women residing in Lebanon. However, through adaptation, and by using various means, Syrians (re)negotiated their way out of the different vulnerabilities. Several of our pictures portrayed this agency and resilience that seemed to vanish under media practices and public discourse.

Moreover, some participants suggested that loopholes within security practices were used and abused by opportunistic agencies and Syrians as well, pushing special interests at the expense of the general communities' well-being. As long as gender-biased laws and security practices emerged, generated, or perpetuated, a cycle of victimhood persisted, and any sustainable solution for the Syrian crisis remained unabated. Despite the many efforts refugees made to escape the horrors of war, governments, international agencies, and nongovernmental organizations seemed to provide little-to-no relief to most of those refugees when looked at from a top-down lens. According to the research participants, the *shawish* phenomenon was living proof of the erection of uncontrollable complex resilience efforts that tended to (re)enforce hierarchies of power relations and discrimination within the local context.

Meanwhile, all participants blamed the Lebanese government officials and humanitarian aid initiatives for the inadequate policies and mixed messages. Instead of providing refugees with secure shelters, as mentioned in the policy planning, Syrians were still discarded in mediocre living conditions on the outskirts of towns, open to all sorts of discrimination. In that case, some participants perceived that most aid techniques were complicated, time-consuming, and mostly sporadic, unreachable by most Syrians. Consequently, many Syrians were pushed into homelessness, sickness, or other types of vulnerability. As seen before, generalizing gendered vulnerabilities creates discriminatory social norms, exclusionary practices and, in some cases, structural violence against refugees with a constitutive power to reinforce, even (re)produce, local anxieties. All participants agreed that reinforcing the misperceptions of residing Syrians as a potential threat or a burden pushed most Syrian women not to report sexual abuse, to provide survival sex, to beg, and to work informally for exploitative wages to survive.[79] Therefore, echoing another feminist argument, all participants believed that without adopting a nuanced approach considering the different sociopolitical sensitivities, refugee management policies become problematic, pushing Syrians' resilience efforts into silence. In effect, Syrian women refugees had to switch gender roles to adapt to the new realities, suffering the brunt and most devastating implications of discriminative securitized practices.

The findings from this project helped this book expand its understandings about the different systems of oppression within the visuals collected and discussed by the research participants. On the one hand, discussing the many negative consequences that come out of these generalized policy processes produced increased empathy and appreciation toward most Syrian refugees. On the other hand, several research participants felt the need to emphasize some positive stories and initiatives, which crucially needed to be expanded on amid what was an extreme negative bias in the coverage of the refugee crisis in Lebanon. In times of hostile refugee political attitudes and practices, all participants felt the need to disseminate accurate stories that had the potential to empower the people whose voices were silenced by channeling the right humanitarian approach. The coresearchers viewed that Lebanese citizens had to get involved as much as Syrian residents did in order to relate more to the individual Syrian insecurities. Consequently, their effort toward working with the diverse Syrian population and connecting with them on an individual level humanized the previously portrayed faceless numbers of refugees, generating sensible questions and, potentially, common sustainable solutions to empower both communities.

To solve the problematic issues with emergency relief, there is a need to reassess the underlying assumptions and approaches. Thereupon, this project helped disrupt some of the stereotypes and inaccuracies that prevailed in the mainstream representations of Syrian refugee insecurities in Lebanon, particularly the victim and threat narratives that flattened and objectified Syrians' issues, especially women's. In that sense, the Photovoice project was conceived as a deliberately transnational project, conducted between an external academic and local refugee volunteers regarding the topic of a transnational Syrian population, that aimed at challenging the stereotype of Syrians as a foreign nuisance, a threat, or vulnerable victimized population in the hopes of promoting self-reliance initiatives for refugees. By thinking through images about the political ramifications of Syrian refugee insecurities, all participants supported the critical engagement of dissecting the problematic issues that the Syrian crisis protracted in the Lebanese context. It is essential to state that the appropriation and generalization of the research findings, applying them to all Syrian refugees in Lebanon, is a practice that this book is keen to avoid.

The findings of this study contested the idea that Syrian refugee (in)security is a zero-sum game where aid assistance and protection services were either available or not. Unfortunately, the portrayal of a "global-local divide" between protecting refugees and protecting host state sovereignty reinforces narrow securitization approaches, in which the advancement of one group's interests would come at the expense of the other group's drawbacks. The outcome leads to what seems like a paradoxical shift from aid to deterrence, detention, and deportation, justifying individual and institutional violence as a means to control the foreign population in a dialectical manner.[80] Contextual dynamics and critical variables thus complicated the Syrian refugee response mechanisms that continually exacerbated their insecurities with the humanitarian, socioeconomic, political, and security practices at hand. As such, the hostility, violence, and hate crimes against Syrians sharply rose during the crisis. And the negative impacts of Syrian refugees portrayed by most Lebanese outlets were exaggerated and misplaced, (re)impowering a vicious cycle that increased the calling for Syrians' return to their home country.

Without meaningful interaction between both communities, these stereotypes would continue to hurt any genuine opportunities to curb the Syrian refugee crisis. Any promising strategy needs to emphasize more intercommunity activities that highlight the commonalities between the diverse groups that make up both Lebanese and Syrian residing communities, halting tensions between both populations with room for solidarity toward positive change.

NOTES

1. Elizabeth Olivius, "Governing Refugees Through Gender Equality: Care, Control, Emancipation." Doctoral dissertation, Umeå Universitet (2014), 38.

2. Olivius, "Governing Refugees Through Gender Equality."

3. Alice Szczepanikova, "Gender Relations in a Refugee Camp: A Case of Chechens Seeking Asylum in the Czech Republic." *Journal of Refugee Studies* 18, no. 3 (2005): 281–98.

4. Sally Engle Merry, *Human Rights and Gender Violence: Translating International Law into Local Justic* (Chicago, IL: University of Chicago Press 2009), 3.

5. Caroline Lenette, Mark Brough, and Leonie Cox, "Everyday Resilience: Narratives of Single Refugee Women with Children." *Qualitative Social Work* 12, no. 5 (2013): 637–53.

6. Michael Ungar, Marion Brown, Linda Liebenberg, and Rasha Othman, "Unique Pathways to Resilience Across Cultures." *Adolescence* 42, no. 166 (2007): 287.

7. Philippe Bourbeau, "Resiliencism: Premises and Promises in Securitisation Research." *Resilience Journal*, no. 1 (2013): 3–17.

8. Susanne Zwingel, *Translating International Women's Rights: The CEDAW Convention in Context* (Palgrave Macmillan, 2016), 33.

9. Mariastella Pulvirenti and Gail Mason, "Resilience and Survival: Refugee Women and Violence." *Current Issues Criminal Justice. HeinOnline* 23 (2011): 37–52.

10. Pulvirenti and Mason, "Resilience and Survival," 37–52.

11. Lenette, Brough, and Cox, "Everyday Resilience," 637–53.

12. Ibid., 637–53.

13. Bourbeau, "Resiliencism," 3–17.

14. Michelle Jarldon, *Photovoice Handbook for Social Workers: Methods, Particularities and Possibilities for Social Change* (Palgrave, 2019), 1–24.

15. Alice McIntyre, *Participatory Action Research*, Vol. 52 (SAGE, 2007): xi.

16. Caroline C. Wang and Yanique A. Redwood-Jones, "Photovoice Ethics: Perspectives from Flint Photovoice." *Health Education & Behavior Sage Journals* 28, no. 5 (2001).

17. Caroline C. Wang, "Photovoice: A Participatory Action Research Strategy Applied to Women's Health." *Journal of Women's Health* 8, no. 2 (1999).

18. Wang, "Photovoice."

19. Lisa M. Given ed., *The SAGE Encyclopedia of Qualitative Research Methods* (SAGE, 2008), 844.

20. ABAAD, "Annual Report 2014," https://www.abaadmena.org/documents/ebook.1476091396.pdf.

21. Caroline Wang and Mary Ann Burris, "Photovoice: Concept, Methodology, and Use for Participatory Needs Assessment." *Health Education & Behavior* 24, no. 3 (1997): 369–87.

22. "Annual Results Report. Water, Sanitation and Hygiene." *UNICEF* (2016), 41.

23. Rola Yasmine and Catherine Moughalian, "Systemic Violence Against Syrian Refugee Women and the Myth of Effective Intrapersonal Interventions." *Reproductive Health Matters* (2016).

24. Claire Harvey, Rosa Garwood, and Roula El-Masri, *Shifting Sands: Changing Gender Roles Among Refugees in Lebanon.* (Oxfam International, 2013), 4.

25. Harvey, Rosa, and El-Masri, *Shifting Sands*, 14.

26. Government of Lebanon and UNHCR, *Lebanon Crisis Response Plan 2017–2020* (2017), 17.

27. Pulvirenti and Mason, "Resilience and Survival," 37–52.

28. "Strengths, Weaknesses and Lessons Learned," Shelter Projects, 2015, https://reliefweb.int/sites/reliefweb.int/ files/resources/ShelterProjects_2015-2016_lowres_web_Part3.pdf.

29. Government of Lebanon and UNHCR, *Lebanon Crisis Response Plan 2017–2020* (2017), 136.

30. Ibid., 137.

31. Mouawad Jamil, "Lebanon's Rubbish Crisis is a Chance to Clean Up the Populated Political System." *The Guardian* (2015).

32. Sima Ghaddar, "Lebanon Treats Refugees as a Security Problem—And It Doesn't Work." *The Century Foundation* (April 4, 2017), https://tcf.org/content/commentary/lebanon-treats-refugees-security-problem-doesnt-work/?agreed=1.

33. Ghaddar, "Lebanon Treats Refugees as a Security Problem—And It Doesn't Work." *The Century Foundation.*

34. Elie Bouri and el-Assad Joseph, "The Lebanese Electricity Woes: An Estimation of the Economical Costs of Power Interruptions." *MDPI Energies* 9, no. 8 (2016): 583.

35. Anne Barnard, "A Refugee Crisis in Lebanon Hides in Plain Sight." *New York Times* (November 12, 2015), https://www.nytimes.com/2015/11/13/world/middleeast/a-refugee-crisis-in-lebanon-hides-in-plain-sight.html.

36. Osama Habib, "Syria Supplying More Electricity to Lebanon." *The Daily Star* (August 8, 2017), https://www.dailystar.com.lb/Business/Local/2017/Aug-08/415279-syria-supplying-more-electricity-to-lebanon.ashx.

37. Habib, "Syria Supplying More Electricity to Lebanon."

38. Lorraine Charles and Kate Denman, "Syrian and Palestinian Syrian Refugees in Lebanon: The Plight of Women and Children." *Journal of International Women's Studies* 14, no. 5 (2013): 96.

39. Ruth Sherlock, "In Lebanon, Syrian Refugees Met with Harassment and Hostility." *NPR* (September 2, 2017), https://www.npr.org/sections/parallels/2017/09/02/547906231/in-lebanon-syrian-refugees-met-with-harassment-andhostility?t=1532003561503.

40. Sherlock, "In Lebanon, Syrian Refugees Met with Harassment and Hostility."

41. "Syria Regional Refugee Response, Information Portal." *United Nations High Commissioner for Refugees (UNHCR)*, http://data.unhcr.org/syrianrefugees/country.php?id=122.

42. Lebanon News, "Lebanon Witnesses Rise in Syrian Refugee Child Labor Over Past Year." *The Daily Star* (June 14, 2018), http://www.dailystar.com.lb/News/Lebanon-News/2018/Jun-14/453154-lebanon-witnesses-rise-in-syrianrefugee-child-labor-over-past-year.ashx.

43. Lebanon News, "Lebanon Witnesses Rise In Syrian Refugee Child Labor Over Past Year."

44. "Growing Up Without an Education: Barriers to Education for Syrian Refugee Children in Lebanon." *Human Rights Watch* (July 2016), https://www.hrw.org/report/2016/07/19/growing-without-education/barriers-education-syrianrefugee-children-lebanon.

45. Julia Craig Romano, "Humanitarian Crisis: Impact of Syrian Refugees in Lebanon." *Middle East Program Wilson Center* (October 29, 2013), https://www.wilsoncenter.org/event/humanitarian-crisis-impact-syrian-refugees-lebanon.

46. Patricia Mouamar, "Viewpoints: Impact of Syrian Refugees on Host Countries." *BBC News* (August 24, 2013), https://www.bbc.com/news/world-23813975.

47. Morgan Meaker, "Syrian Refugee Children Reduced to Selling on Beirut's Streets to Feed Their Families." *The Guardian* (January 25, 2017), https:// www.theguardian.com/global-development/2017/jan/25/syrian-refugee-childrenselling-beirut-streets-lebanon-support-families.

48. "The Situation of Human Rights in Lebanon." *ALEF, Annual Report 2017* (March 2018), 11, https://alefliban.org/wp-content/uploads/2018/04/annual_report_2017_v03_-2.pdf.

49. "Growing Up Without an Education: Barriers to Education for Syrian Refugee Children in Lebanon." *Human Rights Watch* (July 19, 2016).

50. Cherri Zeinab et al., "Early Marriage and Barriers to Contraception Among Syrian Refugee Women in Lebanon: A Qualitative Study." *International Journal of Environmental Research and Public Health*, vol. 8 (2017): 836.

51. "Childhood in the Shadow of War: Voices of Young Syrians." *Save the Children* (2015), http://resourcecentre.savethechildren.se/sites/default/files/documents/childhood-in-the-shadow-of-war.pdf.

52. "Are We Listening? Acting on Our Commitments to Women and Girls Affected by the Syrian Conflict." *International Rescue Committee, IRC* (2014), 15.

53. Ghaddar, "Lebanon Treats Refugees as a Security Problem—And It Doesn't Work."

54. "Syrian Women Rise Above Differences and Forge a Statement of Unity." *UN Women News* (May 23, 2016), http://www.unwomen.org/en/news/stories/2016/5/syrian-women-rise-above-differences-and-forge-a-statement-ofunity.

55. "Syrian Women Rise Above Differences and Forge a Statement of Unity."

56. Maha Yahya, Jean Kassir, and Khalil El-Hariri, *Unheard Voices: What Syrian Refugees Need to Return Home* (Carnegie Endowment for International Peace, 2018), p 12.

57. Geneviève Colas, Secours Catholique-Caritas France, and Peyroux Olivier, "Trafficking in Human Beings." *Caritas* (2016), http://www.caritas.eu/sites/default/files/report_-_trafficking_in_conflict_and_post-conflict_situations_en.pdf.

58. "300 Thousand Syrian Women Pregnant will Give Birth in Lebanon in 2017." *Addiyar News* (March 3, 2017), https://www.addiyar.com/article/1359928-300-2017.

59. Justice Without Borders Expert Interview with Author (May 29, 2017).

60. Mohamed Alloush, "What Is the Truth About the Presence of 300,000 Pregnant Syrian Women in Lebanon?." *ElNashra News* (May 3, 2017), https://www.alaraby.co.uk/english/news/2017/5/5/debunked-300-000-syrian-refugees-arenot-pregnant-in-lebanon.

61. Alloush, "What Is the Truth About the Presence of 300,000 Pregnant Syrian Women in Lebanon?"

62. "Women and the Refugee Crisis: A News Update from Lebanon." *Global Fund for Woman* (2015), https://www.globalfundforwomen.org/news-update-refugee-crisis/#.WVovCoiGPIU.

63. "Women and the Refugee Crisis."

64. Karl Blanchet, Fouad M. Fouad, and Tejendra Pherali, "Syrian Refugees in Lebanon: The Search for Universal Health Coverage." *Conflict and Health* 10 (2016): 12.

65. Blanchet, Fouad, and Pherali, "Syrian Refugees in Lebanon."

66. Goleen Samari, "Syrian Refugee Women's Health in Lebanon, Turkey, and Jordan and Recommendations for Improved Practice." *World Med Health Policy* (June 2017), https://www.ncbi.nlm.nih.gov/pmc/articles/PMC5642924/.

67. Blanchet, Fouad, and Pherali, "Syrian Refugees in Lebanon," 12.

68. Samari, "Syrian Refugee Women's Health in Lebanon, Turkey, and Jordan and Recommendations for Improved Practice."

69. "Food Security Sector, Monthly Dashboard." *UN Inter-Agency Coordination Lebanon* (July 2015), http://data.unhcr.org/syrianrefugees/download.php?id=9506.

70. "Syria Crisis Response, Situation Report." *World Food Programme, Lebanon* (September, 2015), http://data.unhcr.org /syrianrefugees/download.php?id=9670. USJ REPORT

71. Colas, France, and Peyroux, "Trafficking in Human Beings."

72. Clarissa Ward, "Syrian Refugees Sell Daughters in Bid to Survive." *CBS News* (May 15, 2013), http://www.cbsnews.com/news/syrian-refugees-sell-daughters-in-bid-to-survive/.

73. "Identifying the Legislative Gaps that Need to Be Filled for the Application of Security Council Resolution 1325." *United Nations Economic and Social Commission for Western Asia—(ESCWA)* (2000) on Women, Peace and Security in Selected Arab States." E/ESCWA/ECW/2015/Technical Paper.8 (March 17, 2015), women-peace-securitylegisislative-gaps-resolution-1325-english.pdf.

74. Justice Without Borders Expert Interview with Author (May 29, 2017).

75. Ibid.

76. Kareem Shaheen, "Dozens of Syrians Forced Into Sexual Slavery in Derelict Lebanese House." *The Guardian* (April 30, 2016), https://www.theguardian.com/world/2016/apr/30/syrians-forced-sexual-slavery-lebanon.

77. "Syria Regional Refugee Response." *UNHCR* (August 11, 2018), http://data.unhcr.org /syrianrefugees /regional.php.

78. Barnard, "A Refugee Crisis in Lebanon Hides in Plain Sight."

79. Harvey, Garwood, and El-Masri, "Shifting Sands: Changing Gender Roles Among Refugees in Lebanon."

80. Scott D. Watson, "Manufacturing Threats: Asylum Seekers as Threats or Refugees." *Journal International Law & International Relations* 3 (2007): 100.

Chapter 5

A Vicious Cycle of Syrian Refugee Insecurities

As seen throughout this book, the concept of refugee security has provoked intense discussions and criticism, where its depth and breadth pose significant challenges to asylum seekers, neighboring host states, and nongovernmental entities involved with managing crises. While there have been considerable theoretical debates around the notions of security and refugee protection regimes, knowledge of the contextual dynamics of security construction seems to be under-theorized. Exploring the case of Syrian refugees in neighboring Lebanon, a nation populated by roughly four million people, the book investigated the securitization–refugee protection nexus as it permeates a South-South forced migration case of Syrian refugees in Lebanon. This concluding chapter incorporates the interweaving feminist scholarship on security studies and refugee governance to formulate an adequate analytical framework that would critically investigate what seems to be a vicious cycle of multifaceted predicaments across the construction, management, and impact of Syrian refugee (in)security, wherein Lebanon is undergoing a massive demographic transformation.

For the most part, processes of homogenization and practices of objectification play a dominant role in (re)positioning some Syrian refugees at an advantage over others, creating a *"blowback"*—"a metaphor to denote unintended negative consequences"[1] of securitized operations—that (re)affected Syrian refugees' relations with the local population. Borrowing from Sara Meger's article entitled "The Fetishization of Sexual Violence in International Security," her theoretical framework reveals a nonlinear chain of securitization processes of homogenization, objectification, and blowback.[2] By objectifying security problems, state-focused securitization practices tend to decontextualize and homogenize the process, oversimplifying and exploiting specific approaches that fail to adequately address issues such as gender

141

Refugee (In)security

Silenced Insecurities

- Lack of Legal and Social Protection
- Minimal Privacy
- Gendered Livelihood
- Early and Forced Marriage
- GBV: Victims or Felons

Homogenization

- Border control
- Restriction of movement
- Limited access to basic aid and livelihood
- Ad hoc detention/assault/deportation
- Ad hoc Municipal curfews

Sovereignty Through Exclusion

Gendered   *Gendered*

Syrian Women Insecurities

Objectification

- Family separation and disconnection
- Poor living conditions
- Informal work
- Bonded Labor
- Increase in debts, incarceration, and homelessness

Host State Insecurities   General Refugee Insecurities

Blowback

- Overpopulation and lack of commodities
- Increase in Rent/Space sale
- Increase of Physical and Terrorist threats
- Job competition with cheaper Syrian labor

Gendered

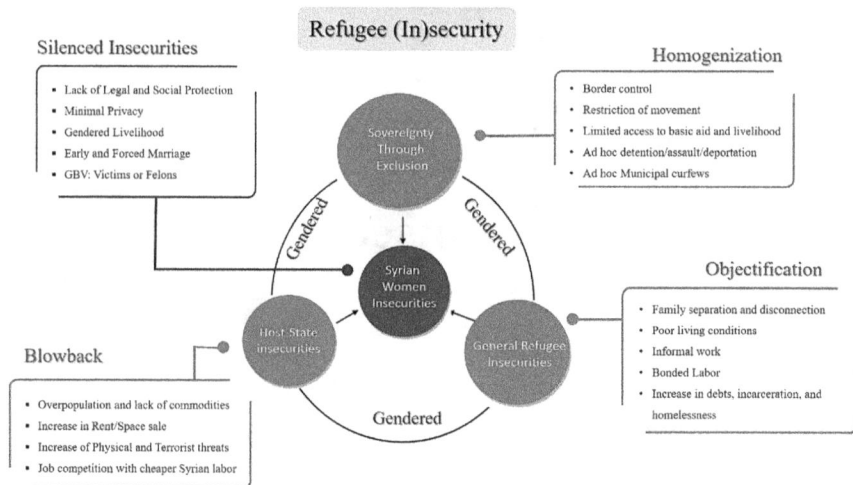

Figure 5.1   The Vicious Cycle Of Refugee (In)security. *Source:* Photo by Author.

violence. Meger's work backs the feminist call for academic and policy practices to go beyond gender-blind refugee management efforts that tend not to address the different types of violence faced by refugee populations. The loss of the contextual meaning of refugees' realities results in their *fetishization*, becoming objects of fascination, consumable by humanitarian and government aid organizations, which maximizes counterintuitive approaches to refugee crisis management.[3]

Women refugees, specifically, tend to be affected the most by securitization discourse, silenced, doubly marginalized, and portrayed as passive victims. According to Meger, women's victimhood only serves as an instrument for patriarchal political interests that silence intersectional gender inequalities. It is crucial to note that women are not one homogenous group that host states discriminate against. Interlocking dynamic systems of privileges such as class, ethnicity, and gender play a dominant role in (re)positioning some at an advantage over others.[4] Through state centered securitized rhetoric, distinct groups of female refugees get exposed to various types of marginalization, often linked to their socioeconomic, cultural, and political backgrounds.

Figure 5.1 synthesizes how different political and socioeconomic elements influence a securitized translation of refugee protection norms in the case of Syrians in Lebanon. It makes visible the various relational processes across numerous spaces, where refugee insecurities are constantly (re)negotiated and translated, (re)impacting their surroundings. This figure highlights how involved *bodies*—host communities, Lebanese government officials, and humanitarian agents—silence Syrian refugees through multiple systems of oppression. By examining the critical gaps within the Lebanese politics of

Syrian forced migration, this interdisciplinary study shows how securitized refugee management practices had intersectional effects on Syrian people with marginalized identities, such as class, ethnicity, and gender. As a matter of fact, Syrian refugee governance policies seem to have affected both Lebanese insecurities and Syrian refugees', especially Syrian women's, livelihoods and self-determination, making the latter's survival increasingly precarious.[5]

Accordingly, this chapter explicitly assesses the implications of this vicious cycle from the research findings, while also integrating them with the study's theoretical framework and methods. This final chapter is thus divided into three different sections, in which the homogenization, objectification, and blowback of Syrian refugees and local insecurities are discussed.

HOMOGENIZATION

As detailed in Chapter 2, geopolitics and biased social attitudes influence the domestic translation and application of universal refugee protection norms. Tracing different critical junctures in Lebanese–Syrian rapport, the study finds that local relations between Lebanese communities and Syrian residents significantly deteriorated in recent years. While Lebanon has shamed developed Western countries by hosting a million and some of the Syrian refugees at a time when most of them closed their borders, the research finds that Syrian refugee insecurities were still (en)gendered with distressing consequences. Even if the main bodies that managed the Syrian crisis in Lebanon were gender-neutral, they seemed to exacerbate a gap between gender-sensitive policies theoretically advertised on paper and their securitized practices in the field.[6] Here gender, as an essential organizing principle, consistently maintained the unequal Lebanese-Syrian relationship, where, Lebanese rhetoric homogenized Syrian de facto refugees as threatening, reigniting a collective memory of an oppressive Assad regime that would want to further Syrian influence on Lebanon's fragile sectarian (im)balance.

On the one hand, like many host countries, Lebanon legitimized its sovereign right to refuse asylum seekers' requests to enter and remain regardless of eligibility.[7] Subsequently, Lebanese law did not extend residency rights to foreigners living in the country except under very limited circumstances, restricting residing Syrians' access to public health care, education, jobs, among many.[8] With such measures in place, refugee insecurities in the case of Lebanon were not prioritized by national governance given the weak, severely divided, and overwhelmed state of the host country. Instead, the Lebanese approach to managing the Syrian crisis became heavily dependent on ad hoc exclusionary (in)security practices.[9]

On the other hand, while the Lebanese government and people welcomed more Syrian refugees than any other country, the presence of so many Syrians became a controversial intersecting political, economic, social, and religious issue for most Lebanese constituents. For instance, numerous Lebanese individuals perceived the presence of Syrians within the country as the cause of their worsened (in)securities and inability to access to work, even though, according to a research survey, only 9 percent said they or their family members were directly affected in their daily lives by the Syrian presence.[10] In fact, as of 2017, 50 percent of registered Syrians operated in construction work and agribusiness—jobs that were traditionally filled by Syrians in Lebanon even before the refugee crisis.[11] The (mis)perceptions of Syrians in Lebanon were thus the result of inflammatory sectarian public discourse against the majority of Syrians (Sunnis) registered with the UNHCR agency. According to Chapter 2, Lebanese concerns were furthered by sporadic (in)security incidences of terrorist attacks and lone crimes such as theft, murder, and gender-based violence led by Syrians within the country.

As stated in Chapter 2, between 1976 and 2005, Syria dominated Lebanon both politically and militarily. Thousands of Lebanese were murdered, kidnapped, or imprisoned by the Syrian authorities, and until this day, thousands remain missing.[12] The crisis in Syria has reversed the power dynamic between the two nations, and while the Lebanese government has welcomed over 1 million and some Syrian refugees, hostility toward them is not uncommon because of historic and deeply rooted animosity, highlighted in Chapter 2. This situation particularly increased the Syrian women refugees' insecurities. According to a Syrian woman called Leila residing in the Bekaa Valley, Lebanon: "Before, Syrians in Lebanon had dignity. Now, after the crisis, all Syrians just walk with our heads down."[13] In politicized contexts such as this one, it is not uncommon for the women of the "other" group to become the objects of eroticized imaging, where host communities tend to objectify women, transforming them into targets of GBV during political conflicts. This process was well documented, for instance, in the context of North Korean refugees residing in South Korea.[14] Although the situation in Lebanon was not like the atrocities of mass rapes committed in many other wars, there were nonetheless some similarities in the manifestation of hostility toward the women of the enemy.[15]

Several Lebanese performative contestations toward the Syrian presence within the country were not only tied to a xenophobic collective memory of Lebanon's subordination to the Syrian Assad regime. Exclusionary tactics were also the product of the refugee host community's fatigue toward a protracted massive Syrian refugee crisis, as well as donor fatigue with a decline in aid funds. Notably, as international funding fell short, the Syrian refugee crisis proved to be very expensive for the Lebanese public, with an estimated cost of $7.5 billion in 2015 alone.[16] A decrease in GDP, an increase in unemployment rates, and a surge of poverty levels resulted in the gradual regression of the economy and the overall living standards of Lebanese citizens. According to Chapter 3, severe cuts of international grants and funding—a reaction to the official decision taken by the Lebanese government to close the borders to Syrian refugees—were also a factor that did not help.[17] The 2017 LCRP states that in 2016, "only 56% of the total appeal for Lebanon's funding requirements" was covered, primarily due to instances of mistrust between several donor communities and governmental agencies.[18] In effect, short-term solutions addressed the protracted Syrian refugee crisis and basic needs of impoverished host communities, reducing any prospects for long-term socioeconomic stability.[19] To this end, Lebanese politicians warned the international community that the shortfall in funding could launch another massive wave of Syrian migrants to Europe, adding to the enduring burden of refugee inflow from a few years prior.[20] Correspondingly, the foreign minister Gebran Bassil severely urged the international community "to quit lecturing Lebanon on humanity and to stop encouraging Syrians to stay in Lebanon."[21] The latter statement triggered aggressive policy measures, reducing all incentives for Syrian refugees to stay in Lebanon, wanting them to return to Syria as soon as possible.

Based on Lene Hansen's definition of "security as silence,"[22] Chapter 3 highlighted a range of securitized mechanisms that the Lebanese government normalized when managing Syrian refugees, reproducing gender hierarchies and hegemonies, affecting residing Syrians asymmetrically. Imprudently, these securitized behaviors became anchoring objectifying practices on how to manage a homogenized refugee crisis. In effect, several practices, highlighted in figure 5.1, homogenized Syrian refugee insecurities, (en)gendering exclusionary refugee insecurity practices—such as visa restrictions and border control, a no-camp policy, curfews, and checkpoints—despite the Syrians clear vulnerabilities. It seems that the Lebanese government's exclusionary measures possessed co-constitutive securitized practices, where only two forms of durable solutions were available for the UNHCR to sustain the legal determination of Syrian refugees in Lebanon: resettlement or repatriation, which were both arduous, somewhat unrealistic options for the one million and some registered Syrian population. Meanwhile, Lebanon's attempt to find temporary solutions to the mass influx of Syrians within the country encompassed a wide range of violations to its human rights obligations, such as limiting refugees' access to livelihood and implementing ad hoc detention, assault, and deportation, all of which hindered humanitarian agencies such as the UNHCR from accurately addressing Syrian refugees' needs.

OBJECTIFICATION

As seen in figure 5.1, Chapter 3 investigated the contextual changes that shape and are shaped by specific refugee crisis response plans between two political institutions with distinct interests and competing goals. The organizational cultural theme analysis teased out how a variety of interests clash between protecting Syrian refugees and protecting the host state's national interests. The focus of the study was on two core institutions with seemingly different knowledge claims and approaches to managing the Syrian crisis: the Lebanese government and the UNHCR. Chapter 3 highlighted how both interested bodies decontextualized the majority of Syrian refugees' specific needs, homogenizing the diverse Syrian groups as both dependent and problematic. Thus, both LCRP documents objectified the many Syrian insecurities through extensive procedural measures of refugee management practices that would hinder a viable translation of global refugee norms into meaningful actions.[23] As highlighted in the vicious cycle of refugee (in)security in figure 5.1, numerous discriminatory incidents projected the host society's conduct of unease and counterproductively enticed exclusionary refugee management practices, which facilitated both bonded and informal labor exploitation, poor living conditions, debts, and homelessness, and incarceration with a chance of deportation due to police and municipal harassment.

In that respect, the UNHCR's struggle to adapt their internationally recognized gender-sensitive norms to local policies distorted their refugee protection and humanitarian assistance goals when translating them into the Lebanese context. Even if the well-intentioned humanitarian agency wanted to provide these essential services to almost 80 percent of the registered Syrian refugee population—Syrian women and children—they ended up objectifying their needs under overgeneralized targeted approaches, failing to empower and protect these 'vulnerable' populations. Chapter 3 traced how humanitarian policies' principles fell short in practice by not enabling and empowering these vulnerable populations and their resilience capabilities. By tracing the significant organizational cultural themes of the two consecutive LCRP documents and their development, the study showed what the expert from Abaad pointed to: "All those response plan mechanisms are mainly designed for the international humanitarian community [and not Syrian refugees themselves]."[24] Instead of involving these targeted groups in crisis response planning, the plan's strategy focused on appealing for more funds for the various projects dependent on donors voluntarily choosing who, what, where, and when to fund.

Consequently, the elaborations, transformations, and changes made between the plans did not advance the necessary protection and assistance that the "targeted" vulnerable groups desperately needed. While both the

Lebanon and the UNHCR genuinely aimed for socioeconomic stability and increase of government services and aid, their selective prioritization of gendered projects, such as targeted approaches, the specific monitoring mechanisms, and the lack of transparency, seemed to affect the management of the Syrian refugee crisis negatively. As such, the study showed that even the second LCRP version failed to provide basic humanitarian services to the majority of the Syrian refugees.

The humanitarian approach seen in both LCRP documents reinforced a mythical construction of the Syrian refugee identity as a burden: disempowered, passive, and helpless.[25] In particular, residing Syrian women were heavily dependent on the framing of the UNHCR, not capable of fully capitalizing on their own skills as self-help mechanisms. Chapter 3 exposed that the elaboration and transformation of the crisis response plan(s) led to a minimal change of approach, where little prioritization of gender-sensitive assistance was made. This increased the gap between theory and actual mitigation of gender-related political or socioeconomic problems regarding the homogenized and objectified refugee population.

Due to several compromises persisting within both Lebanese crisis response plans, none of the LCRP documents fully ensured Syrian refugee safety and self-sufficiency. In that regard, the given compromise that persists within both plans further exacerbated Syrian refugees' insecurities when residing in Lebanon. The dominant governing humanitarian projects counterproductively dehumanized Syrian refugees as part of a larger targeted group of vulnerable people, inaccurately emphasizing their overwhelming numbers and exaggerated statistics ("fake news") that posed a threat to Lebanon's fragile stability, in order to ensure a good amount of aid and funds for their projects. Accordingly, the study found that refugee participation in the planning, implementation, or management of the LCRP operations was absent, increasing the gap between policy management and actual mitigation of gendered political and socioeconomic problems, especially for Syrian women refugees. Consequently, without a gender-sensitive approach, these Syrian women were further marginalized, vulnerable to all types of violence due to a gendered crisis response plan that only allowed three male-dominated low-income industries—construction, sanitation, and agribusiness—and were destined to fail the majority of Syrian refugee women in providing sustainable protection and livelihood. Accordingly, Syrian female heads of households were forced to adapt and work, mostly informally, in domestic service (22 percent) and agricultural labor (55 percent), while many others ventured to work in small service businesses, such as clothing stores and restaurants, to provide for their families.[26]

These types of jobs were typically informal, leaving the majority of Syrian female-headed households economically and socially challenged. The

VASyR estimated that the "level of illiteracy among female heads of house-holds was more than double that of male heads of household (28% and 12% respectively)."[27] Adding to that, Syrian women's limited financial means, due to gendered policy plans and discriminatory government practices, suffered the most under ad hoc policies of excluding them from any viable formal jobs, which caused many to turn to counterintuitive negative coping strate-gies, such as reduction of food intake and expenditure, education, health, debt, informal work, street begging, and even prostitution. Accordingly, almost 30 percent of female-headed households, compared to 15 percent of male-headed households, were forced to live in "non-residential spaces, such as garages or workshops, or in temporary, makeshift shelters" that were below standard, structurally dangerous, not appropriate for living conditions, and "inadequate especially for women and girls."[28] Since most Syrian women refugees were doubly marginalized due to their precarious legal status and due to their gender, access to livelihood and proper housing became even more difficult. The increase of rent in most cities pushed the establishment of informal camps in agricultural areas. Consequently, "informal settlements, collective shelters, substandard dwellings and gatherings," "homelessness, hunger, disease outbreaks, violence, abuse, and exploitation are few of the many consequences that arise."[29]

The UNHCR's refugee crisis responses between 2014 and 2018 increas-ingly institutionalized Syrian refugees' insecurities through standard oper-ating procedures (SOP) for intervention and control in the interests of nationalist donor states, devoid of genuine concerns regarding the multifac-eted needs and risks refugee women experienced in their daily lives. Meticu-lous exercises of counting, calculating, and coding refugees through census and surveys reinforced the inefficient gender-neutral methods of "knowing" the refugees. Thus, their perceptive needs ended up contrasting and contra-dicting the LCRP mission's idea of enhancing gender mainstreaming through protection and assistance that were meant to alleviate various targeted groups from their daily insecurities.[30]

Meanwhile, without gender-inclusive protection measures, the Lebanese government's policy practices engendered extremely precarious administra-tive and legal status for thousands of Syrian women of various ages, making them vulnerable to arrest and deportation. While some progress was made in providing social protection services for women against gender-based vio-lence (GBV) in Lebanon, such as the new domestic violence legislation and the availability of a twenty-four-hour hotline for reporting, these services were barely implemented and generally limited to Lebanese women.[31] Evi-dently, these women were in much worse conditions than those who were registered and thus suffered from much heavier economic burdens than any other refugee group in the country. Because of their intersectional identity as both Syrian refugees and women within exclusionary Lebanese refugee securitized practices, their interests and experiences were frequently marginalized and further complicated depending on gender, class, religion, age, and ethnicity, among many interlinking identities.[32] According to the representative of Justice Without Borders: "Sexual violence is a national crime [in Lebanon], but when you check the national laws, there is no clear definition of what sexual violence is."[33]

The expert interviewee's statement echoed this study's argument that, under Lebanese laws, single, divorced, or widowed Syrian women were not viewed as qualified independent women capable of managing their immediate families. As such, they become easy target for men who find out that they do not have any male support.[34] As highlighted in Chapter 3, public spaces became more dangerous for Syrian women, especially when they were without a male companion. Moreover, while issues related to Lebanese civilians generally involve security forces (e.g., the police), those related to Syrian refugees were managed by a different category of security apparatuses, such as the Lebanese military intelligence, the General Security Directorate, and the Lebanese Information Division. These intelligence entities were rather focused on combating terrorism and dealing with state security threats, and were not specifically trained to deal with gender-sensitive procedures on how to protect women from daily local violence.[35] Meanwhile, under the guise of fighting terrorism, the Lebanese government required humanitarian bodies, such as the UNHCR, to share the registered refugee's information through information-sharing programs between all partner agencies.[36]

Refugee (in)security practices were thus implemented, explicitly or implicitly, by local authorities, who sensed that they had impunity and realized that the targets of their gender violence were powerless with little protection. According to Amnesty International's report on Lebanon, one Syrian woman stated: "After a while, the police would pass by our house or would call us and ask us to go out with them. [. . .] Because we do not have legal [residence] permits, the officers threatened us. They said that they would imprison us if we did not go out with them."[37] This statement reiterates the study's evidence that, in general, victims of prostitution and human trafficking rings do not usually report their predicament or seek help from local authorities even when they may have the opportunity to do so.[38] As a result, the intersection of refugee (in)security practices and sexist Lebanese domestic laws diminished the ability of humanitarian gender-sensitive programs to change the various discriminations that Syrian women experienced in Lebanon. These imposed securitized norms and practices led to a series of Syrian resilience efforts to rely on negative coping skills, resistance, and contempt, to cope with their new status quo, while further exacerbating residing Syrian women's insecurities. Accordingly, uncovering the scholarship on resilience is of the essence in providing a complementary framework to explore the missing link between the current humanitarian and security practices toward Syrian refugees who end up *selling back* those insecurities to the local Lebanese population, and creating a "blowback" that would affect Syrians' relations with the local population.

BLOWBACK

The structural subordination of the status of Syrian refugees, in general, and Syrian women, specifically, leads to the erasure of their agency, (re)enforcing their disproportionate shouldering of their precarious situation through objectified harmful coping mechanisms and increased local (in)securities. As demonstrated in the figure, exclusionary processes of Syrian refugee (in)security homogenization and objectification co-constitute securitized practices that (re)produced social anxieties over the increasing local vulnerabilities. Accordingly, Chapter 4 borrowed Susanne Zwingel's term "impact translation" to shed light on the gendered local repercussions and contextual resilience efforts of Syrian refugees, where the intersectionality of gender, class, and ethnicity played an instrumental role. The analysis revealed that most Syrian refugees, especially women, adopted new coping strategies, (re)impacting their new realities, in turn, Lebanon's (in)security. In fact, residing Syrian girls are at a higher risk of being subjected to "child marriage" because their parents were unable to cater their needs. According to the Women's Refugee Commission, young Syrian girls' parents who were struggling with poverty tended to marry them off immediately when they started menstruating.[39] Accordingly, these married daughters moved to live with their much older husbands and in-laws, thinking that they would be in a safer environment.[40]

In this sense, Chapter 4 traced the gendered impact translation of securitized Syrian refugee management practices through the method of Photovoice. This participatory grassroots methodology provided a "culturally-grounded contextually situated site for reflection on visual images and associated meanings," describing, understanding, and elaborating Syrian resilience efforts within specific communities.[41] Evidently, the intersectionality of Syrian refugees' insecurities was reinforced through exclusionary settings. Consequently, various resilience practices of refugees appropriate, negotiate and modify the little legal provisions they had for personal goals, while "further complicating issues of agency, ownership and humanitarian gender equality interventions."[42] Other instances, such as the *shawish* phenomenon, are living proof of the erection of intersectional systems of oppression and resilience efforts that further (re)enforced hierarchies of relational power and discrimination within already homogenized, vulnerable refugee groups. These facts of gender bias and structural inequalities, thus, created a loop of aggression and exclusion that culminated in the deterioration of local resilience and interactions, completing the vicious cycle in figure 5.1, making it virtually impossible for Syrian refugees to weight productive options.

Several themes were exposed in Chapter 4, such as extreme impoverishment, lack of food, inadequate shelters, legal desperation, and shift of gender roles. As shown earlier, despite all these hardships that the Lebanese research participants highlighted, most Syrians adapted and were determined in doing their best to support themselves and their respective families. Having lost family members, homes, and legal status, the study found that Syrians adopted different types of coping mechanisms to brave through their hostile environments. A mesolevel of resistance became particularly significant to inspect in the case of Lebanon, where Syrians were generally "forbidden from forming or joining formal unions," having little-to-no access to formal institutional protection.[43] Through agency actants, Syrians would thus build support networks and a sustainable resilience system that would relatively enhance their human conditions, thwarting future shocks.

Consequently, the counterintuitive Lebanese approaches toward Syrian refugees created blowbacks, as seen in Chapter 4, with unintended negative consequences on major Lebanese communities.[44] In the photo-elicitation sessions, the research participants underscored several common themes throughout the Syrian ITSs, such as scavenging, informal economies, child labor, excessive waste, and pollution that agonized all residing communities on several levels. Another occurring theme that was not mentioned but is vital to highlight and add to the list is unlawful black-market activities, such as theft, smuggling, human trafficking, prostitution, and drug dealing.[45] In that respect, for refugees who were not fortunate enough, stealing other people's documents was perceived as their only viable solution to acquire freedom of mobility. Small petty crimes became the gateway to larger felonies that Syrians would coopt in their daily (in)security practices. As for the Syrians with a relatively privileged socioeconomic background, they often opted for silent crimes in collaboration with the government, including bribing local authorities to falsify residency papers and forge legal identity documents from Syria, which increased the corruption of local authorities. This affected not only the functioning of concerned Lebanese institutions but also the entire Lebanese social fabric.[46] With dire financial standing, Lebanese nationals complained that they could not find jobs, that local rents were rising, and that wages were falling.[47] Both Syrian refugees and vulnerable Lebanese populations would resort to short-term solutions, such as lending money and buying lower-quality food for lack of finances, which in turn ignited long-term health problems. As seen in the previous chapter, these harsh economic situations obliged Syrians to withdraw their children from schools for them to work and become additional contributors to the household income.

Meanwhile, Syrian women and girls ended up working under exploitative low wages, engaging in dangerous and potentially hazardous work conditions, seeking marriage with Lebanese men, or merely begging on the streets, increasing local anxieties and gendered discriminations. The variety of Syrian women's resilience processes challenged established gendered dichotomies between what is a public and what is a private sphere. As seen in Chapter 4, living in a discriminatory and overwhelmed Lebanese system led Syrian women and girls to increasingly depend upon sporadic emergency aid and adopt harmful coping mechanisms such as illicit work, child labor, child marriage, begging, and prostitution. Some research participants blamed inadequate humanitarian funding, which prevented the possible empowerment of individuals in need. Other coresearchers complained that the legal loopholes and corrupt Lebanese bureaucratic agencies naturally discriminated against disadvantaged individuals, even when adequately funded.

It became clear through this research project that the inherent gender biases and structural inequalities in the Lebanese context created a loop of aggression and exclusion that culminated in the deterioration of local resilience and interactions. The xenophobic Lebanese rhetoric toward Syrians made it virtually impossible for any Syrian refugee to access productive options for livelihood. As a solution to these issues related to the refugee crisis in Lebanon, most of the research participants suggested that drastic changes need to be made in the underlying assumptions and approaches taken by aid organizations, so that these entities learn to work with refugee populations and empower them, rather than "save" and "fix" them. Until such changes are made, a vicious cycle of (in)securities will continue to be (re)produced with practices of mistrust and aggression between Lebanese constituents and residing Syrians.

IMPLICATIONS

Forced displacement due to warfare is one of the most traumatic types of human experiences, where choices made instantly impact different groups of asylum seekers, neighboring host communities, and their power dynamics for the rest of their lives. Highlighting the Syrian women refugee insecurities within a neighboring developing host state adds to the limited literature on South-South refugee crises that have been extensive and protracted. Given the multidisciplinarity of the field of study, this book advanced an innovative research framework built on interweaving feminist scholarships on security studies, refugee politics, and norm translation. This book provides a multidisciplinary account of forced migration, situating my research in a broader range of academic work. It pursued a multileveled approach when exploring the power relations between different bodies, working across local, national, and international levels, that shaped contextual humanitarian norms, security practices, and resilience efforts from residing Syrian refugees. The book involved "bodies"—Lebanese citizens, Lebanese government officials, and humanitarian agents—whose heterogeneity would otherwise be silenced and marginalized through macro decontextualized research practices. As such, the study drew on primary sources, grey literature, human participants, and visual materials to gain in-depth interdisciplinary knowledge of the Syrian refugee crisis in Lebanon by exploring questions about refugee status, refugee rights, gender, and host state's security. It utilized multiple tools such as expert interviews, in-depth longitudinal cultural theme analysis, and a participatory method named Photovoice to understand the multilevel challenges where refugee (in)security is (en)gendered and experienced. By involving local "bodies"—Lebanese volunteers—as coresearchers, the project provided a supportive space for the Lebanese participants, whose voices are often silenced or ascribed to them, to be involved in the exploration of the Syrian refugee crisis. This bottom-up, community-based, participatory exercise led to a fruitful dialogical reconstruction of some of the multiple gendered realities that the Syrian crisis (re)produced in Lebanon with room for both opportunities and misfortunes. Thus, this book provides an original approach to exploring the gender dynamics within the critical scholarship of security studies and refugee governance.

All things considered, this project by no means encompasses a comprehensive understanding of refugee insecurity. Instead, it aims to develop new and more inclusive approaches to gain in-depth knowledge of a compelling case of Syrian refugee (in)security in Lebanon. Accordingly, this transnational feminist research with an intersectional approach considerably filled an empirical and methodological void in refugee scholarship. The gendering of the Syrian refugees' (in)security is multilayered, continually shifting through processes of construction, interpretation, and application that span an array of political, humanitarian, socioeconomic, and security complications. The use of multidisciplinary methods and data adds to the existing feminist literature on securitized refugee governance and expands their visibility by providing a sophisticated understanding of the various spaces where refugee (in)security constructions, management practices, and local experiences materialize, informing the (re)production of refugee insecurities. It reinforces the normative argument that successful refugee management practices of neighboring host states need to acknowledge contextual differences to avoid pathologizing and further stigmatizing the diverse female groups that make up the majority of incoming migrants.[48]

This research has revealed that the insurance of holistic Syrian refugees' protection from gendered violence requires both the Lebanese government and nongovernmental organizations to better understand and coordinate with the diverse groups they are trying to manage. This radical shift in ideological approach would create new opportunities for all groups involved to equally adjust to rising challenges, going beyond the securitized host government practices and the sometimes-counterproductive humanitarian agendas of service providers. By joining forces, these efforts would be a first step in destabilizing the existing power relations previously appropriated and used to limit any form of normative social change. Furthermore, instead of viewing refugee women's insecurities as secondary to the host state's interests and refugee governance in general, refugee women, such as in the Syrian case in Lebanon, need to be prioritized and empowered. Given that women make up the majority of the Syrian refugee population in Lebanon, their issues need to be mainstreamed and dealt with accordingly.

As such, further work and research on Syrian refugee agency and resilience practices could help improve the current efforts in refugee crisis management planning, coordination, innovation, funding, and partnerships by (re)shaping organizational cultures within refugee governance programs. Gender-comprehensive research and policy planning should not just examine refugee politics as a rights-based system, for this tends to disregard local traditions and practices that, till this date, regulate women's rights within the private sphere and not by legal regulations as other parts of social life. After all, universal rights do not automatically translate domestically by excluding silenced voices that influence the active translation of refugee protection norms and local impact. Instead, per Susanne Zwingel's argument, transnational networks of norm entrepreneurs are encouraged to not clash with the local sphere, establishing meaningful connections with the targeted communities through continual long-term processes of (re)negotiation and (re)interpretation.[49] As such, these approaches would serve as an adaptation strategy for refugee empowerment. Policymakers should pay more attention to exploring host state communities' needs, understanding the domestic settings and practices, and involving the marginalized groups of displaced people as purposive subjects with agency, rather than categorizing them based on their vulnerability and special status. Only by doing that can crises be turned into opportunities of (re)constructing favorable conditions for all the affected communities to be empowered and adequately bounce back.

This project equips both academics and practitioners with the necessary tools to understand multilayered social phenomena. It meaningfully contributes to both theory refinement and policy implementation, while also questioning existing paradigms and global structures that tend to homogenize, objectify, and discriminate against women. By conducting a longitudinal cultural theme analysis of crisis response plans, developed by several interest groups with competing goals, future studies could explore the emergence, elaboration, and transformation of their management processes across time. Such studies would, thus, tease out relevant changes and assess these plans' continued engagement with and contribution to empowering their targets. Using the human-centric, bottom-up Photovoice approach to include both host communities and Syrian refugees allowed this study to capture the similarities and differences of perceptions on refugee crises and resilience programs. This approach would assist future projects in highlighting the interlocking systems of oppression and celebrating the gender-inclusive stories of both host communities and people fleeing persecution in their home country. A participatory method would then bridge the present exclusionary practices in refugee crisis response plans and the perceived dichotomy of interests between ensuring host state security and providing a refugee protection mechanism. This approach stimulates a constructive dialogue between all parties involved about local anxieties and refugee management best practices, enhancing cooperation and turning crises into opportunities. Future projects should look beyond copious statistics to the extraordinary everyday experiences of the millions of individuals who are entangled in what is labeled as a "refugee crisis." Such projects would be better equipped to go beyond decontextualized humanitarian agendas and open up new context-specific opportunities that challenge the currently securitized refugee status quo. In that regard, the study is significant in a refugee security context. The critical knowledge on security studies, refugee protection regimes, and women and gender studies, advanced within this book, provides useful tools for any future inquiry project on the contested politics of refugee (in)security and gender norm translations.

NOTES

1. Sara Meger, "The Fetishization of Sexual Violence in International Security," *International Studies Quarterly* 60, no. 1 (2016): 149–59.

2. Meger, "The Fetishization of Sexual Violence in International Security," 149–59.

3. Ibid., 53.

4. Sumi Cho, Kimberlé Williams Crenshaw, and Leslie McCall, "Toward a Field of Intersectionality Studies: Theory, Applications, and Praxis." *Signs: Journal of Women in Culture and Society* 38, no. 4 (2013): 785–810.

5. Richard Hall, "After Trump's Ban, Lebanon Renews Calls to Send Back Syrian Refugees," *Public Radio International* (February 6, 2017), www.pri.org/stories/2017-02-06/after-trump-s-ban-lebanon-renews-calls-send-backsyrian-refugees.

6. Julie Mertus, "Sovereignty, Gender, and Displacement," in *Refugees and Forced Displacement. International Security, Human Vulnerability and the State*, ed. Edward Newman and Joanne Van Selm (Tokyo United Nations University Press, 2003), 252.

7. Susan M. Akram, Sarah Bidinger, Aaron Lang, Danielle Hites, Yoana Kuzmova, and Elena Noureddine, "Protecting Syrian Refugees: Laws, Policies, and Global Responsibility Sharing," *Middle East Law and Governance* 7, no. 3 (2015): 287–318.

8. Ruth Pollard, "Lebanese Citizenship Law Strips Women of Identity and Property." *Reuters* (May 25, 2016), https://www.reuters.com/article/us-lebanon-women-p roperty-rights/lebanese-citizenship-law-strips-women-of-identityand-property-idU SKCN0YH03O

9. Filippo Dionigi, "The Syrian Refugee Crisis in Lebanon: State Fragility and Social Resilience," *LSE Middle East Centre Paper Series, 15.* Middle East Centre, LSE, London, UK (2016).

10. Carole Alsharabati and Jihad Nammour, "Survey on Perceptions of Syrian Refugees in Lebanon," *Université Saint Joseph* (August, 2015): 33–4.

11. "VASyR: Vulnerability Assessment of Syrian Refugees in Lebanon," *World Food Program, UNICEF, and UNHCR* (December 2017), https://reliefweb.int/report/ lebanon/vasyr-2017-vulnerability-assessment-syrian-refugeeslebanon.

12. Nisan Mordechai, "The Syrian Occupation of Lebanon." *Coalition for Responsible Peace in the Middle East* (2000).

13. Amnesty International Focus Group Discussion (October 6, 2015), Saadnyal, Bekaa Valley.

14. Kim Mikyoung, *Securitization of Human Rights: North Korean Refugees in East Asia* (ABC-CLIO, 2012), 73.

15. Meger, "The Fetishization of Sexual Violence in International Security," 149–59.

16. "Lebanon: Economic and Social Impact Assessment of the Syrian Conflict." *World Bank Report,* http://documents.worldbank.org/curated/en/2013/09/18292074/l ebanon-economic-social-impact-assessment-syrianconflict.

17. "Lebanon and Jordan Close Their Borders to Syrian Refugees," *The Chronicle* (December 22, 2014), https://chronicle.fanack.com/refugees/lebanon-and-jordan-clo se-their-borders-to-syrian-refugees/.

18. "Following the Money: Lack of Transparency in Donor Funding for Syrian Refugee Education," *Human Rights Watch* (September 14, 2017), https://www.hrw .org/report/2017/09/14/following-money/lack-transparency-donorfunding-syrian-ref ugee-education.

19. "UNHCR 2016 Regional Refugee & Resilience Plan—Funding Snapshot as of End of 2016," *UNHCR* (December 31, 2016), https://alefliban.org/wp-content/up loads/2017/03/ALEF_AnnualReport_2016.pdf

20. "International Plea for Syrian Refugee Jobs Sparks Anger in Lebanon." *Arab News* (June 24, 2018), http://www.arabnews.com/node/1292241/middle-east.

21. "International Plea for Syrian Refugee Jobs Sparks Anger in Lebanon."

22. Ibid.

23. Olivius Elisabeth, "(Un) Governable Subjects: The Limits of Refugee Participation in the Promotion of Gender Equality in Humanitarian Aid." *Journal of Refugee Studies* 27, no. 1 (2013): 42–61

24. Abaad Expert Interview with Author (June 20, 2017).

25. Heather L. Johnson, "Click to Donate: Visual Images, Constructing Victims and Imagining the Female Refugee." *Third World Quarterly* 32, no. 6 (2011): 1015–37.

26. Johnson, "Click to Donate."

27. "VASyR 2017: Vulnerability Assessment of Syrian Refugees in Lebanon," *World Food Program, United Nations Children's Fund (UNICEF), and UNHCR* (2016), http://documents.wfp.org/stellent/groups/public /documents/ ena/ wfp289533.pdf.

28. Government of Lebanon and UNHCR, *Lebanon Crisis Response Plan 2017–2020* (2017), 137.

29. Government of Lebanon and UNHCR, *Lebanon Crisis Response Plan 2017–2020,* 17.

30. Ibid.

31. "Lebanon Annual Report 2014 Highlights." *KAFA* (2014), http://www.kafa .org.lb/StudiesPublicationPDF/ PRpdf82-635689245975040950.pdf.

32. Abaad Report 2014.

33. Justice Without Borders Expert Interview with Author (May 29, 2017).

34. "I Want a Safe Place: Refugee Women from Syria Uprooted and Unprotected in Lebanon." *Amnesty International* (2015), https://www.amnesty.org/download/Do cuments/MDE2417852015ENGLISH.PDF.

35. "Lebanon Annual Report 2014 Highlights."

36. Jennifer Hyndman, *Managing Displacement: Refugees and the Politics of Humanitarianism* (University of Minnesota Press, 2000), 61.

37. "I Want a Safe Place."

38. Kareem Shaheen, "Lebanon Sex Trafficking: Syrian Woman Describes Nine-Month Ordeal." *The Guardian* (August 1, 2016), https://www.theguardian.com/wo rld/2016/aug/01/lebanon-sex-trafficking-syrian-woman-describes-ninemonth-ordeal.

39. Cherri Zeinab et al., "Early Marriage and Barriers to Contraception Among Syrian Refugee Women in Lebanon: A Qualitative Study." *International Journal of Environmental Research and Public Health* 8 (2017): 836.

40. "Childhood in the Shadow of War: Voices of Young Syrians." *Save the Children* (2015), http://resourcecentre.savethechildren.se/sites/default/files/documents/ childhood-in-the-shadow-of-war.pdf.

41. Camille A. Sutton-Brown, "Photovoice: A Methodological Guide." *Photography and Culture* 7, no. 2 (2014): 169–85

42. Elisabeth Olivius, "Constructing Humanitarian Selves and Refugee Others: Gender Equality and the Global Governance of Refugees." *International Feminist Journal of Politics* 18, no. 2 (2016): 270–90.

43. Amrita Pande, "From 'Balcony Talk' and 'Practical Prayers' to Illegal Collectives: Migrant Domestic Workers and Meso-Level Resistances in Lebanon." *Gender & Society* 26, no. 3 (2012): 382–405.

44. Pande, "From 'Balcony Talk' and 'Practical Prayers' to Illegal Collectives."

45. Lebanon News, "Small Drug Cartel Operating in Dora, Jounieh Arrested." *The Daily Star* (April 5, 2018), http://www.dailystar.com.lb/News/Lebanon-News/2018/ Apr-05/444244-small-drug-cartel-operating-in-dora-jouniehharrested.ashx.

46. Conflict Analysis Report, "The Burden of Scarce Opportunities: The Social Stability Context in Central and West Bekaa." *UN Development Program* (March 2017), https://reliefweb.int/report/lebanon/burden-scarce-opportunitiessocial-stab ility-context-central-and-west-bekaa-conflict.

47. "Syrians Entering Lebanon Face New Restrictions." *BBC News* (January 5, 2015): https://www.bbc.com/news/worldmiddle-east-30657003

48. Elisabeth Olivius, "Governing Refugees Through Gender Equality: Care, Control, Emancipation." PhD dissertation., Umeå Universitet (2014), 8.

49. Susanne Zwingel, *Translating International Women's Rights* (Palgrave Macmillan UK, 2016), p 32.

Bibliography

Abels, Gabriele and Maria Behrens. "Interviewing Experts in Political Science: A Reflection on Gender and Policy Effects Based on Secondary Analysis." *Interviewing Experts,* 140. London: Palgrave Macmillan, 2009.

Abramson, Scott. "Lebanese Armenians: A Distinctive Community in the Armenian Diaspora and in Lebanese Society." *The Levantine Review* 2, no. 2 (2013): 188–216.

Acharya, Amitav. "The Limitations of Mainstream International Relations Theories for Understanding the Politics of Forced Migration." *Centre for International Studies,* 27. Oxford University, 2008.

Adler, Emanuel and Vincent Pouliot. "International Practices." *International Theory* 3, no. 1 (2011): 1–36.

Adler, Emanuel and Vincent Pouliot. "The Practice Turn in International Relations: Introduction and Framework," in *International Studies Association 49th Annual Convention,* 26–9. San Francisco, 2008.

Agosti, Marta. "The Nationality Law in Light of the Refugee Crisis in Lebanon: Old Battles, New Consequences." *Contemporary Levant* 1, no. 2 (2016): 148–51.

Akram, Susan M., Sarah Bidinger, Aaron Lang, Danielle Hites, Yoana Kuzmova, and Elena Noureddine. "Protecting Syrian Refugees: Laws, Policies, and Global Responsibility Sharing." *Middle East Law and Governance* 7, no. 3 (2015): 287–318.

Alexievich, Svetlana. *The Unwomanly Face of War: An Oral History of Women in World War II.* New York: Random House, 2017.

Alfred, Charlotte. "Dangerous Exit: Who Controls How Syrians in Lebanon Go Home." *News Deeply* (August 8, 2018), https://www.newsdeeply.com/refugees/articles/2018/08/08/dangerous-exit-whocontrols-how-syrians-in-lebanon-go-home.

Alloush, Mohamed. "What is the Truth About the Presence of 300,000 Pregnant Syrian Women in Lebanon?" *El-Nashra News* (May 3, 2017), https://www.alaraby.co.uk/english/news/2017/5/5/debunked-300-000-syrianrefugees-are-not-pregnant-in-lebanon.

Al-Saadi, Yazan. "The Diversion Strategy: Lebanese Racism, Classism, and the Refugees." *Al-Akhbar* (June 10, 2014), https://english.alakhbar.com/node/20121.

Alsharabati, Carole and Jihad Nammour. "Survey on Perceptions of Syrian Refugees in Lebanon." *Université Saint Joseph,* 33–4, 2015.

Amnesty International. *Interviews with Refugee Women from Syria and with NGOs Working with Refugees.* Lebanon: Amnesty International, June and October 2015.

Anani, Ghida. "Syria Crisis – Dimensions of Gender-Based Violence Against Syrian Refugees in Lebanon." *Forced Migration Review*, no. 44 (2013), http://www.fmre view.org/en/detention/anani.pdf.

Anderson, Benedict. *Imagined Communities: Reflections on the Origin and Spread of Nationalism.* London: Verso, 2006.

Arendt, Hannah. *The Origins of Totalitarianism*, vol. 244, 464. Houghton Mifflin Harcourt, 1973.

Armstrong, Martin. "Lebanon Resists Granting Work Permits to Syrian Refugees." *Middle East Eye* (February 4, 2016), http://www.middleeasteye.net/news/lebano nsyria-refugees-jobs-554259285.

Astih, Paula. "Lebanon: Public Discontent over Continuous Power Cuts." *Asharq Al-Awsat Newspaper* (December 23, 2017), https://aawsat.com/english/home/article/1121661/lebanon-public-discontent-overcontinuous-power-cuts?amp.

Atallah, Sami and Dima Mahdi. "Law and Politics of 'Safe Zones' and Forced Returns to Syria: Refugee Politics in Lebanon." *The Lebanese Center for Policy Studies*, no. 39 (2017): 36.

Atassi, Bassma. "Syria's War Widows Fight for Survival." *Al Jazzera News* (July, 2014), https://www.aljazeera.com/humanrights/2014/07/syrian-women-struggle-as -soleproviders-201478122435631439.html.

Avis, William. "Gender Equality and Women's Empowerment in Lebanon." *University of Birmingham: Helpdesk Report* (2017), https://www.alnap.org/system/files/content/resource/files/main/175-gender-equalityand-womens-empowerment-in-le banon.pdf.

Ayoub, Bachir and Dima Mahdi. "Making Aid Work in Lebanon: Promoting Aid Effectiveness and Respect for Rights in Middle-Income Countries Affected by Mass Displacement." *OXFAM* (2018).

Azar, Georgi. "Lebanese President Draws Fire with Naturalization Decree." *Annahar News* (June 1, 2018), https://en.annahar.com/article/812753-lebanese-presiden tdraws-fire-with-naturalization-decree.

Bach, Hedy. "Composing a Visual Narrative Inquiry," in *Handbook of Narrative Inquiry Mapping a Methodology,* ed. Jean Clandinin. SAGE, 2006.

Baines, Erin K. *Vulnerable Bodies: Gender, the UN and the Global Refugee Crisis.* London: Routledge, 2017.

Bajec, Alessandra. "Lebanon's Political Crisis Drags on as Politicians Agree to Extend their Mandate a Third Time." *Al-Araby News* (June 20, 2017), https://ww w.alaraby.co.uk/english/indepth/2017/6/20/lebanons-political-crisis-dragson-with -third-term-extension.

Baldwin, David. "The Concept of Security." *Review of International Studies*, no. 23 (1997): 5–26.

Balzacq, Thierry. "Constructivism and Securitization Studies," in *The Routledge Handbook of Security Studies*, 56–72. Routlege, 2016.

Barnard, Anne. "A Refugee Crisis in Lebanon Hides in Plain Sight." *New York Times* (November 12, 2015), https://www.nytimes.com/2015/11/13/world/middleeast/are fugee-crisis-in-lebanon-hides-in-plain-sight.html.

Barnett, Laura. "Global Governance and the Evolution of the International Refugee Regime." *International Journal of Refugee Law* 14, no. 2/3 (2002): 238–62.

Barnett, Michael. "Humanitarianism Transformed." *Perspectives on Politics* 3, no. 4 (2005): 723–40.

Bergold, Jarg and Stefan Thomas. "Particpatory Research Methods: A Methodological Approach in Motion." *Forum Qualitative Social Research* (2012): 191–222.

Berti, Benedetta. "The Syrian Refugee Crisis: Regional and Human Security Implications." *Strategic Assessment* 17, no. 4 (2015): 41–53.

Betts, Alexander. *Forced Migration and Global Politics* New York: John Wiley & Sons, 2009.

Bigo, Didier. "Security and Immigration: Toward a Critique of the Governmentality of Unease." *Alternatives* 27, no. 1 (2002): 63–92.

Binder, Werner and Bernadette Nadya Jaworsky. "Refugees as Icons: Culture and Iconic Representation." *Sociology Compass* 12, no. 3 (2018): e12568.

Black, Ian. "Syria and Lebanon to Establish Diplomatic Relations." *The Guardian* (October 2008), https://www.theguardian.com/world/2008/oct/14/syria-lebanon.

Blanchet, Karl, Fouad M. Fouad and Tejendra Pherali. "Syrian Refugees in Lebanon: The Search for Universal Health Coverage." *Conflict and Health* 10 (2016): 12.

Boed, Roman. "The State of the Right of Asylum in International Law." *Duke Journal of Comparative & International Law* 5, no. 1 (1994): 5.

Bogner, Alexander, Beate Littig and Wolfgang Menz. "Interviewing the Elite— Interviewing Experts: Is there a Difference?" in *Interviewing Experts*, 98–139. London: Palgrave Macmillan, 2009.

Borgmann, Monika and Lokman Slim. "Fewer Refugees More Refugeeism." *UMAM D&R Documentation and Research* (2018), https://umamdr.org/en/home/projects /14/advance-contents/188/fewer-refugees-more-refugeeism.

Bourbeau, Philippe. "Migration and Security: Securitization Theory and Its Refinement," in *Annual Meeting of the International Studies Association*. Town & Country Resort and Convention Center, San Diego, California, USA, 2006.

Bourbeau, Philippe. "Resiliencism: Premises and Promises in Securitisation Research." *Resilience Journal*, no.1 (2013): 3–17.

Bourbeau, Philippe. "The Practice Approach in Global Politics." *Journal of Global Security Studies* 2, no. 2 (2017): 170–82.

Bouri, Elie and Joseph El-Assad. "The Lebanese Electricity Woes: An Estimation of the Economical Costs of Power Interruptions." *MDPI Energies* 9, no. 8 (2016): 583.

Bryson, John M. *Strategic Planning for Public and Nonprofit Organizations: A Guide to Strengthening and Sustaining Organizational Achievement*. Hoboken: John Wiley & Sons, 2018.

Bulos, Nabih. "In Lebanon, a Rape and Murder Galvanize Anti-Syrian Fervor." *Los Angeles Times* (October 2017), http://www.latimes.com/world/middleeast/la-fg lebanon-syria-slaying-2017-story.html.

Butler, Judith. *Gender Trouble: Feminism and the Subversion of Identity.* New York: Routledge, 1990.

Butler, Judith and Gayatri Chakravorty Spivak. *Who Sings the Nation-State?: Language, Politics, Belonging.* London: Seagull Books, 2007.

Buzan, Barry. "Peace, Power and Security: Contending Concepts in the Study of International Relations." *Journal of Peace Research*, no. 21 (1984): 109–25.

Buzan, Barry. *People. States & Fear: An Agenda for International Security Studies in the Post-Cold War Era.* Colchester: ECPR Press, 2008.

Buzan, Barry, Ole Wæver, and Jaap DeWilde. *Security: A New framework for Analysis.* Harvard: Lynne Rienner Publishers, 1998.

Byman, Daniel and Sloane Speakman. "The Syrian Refugee Crisis: Bad and Worse Options." *The Washington Quarterly* 39, no. 2 (2016).

Capoccia, Giovanni and R. Daniel Kelemen. "The Study of Critical Junctures: Theory, Narrative, and Counterfactuals in Historical Institutionalism." *World Politics* 59, no. 3 (2007): 341–69.

Carpenter, R. Charli. "Women, Children, and Other Vulnerable Groups: Gender, Strategic Frames, and the Protection of Civilians as a Transnational Issue." *International Studies Quarterly* 49, no. 2 (June 2005): 295–355.

Chaaban, Jad. "Should Lebanon Get More Funds for Hosting Refugees?" In *Al Jazeera* (April 2017), https://www.aljazeera.com/indepth/features/2017/04/leba non-fundshosting-refugees-170405082414586.html.

Chandler, David and Nik Hynek, eds. *Critical Perspectives on Human Security: Rethinking Emancipation and Power in International Relations.* New York: Routledge, 2010.

Charles, Lorraine and Kate Denman. "Syrian and Palestinian Syrian Refugees in Lebanon: The Plight of Women and Children." *Journal of International Women's Studies* 14, no. 5 (2013): 96.

Chatty, Dawn. "Bedouin in Lebanon: The Transformation of a Way of Life or an Attitude?" *International Journal of Migration, Health and Social Care* 6, no. 3 (2011): 21–30.

Chatty, Dawn, Nisrine Mansour, and Nasser Yassin. "Statelessness and Tribal Identity on Lebanon's Eastern Borders." *Mediterranean Politics* 18, no. 3 (2013): 411–26.

Chia, Joy L. "Piercing the Confucian Veil: Lenagan's Implications for East Asia and Human Rights." *American University Journal of Gender, Social Policy & the Law* 21 (2012): 379.

Chick, Kristen. "To Fight Domestic Violence among Syrian Refugees, an Outreach to Men." *The Christian Science Monitor* (August 26, 2017), https://www.csmonito r.com/World/Middle-East/2017/0426/To-fight-domesticviolence-among-Syrian-re fugees-an-outreach-to-men.

Chit, Mohamad Ali Nayel Bassem. "Understanding Racism Against Syrian Refugees in Lebanon." *Civil Society Knowledge Centre, Lebanon Support* (November

1, 2013), http://cskc.daleel-madani.org/paper/understanding-racism-against-syria n-refugeeslebanon.

Cho, Sumi, Kimberlé Williams Crenshaw, and Leslie McCall. "Toward a Field of Intersectionality Studies: Theory, Applications, and Praxis." *Signs: Journal of Women in Culture and Society* 38, no. 4 (2013): 785–810.

Colas, Geneviève, Secours Catholique-Caritas France, and Peyroux Olivier. "Trafficking in Human Beings." *Caritas* (2016), http://www.caritas.eu/sites/default/file s/report__trafficking_in_conflict_and_post-conflict_situations_en.pdf.

Conflict Analysis Report. "The Burden of Scarce Opportunities: The Social Stability Context in Central and West Bekaa." *UN Development Program* (March 2017), https://reliefweb.int/report/lebanon/burden-scarce-opportunities-social-sta bilitycontext-central-and-west-bekaa-conflict.

Cox, Robert W. "Social Forces, States, and World Orders: Beyond International Relations Theory." *Millennium* 10, no. 2 (1981): 126–55.

Creswell, John W. *Qualitative Inquiry and Research Design: Choosing Among Five Approaches.* SAGE, 2007.

Culbertson, Shelly, Olga Oliker, Ben Baruch, and Ilana Blum. *Rethinking Coordination of Services to Refugees in Urban Areas: Managing the Crisis in Jordan and Lebanon.* Rand Corporation, 2016.

Dabbagh, Salah, George Deeb, Farid El-Khazen, and Maroun Kisirwani. "The Lebanese Constitution." *Arab Law Quarterly* 12, no. 2 (1997): 224–61.

David, E. J. R. and Annie O. Derthick. "What Is Internalized Oppression, and so What." in *Internalized Oppression: The Psychology of Marginalized Groups*, 1–30. Springer Publishing Co., 2014.

Davison, John. "Redrawing the Middle East: A Generation of Syrian Children Who Don't Count." *Thompson Reuters* (May 3, 2016), http://www.reuters.com/investi gates/special-report/syria-refugeesstateless/.

Davison, John. "Syrians in Lebanon Hit by Arrests, Curfews and Hostility after Bombing." *Reuters* (July 25, 2016), www.reuters.com/article/us-mideast-crisis-syr ialebanon/syrians-in-lebanon-hit-by-arrests-curfews-and-hostility-after-bombings idUSKCN1051KO.

Deeb, Marius. *Syria's Terrorist War on Lebanon and the Peace Process.* New York: Palgrave Macmillan, 2003.

DeGhett, Torie Rose. "Is Syria About to Become Iran's New Vietnam?" *Vice News* (October 7, 2015), https://news.vice.com/article/is-syria-about-to-become-irans vietnam.

DeJong, Jocelyn, Farah Sbeity, Jennifer Schlecht, Manale Yamout Harfouche, Fouad M. Fouad Rouham, Seema Manohar, and Courtland Robinson. "Young Lives Disrupted: Gender and Well-Being Among Adolescent Syrian Refugees in Lebanon." *Conflict and Health* 11, no. 23 (2017).

Dionigi, Filippo. "Rethinking Borders: The Dynamics of Syrian Displacement to Lebanon." *Middle East Law and Governance* 9, no. 3 (2017): 232–48.

Dionigi, Filippo. "The Syrian Refugee Crisis in Lebanon: State Fragility and Social Resilience." *LSE Middle East Centre Paper Series, 15.* London: Middle East Centre, LSE, 2016.

El-Husseini, Rola. "Pax Syriana," in *Elite Politics in Postwar Lebanon.* Syracuse University Press, 2012.

El Khazen, Farid. "Permanent Settlement of Palestinians in Lebanon: A Recipe for Conflict." *Journal of Refugee Studies* 10, no. 3 (1997): 275–93.

El Khazen, Farid. "Political Parties in Postwar Lebanon: Parties in Search of Partisans." *Middle East Journal* 57, no. 4 (2003): 605–24.

El-Masri, Roula, C. Harvey, and R. Garwood. "Shifting Sands: Changing Gender Roles Among Refugees in Lebanon." *Joint Research Report: Oxfam and Resource Center for Gender Equality* (2013).

Enders, David. "Merkel Finds a Familiar Attitude to Refugees in Lebanon." *The National* (June 23, 2018), https://www.thenational.ae/world/mena/merkel-finds -afamiliar-attitude-to-refugees-in-lebanon-1.743220.

Ensor, Josie. "The Muslim Refugees Converting to Christianity to Find Safety." *The Telegraph* (January 30, 2017), https://www.telegraph.co.uk/news/2017/01/30/m uslim-refugees-convertingchristianity-find-safety.

Estatie, Lamia. "Lebanon Detains Men Behind Assault on Syrian Refugee." *BBC News* (July 19, 2017), http://www.bbc.com/news/blogs-trending-40653714.

Evans, Dominic. "Syria War, Refugees to Cost Lebanon $7.5 Billion: World Bank." *Reuters* (September 19, 2013), https://www.reuters.com/article/us-syria-crisisleb anon-idUSBRE98I0T320130919.

Fakhreddin, Lina. "Lebanon Between the Largest Displacement and the Least Aid." *Assafir News* (January 6, 2015), http://assafir.com/Article/2/394120.

Faletar, Sanjica, Maja Krtalić Tanacković, and Darko Lacović. "Newspapers as a Research Source: Information Needs and Information Seeking of Humanities Scholars." *Digital Transformation and the Changing Role of News Media in the 21st Century.* IFLA Newspapers Section Pre-Conference, 2014.

Fassin, Didier. "Humanitarianism: A Nongovernmental Government." in *Nongovernmental Politics*, ed. M. Feher, 149–60. New York: Zone Books, 2007.

Fawaz, Mona. "Planning and the Refugee Crisis: Informality as a Framework of Analysis and Reflection." *Planning Theory* 16, no. 1 (2017): 99–115.

Feller, Erika. "The Evolution of the International Refugee Protection Regime." *Washington University Journal of Law and Policy* 5 (2001): 129.

Filippo, Dionigi. "The Syrian Refugee Crisis in Lebanon: State Fragility and Social Resilience." *LSE, Middle East Centre Paper Series 15* (2016), 25.

Filippo, Dionigi. "The Syrian Refugee Crisis in Lebanon: State Fragility and Social Resilience." *LSE, Middle East Centre Paper Series 15*, 6–37. London, UK: Middle East Centre, LSE, 2016.

Finnemore, Martha and Kathryn Sikkink. "Taking Stock: The Constructivist Research Program in International Relations and Comparative Politics." *Annual Review of Political Science* 4, no. 1 (2001): 391–416.

Foran, Siobhán, Aisling Swaine, and Kate Burns. "Improving the Effectiveness of Humanitarian Action: Progress in Implementing the Inter-Agency Standing Committee (IASC) Gender Marker." *Gender & Development* 20, no. 2 (2012): 233247.

Francis, Ellen. "Hostility Grows Towards Syrian Refugees in Lebanon." *Reuters* (August 28, 2017), https://www.reuters.com/article/us-lebanon-refugees-ten sionidUSKCN1B8128.Frangieh, Ghida. "Lebanon Places Discriminatory Entry

Restrictions on Syrians." *Legal Agenda* 22 (2015), http://legalagenda.com/en/arti cle.php?id=679&folder=articles&lang=en.

Frangieh, Ghida. "Relations Between UNHCR and Arab Governments: Memoranda of Understanding in Lebanon and Jordan." *Middle East Centre Blog* (2016).

Freedman, Jane. *Gendering the International Asylum and Refugee Debate*. Basingstoke: Palgrave Macmillan, 2015.

Freedman, Jane. "Mainstreaming Gender in Refugee Protection." *Cambridge Review of International Affairs* 23, no. 4 (2010): 589–607.

Gade, Tine. "Lebanon on the Brink." *Norwegian Institute of International Affairs, Policy Brief 23* (2016), https://core.ac.uk/download/pdf/154676181.pdf.

Gallagher, Ashley. "Syrian Refugees Are Turning to Prostitution at Super Nightclubs." *Vice News* (June 11, 2014), https://news.vice.com/article/syrian-refugees -are-turningto-prostitution-at-super-nightclubs.

Gerard, Alison and Sharon Pickering. "Gender, Securitization and Transit: Refugee Women and the Journey to the EU." *Journal of Refugee Studies* 27, no. 3 (2014): 338–59.

Ghaddar, Sima. "Lebanon Treats Refugees as a Security Problem—and It Doesn't Work." *The Century Foundation* (April 4, 2017), https://tcf.org/content/commen tary/lebanontreats-refugees-security-problem-doesnt-work/?agreed=1.

Ghezelbash, Daniel. *Refuge Lost: Asylum Law in an Interdependent World*. Cambridge: University Press, 2018.

Gibson, Sarah. "Abusing Our Hospitality: Inhospitableness and the Politics of Deterrence," in *Mobilizing Hospitality: The Ethics of Social Relations in a Mobile World*, 159–77. Aldershot, UK: Ashgate Publishing, 2007.

Given, Lisa M. ed. *The SAGE Encyclopedia of Qualitative Research Methods*, 844. SAGE, 2008.

Golder, Ben and George Williams. "Balancing National Security and Human Rights: Assessing the Legal Response of Common Law Nations to the Threat of Terrorism." *Journal of Comparative Policy Analysis* 8, no. 1 (2006): 43–62.

Government of Lebanon and the United Nations. *Lebanon Crisis Response Plan: 2015–2016* (2015).

Government of Lebanon and the United Nations. *Lebanon Crisis Response Plan: 2017–2020* (2017).

Grip, Lina. "Coping with Crises: Forced Displacement in Fragile Contexts," in *SIPRI Yearbook 2017: Armaments, Disarmament and International Security*, 256. Oxford: Oxford University Press, 2016.

Habib, Osama. "Tax Evasion Close to $4.2B Annually: Economist." *The Daily Star News* (March 2, 2017), http://www.dailystar.com.lb/Business/Local/2017/Mar02/3 95690-tax-evasion-close-to-42b-annually-economist.ashx.

Haddad, Emma. *The Refugee in International Society: Between Sovereigns*, vol. 106, 35. Cambridge: Cambridge University Press, 2008.

Haddad, Simon. "The Origins of Popular Opposition to Palestinian Resettlement in Lebanon." *International Migration Review* 38, no. 2 (2004): 470–92.

Haines-Young, James. "Lebanon's Bassil Meets UNHCR to Defuse Refugee Row." *The National* (June 17, 2018), https://www.thenational.ae/world/mena/lebanon -s-bassilmeets-unhcr-to-defuse-refugee-row-1.741039.

Hall, Richard. "After Trump's Ban, Lebanon Renews Calls to Send Back Syrian Refugees." *Public Radio International* (February 6, 2017), www.pri.org/stories/201702-06/after-trump-s-ban-lebanon-renews-calls-send-back-syrian-refugees.

Hall, Richard. "Lebanon Doesn't Want Syrian Refugees Getting Too Comfortable, Even in Winter." *Agence France-Presse* (February 15, 2016), https://www.pri.org/stories/2016-02-15/lebanon-doesnt-want-syrian-refugees-gettingtoo-comfortable-even-winter.

Hammerstad, Anne. *The Rise and Decline of a Global Security Actor: UNHCR, Refugee Protection, and Security.* Oxford: Oxford University Press, 2014.

Hanafi, Sari and Taylor Long. "Governance, Governmentalities, and the State of Exception in the Palestinian Refugee Camps of Lebanon." *Journal of Refugee Studies* 23, no. 2 (2010): 134–59.

Hansen, Lene. "The Little Mermaid's Silent Security Dilemma and the Absence of Gender in the Copenhagen School." *Millennium: Journal of International Relations* 29, no. 2 (2000): 285–306.

Hansen, Lene. "Theorizing the Image for Security Studies: Visual Securitization and the Muhammad Cartoon Crisis." *European Journal of International Relations* 17, no. 1 (2011): 51–74.

Harb, Imad K. *The Hezbollah-Iran Pivot: The Controlling Agencies Behind Lebanon's Sectarian Politics.* SAGE International Australia, 2016.

Harriso, Lisa and Theresa Callan. *Key Research Concepts in Politics and International Relations.* SAGE Publications, 2013.

Harvey, Claire, Rosa Garwood, and Roula El-Masri. "Shifting Sands: Changing Gender Roles Among Refugees in Lebanon." *OXFAM International* (2013).

Hasselbarth, Sarah. *Islamic Charities in the Syrian Context in Jordan and Lebanon.* Beyrouth: Friedrich Ebert Stiftung, 2014.

Helou, Marguerite. "Lebanese Women and Politics: A Comparison Between Two Field Studies." *Al-Raida Journal, 0,* (2001): 33–40.

Helou, Marguerite. "Women's Political Participation in Lebanon: Gaps in Research and Approaches." *Al-Raida Journal, 0,* (2014): 74–84.

Ho, Anita and Carol Pavlish. "Indivisibility of Accountability and Empowerment in Tackling Gender-Based Violence: Lessons from a Refugee Camp in Rwanda." *Journal of Refugee Studies* 24, no. 1 (2011): 88–109.

Hodeib, Mirella. "Hezbollah Fighters Find Nusra's Tactics in Qusair 'Irritatingly Familiar.'" *Daily Star Lebanon* (May 31, 2013), http://www.dailystar.com.lb/News/Local-News/2013/May31/218984-hezbollahfighters-find-nusras-tactics-in-qusair-irritatingly-familiar.ashx.

Hoffman, John. *Gender and Sovereignty: Feminism, the State and International Relations.* Springer, 2001.

Holmes, Oliver. "New Restrictions in Lebanon Mean Syrian Refugees Live in Fear." *Reuters* (April 17, 2015), www.reuters.com/article/us-mideast-crisis-lebanonrefugees/new-restrictions-in-lebanon-mean-syrian-refugees-live-in-fear.

Human Rights Watch. "Our Homes Are Not for Strangers: Mass Evictions of Syrian Refugees by Lebanese Municipalities" (April 20, 2018), https://www.hrw.org/report/2018/04/20.

Husem, Erik. "The Syrian Involvement in Lebanon: An Analysis of the Role of Lebanon in Syrian Regime Security, From Ta'if to the Death of Hafiz al-Assad (1989–2000)." *FORSVARETS FORSKNINGSINSTITUTT (FFI) Norwegian Defense Research Establishment* (2002), https://admin.ffi.no/no/Rapporter/02-03005.pdf.

Huysmans, Jef. *The Politics of Insecurity: Fear, Migration and Asylum in the EU.* Routledge, 2006.

Hyndman, Jennifer. "Managing Difference: Gender and Culture in Humanitarian Emergencies." *Gender, Place and Culture: A Journal of Feminist Geography* 5, no. 3 (1998): 241–60.

Hyndman, Jennifer. *Managing Displacement: Refugees and the Politics of Humanitarianism.* University of Minnesota Press, 2000.

Hyndman, Jennifer and Wenona Giles. "Waiting for What? The Feminization of Asylum in Protracted Situations." *Gender, Place & Culture* 18, no. 3 (2011): 361–79.

Ibrahim, Arwa. "Syria: 'Absentees Law' Could See Millions of Refugees Lose Lands." *AlJazeera News* (April 7, 2018), www.aljazeera.com/news/2018/04/syria-absenteeslaw-millions-refugees-lose-lands180407073139495.html.

Institut Des Sciences Politiques USJ. "Survey on Perceptions of Syrian Refugees in Lebanon." (March, 2015), http://www.sciences-po.usj.edu.lb/ pdf/Executive%20 Summary.pdf.

Irshaid, Faisal. "Anti-Syrian Hostility in Lebanon Spawns Social Media Backlash." *BBC News* (April 4, 2014), https://www.bbc.coober m/news/world-middle-east-26871736.

Jacobsen, Karen and Loren B. Landau. "The Dual Imperative in Refugee Research: Some Methodological and Ethical Considerations in Social Science Research on Forced Migration." *Disasters* 27, no. 3 (2003): 185–206.

Jacobsen, Katja Lindskov. *The Politics of Humanitarian Technology: Good Intentions, Unintended Consequences and Insecurity.* Routledge 2015.

Janmyr, Maja. "No Country of Asylum: Legitimizing Lebanon's Rejection of the 1951 Refugee Convention." *International Journal of Refugee Law* 29, no. 3 (2017): 438465.

Janmyr, Maja. "Precarity in Exile: The Legal Status of Syrian Refugees in Lebanon." *Refugee Survey Quarterly* 35, no. 4 (2016): 58–78.

Janmyr, Maja. "UNHCR and the Syrian Refugee Response: Negotiating Status and Registration in Lebanon." *The International Journal of Human Rights* 22, no. 3 (2018): 393–419.

Janmyr, Maja and Lama Mourad. "Modes of Ordering: Labelling, Classification and Categorization in Lebanon's Refugee Response." *Journal of Refugee Studies* 31, no. 4 (2017): 544–65.

Jaulin, Thibaut. "Citizenship, Migration, and Confessional Democracy in Lebanon." *Middle East Law and Governance* 6, no. 3 (2014): 250–71.

Johnson, Heather L. "Click to Donate: Visual Images, Constructing Victims and Imagining the Female Refugee." *Third World Quarterly* 32, no. 6 (2011): 1015–37.

Jones, Katharine. "Syrian Refugees in Lebanon Are Falling into Slavery and Exploitation." *The Conversation* (April 13, 2016), https://theconversation.com/syrianrefugees-in-lebanon-are-falling-into-slavery-and-exploitation-57521.

Jones, Katharine and Ksaifi, Leena. *Struggling to Survive: Slavery and Exploitation of Syrian Refugees in Lebanon.* London, England: Freedom Fund, 2016, http://fre edomfund.org/wp-content/uploads/Lebanon-Report-FINAL-8April16.pdf.

Jureidini, Ray. "An Exploratory Study of Psychoanalytic and Social Factors in the Abuse of Migrant Domestic Workers by Female Employers in Lebanon." *KAFA (Enough) Violence & Exploitation* (2011).

Kail, C. Ellis. "Lebanon: The Struggle of a Small Country in a Regional Context." *Arab Studies Quarterly* (1999): 5–25.

Kamal, Dib. *Warlords and Merchants: The Lebanese Business and Political Establishment.* Ithaca Press, 2004.

Katzenstein, Peter J., ed. *The Culture of National Security: Norms and Identity in World Politics.* Columbia University Press, 1996, 26.

Kneebone, Susan. "Women Within the Refugee Construct: 'Exclusionary Inclusion' in Policy And Practice – The Australian Experience." *International Journal of Refugee Law* 17, no. 1 (2005): 7–42.

Knudsen, Are John. "Syria's Refugees in Lebanon: Brothers, Burden, and Bone of Contention," in *Lebanon Facing the Arab Uprisings*, 135–54. Palgrave Pivot, London, 2017.

Koning, Edward Anthony. "The Three Institutionalisms and Institutional Dynamics: Understanding Endogenous and Exogenous Change." *Journal of Public Policy* 36, no. 4 (2016): 639–64.

Krayem, Hassan. "The Lebanese Civil War and the Taif Agreement." *Conflict Resolution in the Arab World: Selected Essays* (1997): 411–36. Digital documentation center, American University of Beirut.

Lansing, Melissa. "Terrorism, Securitization of the Nation and Refugee Flows: Implications of Policies and Practices in a Post-911 Era." PhD dissertation, University of Ottawa (Canada), 2007.

Latour, Bruno. "On Actor-Network Theory: A Few Clarifications Plus More Than a Few Complications." *Soziale welt* 47, no. 4 (1996): 1–16.

Lautze, Sue and John Hammock. *Saving Lives and Livelihoods: The Fundamentals of a Livelihood Strategy.* Medford, MA: Feinstein International Famine Center, Tufts University, 1997.

Lebanon News. "Bassil Calls on Expats to Reclaim Citizenship." *The Daily Star* (February 4, 2017), http://www.dailystar.com.lb/News/Lebanon-News/2017/Feb0 4/392246-bassil-calls-on-expats-to-reclaim-citizenship.ashx.

Lebanon News. "Lebanon Witnesses Rise in Syrian Refugee Child Labor over Past Year." *The Daily Star* (June 14, 2018), http://www.dailystar.com.lb/News/Le banonNews/2018/Jun-14/453154-lebanon-witnesses-rise-in-syrian-refugee-child -laborover-past-year.ashx.

Lebanon News. "Small Drug Cartel Operating in Dora, Jounieh Arrested." *The Daily Star* (April 5, 2018), http://www.dailystar.com.lb/News/Lebanon-News/2018/Apr0 5/444244-small-drug-cartel-operating-in-dora-jounieh-arrested.ashx.

Lebanon News. "UNHCR to Cross 5,500 Syrian Refugees: Derbas." *The Daily Star* (August 29, 2015), https://www.dailystar.com.lb/News/LebanonNews/2015/Apr2 9/296164-unhcr-to-cross-off-5500-syrian-refugeesderbas.ashx.

Lenette, Caroline, Mark Brough, and Leonie Cox. "Everyday Resilience: Narratives of Single Refugee Women with Children." *Qualitative Social Work* 12, no. 5 (2013): 637–53.

Lischer, Sarah Kenyon. *Dangerous Sanctuaries: Refugee Camps, Civil War, and the Dilemmas of Humanitarian Aid*, 26. Ithaca, NY: Cornell University Press, 2015.

Locher, Birgit and Elisabeth Prügl. "Feminism and Constructivism: Worlds Apart or Sharing the Middle Ground?" *International Studies Quarterly* 45, no. 1 (2001): 111–29.

Loveday, Morris, and Suzan Haidamous. "Beirut Car Bomb Kills at least 21." *The Washington Post* (August 15, 2013), http://articles.washingtonpost.com.

Loveless, Jeremy. "Crisis in Lebanon: Camps for Syrian Refugees?" *Forced Migration Review*, no. 43 (May, 2013): 66–8, www.fmreview.org/en/fragilestates/loveless.pdf.

Manly, Mark. "UNHCR's Mandate and Activities to Address Statelessness in Europe." *European Journal of Migration and Law* 14, no. 3 (2012): 261–77.

Mansour, Kholoud. "UN Humanitarian Coordination in Lebanon the Consequences of Excluding Syrian Actors International." *Chatham House the Royal Institute of International Affairs* (March 2017): 1–23.

Mahmoud, Haytham. "Syrian Refugees Change the Lebanese Labor Scene." *Al-Arabiya* (July 8, 2016), http://english.alarabiya.net/en/business/economy/2016/0 7/08/Syrianrefugees-change-the-Lebanese-labor-scene.html.

Mansour, Maya and Sarah Abou-Aad. "Women's Citizenship Rights in Lebanon." *Research and Policy-Making in the Arab World,* Issam Fares Institute for Public Policy and International Affairs at the American University of Beirut, Working Paper Series #8, (2012).

Mansour-Ille, Dina and Maegan Hendow. "From Exclusion to Resistance: Migrant Domestic Workers and the Evolution of Agency in Lebanon." *Journal of Immigrant & Refugee Studies* (2018): 1–21.

Marks, Jesse. "Pushing Syrian Refugees to Return." *Carnegie Middle East Center* (March 1, 2018), http://carnegie-mec.org/sada/75684.

Marsella, Anthony and Erin Ring. "Human Migration and Immigration: An Overview." in *Migration: Immigration and Emigration in International Perspective*, ed. L. L. Adler and U. P. Gielen, 3–22. Westport, CT: Praeger, 2003.

McAuliffe, Marie. "Lebanon: Struggling on in the Face of Donor Fatigue." *The Interpreter, LOWY Institute* (May 18, 2016), https://www.lowyinstitute.org/theinterpr eter/lebanon-struggling-face-donor-fatigue.

McCormack, Tara. "Power and Agency in the Human Security Framework." *Cambridge Review of International Affairs* 21, no. 1 (2008): 113–28.

McCourt, David M. "Practice Theory and Relationalism as the New Constructivism." *International Studies Quarterly* 60, no. 3 (2016): 475–85.

McDonald, Mark. "Securitization and the Construction of Security." *European Journal of International Relations* 14, no 4. (2008): 563–87.

McIntyre, Alice. *Participatory Action Research*, vol. 52. SAGE, 2007.

Meaker, Morgan. "Syrian Refugee Children Reduced to Selling on Beirut's Streets to Feed their Families." *The Guardian* (January 25, 2017), https://www.theguard ian.com/global-development/2017/jan/25/syrian-refugee-childrenselling-beirut-str eets-lebanon-support-families.

Meaker, Morgan. "When Aid Funds a Country — Not Its Refugees." *Devex News* (March 10, 2017), https://www.devex.com/news/when-aid-funds-a-country-not -its-refugees89744.

Meger, Sara. "The Fetishization of Sexual Violence in International Security." *International Studies Quarterly* 60, no. 1 (2016): 149–59.

Meier, Daniel. "La Strategie Du Regime Assad Au Liban Entre 1970 Et2013. Du Pouvoir Symbolique A La Coercion." *Revue EurOrient*, no. 41 (2013): 171–88.

Meier, Daniel. "Lebanon: The Refugee Issue and the Threat of a Sectarian Confrontation." *Oriente moderno* 94, no. 2 (2014): 382–401.

Merry, Sally Engle. *Human Rights and Gender Violence: Translating International Law into Local Justic.* Chicago, IL: University of Chicago Press, 2009.

Merry, Sally Engle and Peggy Levitt. "The Vernacularization of Women's Human Rights." in *Human Rights Futures*, ed. S. Hopgood, J. Snyder, and L. Vijamuri, 213–36. Cambridge: Cambridge University Press, 2017.

Mertens, Donna M. and Sharlene Hesse-Biber. "Triangulation and Mixed Methods Research: Provocative Positions." *Sage Journals* (2012): 75–9.

Mertus, Julie. "Sovereignty, Gender, and Displacement," in *Refugees and Forced Displacement. International Security, Human Vulnerability and the State*, ed. Newman Edward and Joanne Van Selm. Tokyo United Nations University Press, 2003.

Mikyoung, Kim. *Securitization of Human Rights: North Korean Refugees in East Asia*, 73. ABC-CLIO, 2012.

Milner, James. "Introduction: Understanding Global Refugee Policy." *Journal of Refugee Studies* 27, no. 4 (2014): 477–94.

Mitri, Dalya. "Challenges of Aid Coordination in a Complex Crisis: An Overview of Funding Policies and Conditions Regarding Aid Provision to Syrian Refugees in Lebanon." *Civil Society Knowledge Center* (2014).

Mordechai, Nisan "The Syrian Occupation of Lebanon." *Coalition for Responsible Peace in the Middle East* (2000): 59–110.

Mouamar, Patricia. "Viewpoints: Impact of Syrian Refugees on Host Countries." *BBC News* (August 24, 2013), https://www.bbc.com/news/world-23813975.

Mourad, Lama. "Inaction as Policy-Making: Understanding Lebanon's Early Response to the Refugee Influx." *POMEPS Studies* no. 25 (March, 2017): 49–55.

Mufti, Karim El. "Official Response to the Syrian Refugee Crisis in Lebanon: The Disastrous Policy of No-Policy." *Civil Society Knowledge Center, Lebanon Support* (January 10, 2014), http://civilsociety-centre.org/paper/official-response-syria nrefugee-crisis-lebanon-disastrous-policy-no-policy.

Naber, Nadine. "Arab American Femininities: Beyond Arab Virgin/American(ized) Whore." *Feminist Studies* 32, no. 1 (2006): 87–111.

Nachmias, David and Chava Nachmias. "Content Analysis," in *Research Methods in the Social Sciences*, ed. Edward Arnold. London, England, 1976, 132–9.

Naimou, Angela. "Double Vision: Refugee Crises and the Afterimages of Endless War." *College Literature* 43, no. 1 (2016): 226–33.

Nakhoul, Samia. "Analysis: Killing of Security Chief Raises Fears for Lebanon." *Reuters. Beirut* (October 22, 2012), https://en.wikipedia.org/wiki/Wissam_alH assan#cite_note-samia2212-19.

Naufal, Hala, "Syrian Refugees in Lebanon: The Humanitarian Approach Under Political Divisions." *Migration Policy Centre Research Report*, 2012/13, 16, http://cadmus.eui.eu/bitstream/handle.

Ní Aoláin, Fionnuala. "Women, Vulnerability, and Humanitarian Emergencies." *Michigan Journal Gender & Law* 18 (2011): 1–23.

Noll, Gregor. "Securitizing Sovereignty? States, Refugees, and the Regionalization of International Law." in *Refugees and Forced Displacement: International Security, Human Vulnerability, and the State*, ed. E. Newman and J. van Selm, 277–305. Tokyo, New York and Paris: United Nations University Press, 2003.

Northam, Jackie. "For Syrian Refugees, Needs Are Growing and Aid Is Declining." *National Public Radio* (September 14, 2015), https://www.npr.org/sections/parallels/2015/09/14/440280540/for-syrian-refugeesneeds-are-growing-and-aid-is-declining.

Norton, Augustus Richard. "Lebanon After Ta'if: Is the Civil War Over?" *Middle East Journal* 45, no. 3 (1991): 457–73.

Olivius, Elisabeth. "Constructing Humanitarian Selves and Refugee Others: Gender Equality and the Global Governance of Refugees." *International Feminist Journal of Politics* 18, no. 2 (2016): 276.

Olivius, Elisabeth. "Governing Refugees Through Gender Equality: Care, Control, Emancipation." PhD dissertation, Umeå universitet (2014), 2.

Olivius, Elisabeth. "(Un)Governable Subjects: The Limits of Refugee Participation in the Promotion of Gender Equality in Humanitarian Aid." *Journal of Refugee Studies* 27, no. 1 (2013): 42–61.

Ostrand, Nicole. "The Syrian Refugee Crisis: A Comparison of Responses by Germany, Sweden, the United Kingdom, and the United States." *Journal on Migration & Human Security* 3 (2015): 255.

OXFAM Discussion Paper, *Lebanon: Looking Ahead in Times of Crisis* (December 2015), https://www.oxfam.org/sites/www.oxfam.org/files/file_attachments/dpleb anon-looking-ahead-time-crisis-141215-en_0.pdf.

Pande, Amrita. "From 'Balcony Talk' and 'Practical Prayers' to Illegal Collectives: Migrant Domestic Workers and Meso-level Resistances in Lebanon." *Gender & Society* 26, no. 3 (2012): 382–405.

Pasquetti, Silvia, and Giovanni Picker. "Urban Informality and Confinement: Toward a Relational Framework." *International Sociology* 32, no. 4 (2017): 532–44.

Patrick, Stewart. "Are Ungoverned Spaces a Threat?" *Council on Foreign Relations* (2010), https://www.cfr.org/expert-brief.

Perry, Tom. "Lebanon near 'Breaking Point' Over Syrian Refugee Crisis: PM Hariri." *Reuters* (March 31, 2017), http://www.reuters.com/article/us-mideast-crisis-syrial ebanon-idUSKBN1722JM.

Perthes, Volker. "From Front State to Backyard? Syria and the Risks of Regional Peace," in *Economic and Political Impediments to Middle East Peace*, ed. J. W. Wright and L. Drake, 225–40. London, England: Palgrave Macmillan, 2000.

Pickering, Sharon. "Women and Extra Legal Border Crossing," in *Women, Borders, and Violence*, 1–16. New York, NY: Springer, 2011.

Pollard, Ruth. "Lebanese Citizenship Law Strips Women of Identity and Property." *Reuters* (May 25, 2016), https://www.reuters.com/article/us-lebanon-womenproperty-rights/l ebanese-citizenship-law-strips-women-of-identity-and-propertyidUSKCN0YH03O.

Porter, Lizzie and Kareem Chehayeb. "EXCLUSIVE: Lebanese Army Accused of Torturing Syrian Refugees." *Middle East Eye* (July 17, 2017), http://www.midd leeasteye.net/news/exclusive-syrian-refugees-tortured-deathlebanese-army-48 1522780.

Preston, Scott. "The Confessional Model and Sectarian Politics: Lessons from Lebanon and the Future of Iraq." Honors Theses, Paper 2281. Kalamazoo: Western Michigan University, 2013.

Price, Richard and Christian Reus-Smit. "Dangerous Liaisons? Critical International Theory and Constructivism." *European Journal of International Relations* 4, no. 3 (1998): 259–94.

Prügl, Elisabeth. "Social Mechanisms: A Methodological Tool for Feminist IR," in *The Art of World-Making*, 160–74, 302. Routledge, 2017.

Pulvirenti, Mariastella and Gail Mason. "Resilience and Survival: Refugee Women and Violence." *Current Issues Criminal Justice HeinOnline* 23 (2011): 37–52.

Rabil, Robert. *The Syrian Refugee Crisis in Lebanon: The Double Tragedy of Refugees and Impacted Host Communities.* Lexington Books, 2016.

Raffaela, Puggioni. "Refugees, Institutional Invisibility, and Self-Help Strategies: Evaluating Kurdish Experience in Rome." *Journal of Refugee Studies* 18, no. 3 (2005): 319–39.

Raymond, Janice G. "Pity the Nations: Women Refugees in Lebanon." *Coalition against Trafficking in Women Report* (December 6, 2017), http://www.catwinter national.org/Home/Article/727-pity-the-nations-womenrefugees-in-lebanon.

Riedel, Bruce and Bilal Y. Saab. "Lessons for Lebanon from Nahr El-Bared." *Op-Ed, Brookings* (October 4, 2007).

Riskedahl, Diane. "The Sovereignty of Kin: Political Discourse in Post-Ta'if Lebanon." *PoLAR: Political and Legal Anthropology Review* 34, no. 2 (2011): 233–50.

Roland, Paris. "Human Security: Paradigm Shift or Hot Air?" *International Security* 26, no. 2 (2001): 87–102.

Romano, Julia Craig. "Humanitarian Crisis: Impact of Syrian Refugees in Lebanon." *Middle East Program Wilson Center* (October 29, 2013), https://www.wilsonce nter.org/event/humanitarian-crisis-impact-syrian-refugeeslebanon.

Romany, Celina "Women as Aliens: A Feminist Critique of the Public/Private Distinction in International Human Rights Law." *Harvard Human Rights Journal* 6 (1993).

Romola, Sanyal. "A No-camp Policy: Interrogating Informal Settlements in Lebanon." *Geoforum* 84 (2017): 117–25.

Rosenow-Williams, Kerstin and Katharina Behmer. "A Gendered Human Security Perspective on Humanitarian Action in IDP and Refugee Protection." *Refugee Survey Quarterly* 34, no. 3 (2015): 1–23.

Ruggie, John Gerard. "What Makes the World Hang Together? Neo-Utilitarianism and the Social Constructivist Challenge." *International Organization* 52, no. 4 (1998): 855–85.

Runyan, Anne Sisson. *Global Gender Issues in the New Millennium.* Routlege, 2018.

Rustum Shehadeh, Lamia. "Gender-Relevant Legal Change in Lebanon." *Feminist Formations* 22, no. 3 (2010): 210–28.

Sadliwal, Batl. "Including Women, Excluding Migrants, and Reimagining National Belonging in the GCC." *World Peace Foundation* (March 12, 2018), https://sites. tufts.edu/reinventingpeace/2018/03/12/including-women-excludingmigrants-and-reimagining- national-belonging-in-the-gcc/.

Saldaña, Johnny. *The Coding Manual for Qualitative Researchers.* SAGE, 2015.

Saldaña, Johnny. *The Coding Manual for Qualitative Researchers.* SAGE, 2016.

Salem, Paul. "The Future of Lebanon." *Foreign Affairs* 85, no. 6 (2006): 13–22.

Saliba, Issam M. "Refugee Law and Policy in Selected Countries." *The Law Library of Congress, Global Legal Research Center* (March 2016).

Samari, Goleen. "Syrian Refugee Women's Health in Lebanon, Turkey, and Jordan and Recommendations for Improved Practice." *World Med Health Policy* (June, 2017), https://www.ncbi.nlm.nih.gov/pmc/articles/PMC5642924/

Sanyal, Romola. "A No-Camp Policy: Interrogating Informal Settlements in Lebanon." *Geoforum* 84 (2017): 117–25.

Schneider, Anne and Helen Ingram. "Social Construction of Target Populations: Implications for Politics and Policy." *American Political Science Review* 87, no. 2 (1993): 334–47.

Schultz, Tim. "Combating Statelessness in the Wake of the Syrian Conflict: A Right Without a Remedy." *Notre Dame Journal of International & Comparative Law* 8, no. 2 (2018): 131–56.

Selin, Akyüz and Bezen Balamir Coşkun. "Gendered (In) Securities: Refugee Camps in Southeastern Turkey." *Journal of Conflict Transformation and Security* 4, nos. 1–2 (2014): 7–22.

Sfeir, Rita. "Migration Is Increasing and the 'Specter' Of Bosnia and Rwanda Present any Repercussions of Russian Military Intervention on Asylum?" *Annahar News* (September 20, 2015). https://newspaper.annahar.com/article/276860

Shaheen, Kareem. "Dozens of Syrians Forced Into Sexual Slavery in Derelict Lebanese House." *The Guardian* (April 30, 2016), https://www.theguardian.com/wo rld/2016/apr/30/syrians-forced-sexual-slaverylebanon.

Shaheen, Kareem. "Lebanon Sex Trafficking: Syrian Woman Describes Nine-Month Ordeal." *The Guardian* (August 1, 2016), https://www.theguardian.com/world/2 016/aug/01/lebanon-sex-trafficking-syrianwoman-describes-nine-month-ordeal.

Shawaf, Nour and Francesca El Asmar. "We Are Not There Yet: Voices of Refugees from Syria in Lebanon." *OXFAM* (May, 2017), https://d1tn3vj7xz9fdh.cloudfront.net/s3 fs-public/file_attachments/rr-voices-syrialebanon-refugees-protection-310517-en.pdf.

Sikkink, Kathryn. *The Justice Cascade: How Human Rights Prosecutions Are Changing World Politics*, 236. WW Norton & Company, 2011.

Singleton Royce A. Jr. and Bruce C. Straits. *Approaches to Social Research.* Oxford University Press, 2005.

Slaughter, Amy et al., *Refugee Self-Reliance: Moving Beyond the Marketplace.* Oxford, England: Refugee Studies Center, 2017.

Steans, Jill. *Gender and International Relations: An Introduction.* New Jersey: Rutgers University Press, 1998.

Steele, Brent J. *Alternative Accountabilities in Global Politics: The Scars of Violence.* Routledge, 2013.

Stent, Angela. "Putin's Power Play in Syria: How to Respond to Russia's Intervention." *Foreign Affairs* 95 (2016): 106.

Sutton-Brown, Camille "Photovoice: A Methodological Guide." *Photography and Culture* 7, no. 2 (2014):169–85.

Sylvester, Christine. *War as Experience: Contributions from International Relations and Feminist Analysis.* London, England: Routledge, 2013.

Syrian American Society Foundation. "The Need for Chronic Disease Support for Refugees." *Relief Web* (May 21, 2018), https://reliefweb.int/report/lebanon/nee dchronic-disease-support-refugees.

Szczepanikova, Alice. "Gender Relations in a Refugee Camp: A Case of Chechens Seeking Asylum in the Czech Republic." *Journal of Refugee Studies* 18, no. 3 (2005): 281–98.

Szczepanikova, Alice. "Performing Refugeeness in the Czech Republic: Gendered Depoliticisation Through NGO Assistance." *Gender, Place & Culture* 17, no. 4 (2010): 461–77.

Tamang, Dipti. "Gendering International Security: Seeing Feminist Theories as International Relations." *International Studies* 50, no. 3 (2013): 226–39.

Tarazi, Leila. Fawaz. *An Occasion for War: Civil Conflict in Lebanon and Damascus in 1860.* University of California Press, 1994.

Thaddeus, Patrick Jackson. "Foregrounding Ontology: Dualism, Monism, and IR Theory." *Review of International Studies* 34, no. 1 (2008): 129–53.

Thibaut, Jaulin. "Citizenship, Migration, and Confessional Democracy in Lebanon." *Middle East Law and Governance* 6, no. 3 (2014): 250–71.

Thompson, Elizabeth. "Public and Private in Middle Eastern Women's History." *Journal of Women's History* 15, no. 1 (2003): 52–69.

Tickner, J. Ann. "Re-Visioning Security." *International Relations Theory Today*, 175–97. University Park, PA: Pennsylvania State University, 1995.

Tickner, J. Ann. "You Just Don't Understand: Troubled Engagements Between Feminists and IR Theorists." *International Studies Quarterly* 41, no. 4 (1997): 611–32.

Tickner, J. Ann and Laura Sjoberg. "Feminism," in *International Relations Theory, Discipline and Diversity*, 3rd ed., ed. Tim Dunne, Milja Kurki, and Steve Smith. Oxford: Oxford University Press, 2013.

Traboulsi, Fawwaz. *A History of Modern Lebanon.* Pluto Press, 2007.

Tueni, Nayla. "Lebanon's Baabda Declaration, A National Necessity." *Al-Arabiya News* (June 26, 2015), http://english.alarabiya.net/en/views/news/middleeast/2 015/06/26/Lebanon-s-Baabda-Declaration-a-national-necessity.html.

Turk, Volker and Elizabeth Eyster. "Strengthening Accountability in UNHCR." *International Journal of Refugee Law* 22, no. 2 (2010): 159–72.

Tyab, Imtiaz. "Anti-Syrian Hostility Surges in Lebanon." *Al-Jazeera* (October 25, 2017), https://www.aljazeera.com/news/2017/10/anti-syrian-hostility-surges-le banon171025105854684.html.

Ungar, Michael, Marion Brown, Linda Liebenberg, and Rasha Othman. "Unique Pathways to Resilience Across Cultures." *Adolescence* 42, no. 166 (2007): 287.

UNHCR, "Country Operations Plan" (2004), http://www.unhcr.org/3fd9c6a14.pdf.

UNHCR and International Rescue Committee. "Vulnerability Assessment of Syrian Refugee Men in Lebanon." *International Rescue Committee* (January 2016), https ://www.rescue.org/sites/default/files/document/464/irclebanonrefugeemensvulne rabilityassessment.pdf.

UNHCR Regional Office in Lebanon, Country Operations Plan 1 (2004), http://www. unhcr.org/3fd9c6a14.pdf.

United Nations Children's Fund (UNICEF), United Nations High Commissioner for Refugees (UNHCR), and the United Nations World Food Programme (WFP), *Vulnerability Assessment of Syrian Refugees in Lebanon Report, VASyR-2017*, 2017, https://data2.unhcr.org/fr/documents/download/61312.

United Nations Program, United Nations Children's Fund (UNICEF), and UNHCR (2016), http://documents.wfp.org/stellent/groups/public/documents/ena/ wfp289533.pdf.

Walsh, Bryan. "Alan Kurdi's Story: Behind the Most Heartbreaking Photo of 2015." *TIME Magazine* (December 29, 2015), http://time.com/4162306/alan-kurdi-syria drowned-boy-refugee-crisis.

Wang, Caroline and Mary Ann Burris. "Photovoice: Concept, Methodology, and Use for Participatory Needs Assessment." *Health Education & Behavior* 24, no. 3 (1997): 369–87.

Wang, Caroline C. "Photovoice: A Participatory Action Research Strategy Applied to Women's Health." *Journal of Women's Health* 8, no. 2 (1999): 185–92.

Wang, Caroline C. and Yanique A. Redwood-Jones. "Photovoice Ethics: Perspectives from Flint Photovoice." *Health Education & Behavior* 28, no. 5 (2001): 560–72.

Ward, Clarissa. "Syrian Refugees Sell Daughters in Bid to Survive." *CBS News* (May 15, 2013), http://www.cbsnews.com/news/syrian-refugees-sell-daughters-in-bid -tosurvive/.

Watson, Adam. "Hedley Bull, States Systems and International Societies." *Review of International Studies* 13, no. 2 (1987): 147–53.

Watson, Scott D. "Manufacturing Threats: Asylum Seekers as Threats or Refugees." *Journal of International Law & International Relations* 3 (2007): 95–117.

Wendt, Alexander. *Social Theory of International Politics.* Cambridge University Press, 1999.

Wiedman, Dennis and Iveris L. Martinez. "Organizational Culture Theme Theory and Analysis of Strategic Planning for a New Medical School." *Human Organization* 76, no. 3 (2017).

Williams, Michael C. "Securitization as Political Theory: The Politics of the Extraordinary." *International Relations* 29, no. 1 (2015): 114–20.

Wilmott, Annabelle Cathryn. "The Politics of Photography: Visual Depictions of Syrian Refugees in UK Online Media." *Visual Communication Quarterly* 24, no. 2 (2017): 67–82.

Wood, Josh. "Syrian War Deals Heavy Blow to Lebanon's Export Business." *The National News* (September 26, 2015), https://www.thenational.ae/world/syrian- wardeals-heavy-blow-to-lebanon-s-export-business-1.127856.

Yarzeh, Ruth Sherlock. "Expat Syrians Join the Crush to Support Assad in Parody Election." *Telegraph UK* (May 28, 2014).

Yarzeh, Ruth Sherlock, "In Lebanon, Syrian Refugees Met with Harassment and Hostility." *NPR* (September 2, 2017), https://www.npr.org/sections/parallels/2017/0 9/02/547906231/in-lebanon-syrianrefugees-met-with-harassment-and-hostility.

Yasmine, Rola and Catherine Moughalian. "Systemic Violence Against Syrian Refugee Women and the Myth of Effective Intrapersonal Interventions." *Reproductive Health Matters* 24, no. 47 (2016): 27–35.

Yuval-Davis, Nira, Floya Anthias, and Eleonore Kofman. "Secure Borders and Safe Haven and the Gendered Politics of Belonging: Beyond Social Cohesion." *Ethnic and Racial Studies* 28, no. 3 (2005): 513–35.

Zahar, Marie-Joëlle. "Peace by Unconventional Means: Lebanon's Ta'if Agreement." in *Ending Civil Wars: The Implementation of Peace Agreements*, ed. Stephen Stedman, Donald Rothchild, and Elizabeth Cousens, 567–97. Lynne Rienner Press, 2002.

Zeinab, Cherri et al. "Early Marriage and Barriers to Contraception Among Syrian Refugee Women in Lebanon: A Qualitative Study." *International Journal of Environmental Research and Public Health* vol. 8 (2017), 14.

Zeinab, Cherri, Pedro Arcos González, and Rafael Castro Delgado. "The Lebanese–Syrian Crisis: Impact of Influx of Syrian Refugees to an Already Weak State." *Risk Management and Healthcare Policy* 9 (2016).

Zetter, Roger and Héloïse Ruaudel. "Development and Protection Challenges of the Syrian Refugee Crisis." *Forced Migration Review* 47 (September 2014): 6–10.

Zwingel, Susanne. "How Do Norms Travel? Theorizing International Women's Rights in Transnational Perspective." *International Studies Quarterly* 56, no. 1 (2012): 115–29.

Zwingel, Susanne. *Translating International Women's Rights*. Palgrave Macmillan UK, 2016.

Zwingel, Susanne. *Translating International Women's Rights: The CEDAW Convention in Context*. Palgrave Macmillan, 2016.

"300 Thousand Syrian Women Pregnant Will Give Birth in Lebanon in 2017." *Addiyar News* (March 3, 2017), https://www.addiyar.com/article/1359928-300-2017.

"A Convoy of 300 Syrian Displaced Returned from the Town of Arsal to the Syrian Town Isal Al-Ward," *An-Nahar* (July 12, 2017), https://www.annahar.com/article/617319F.

"Abu Khalil: Without the Syrian Crisis, Electricity Would Have Been 24/24." *Lebanon News*, *LBC News* (February 21, 2017), www.lbcgroup.tv/news/d/lebanon/3040 03/24/24.

"Bou Saab Continued with Lazarene Preparations for the Donor Conference and the IDP Education Plan." *Lebanonfiles Local News* (January 13, 2016), http://www.lebanonfiles.com/news/985407.

"Effective Intrapersonal Interventions." *Reproductive Health Matters* 24, no. 47, https://www.tandfonline.com/doi/pdf/10.1016/j.rhm.2016.04.008.

"Extremist Ain El Hilweh Group Threatens Escalation." *The Daily Star* (May 8, 2017), http://www.dailystar.com.lb/News/Lebanon-News/2017/May-08/404971-extremistain-al-hilweh-group-threatensescalation.ashx.

"International Plea for Syrian Refugee Jobs Sparks Anger in Lebanon." *Arab News* (June 24, 2018), http://www.arabnews.com/node/1292241/middle-east.

"Lebanon and Jordan Close Their Borders to Syrian Refugees." *The Chronicle* (December 22, 2014), https://chronicle.fanack.com/refugees/lebanon-and-jorda nclose-their-borders-to-syrian-refugees/.

"Lebanon between the Largest Displacement and the Least Aid." *Emirates News Agency* (June 6, 2017), https://www.zawya.com/mena/en/story/Some _60000_Syrian_refugees_in_Lebanon__ Jordan_could_lose_assistance_ warns_UNHCR-WAM20170606192048379.

"Lebanon Cabinet Votes to Stop Accepting Syrian Refugees." *Daily Star* (October 23, 2014), www.dailystar.com.lb/News/Lebanon-News/2014/Oct-23/275075-re fugeecrisis-tops-lebanoncabinetagenda.ashx.

"Lebanon Elects Six Women to Parliament." *The Daily Star* (May 09, 2018), http:// www.dailystar.com.lb /News/Lebanon-Elections/2018/May-09/448633lebanon-elects-six-women-to-parliament.ashx.

"Lebanon First Ever Womens Affairs Minister Man Jean Ogasapian Rights Equal." *Independent* (December 19, 2016), https://www.independent.co.uk/news/world/ middle-east/lebanon-first-ever-womensaffairs-minister-man-jean-ogasapian-rights -equal-a7484221.html.

"Lebanon Freezes UNHCR Staff Residency Applications in Row Over Syrian Refu-gees." *Reuters* (June 8, 2018), https://www.reuters.com/article/us-lebanon-syria-r efugeesunhcr/lebanon-freezes-unhcr-staff-residency-applications-in-row-over-syri anrefugees-idUSKCN1J41JE.

"Lebanon 'Moves Right Way' on ID." *BBC News*, February 24, 2009, http://news.bbc .co.uk/2/hi/middle_east/7906125.stm.

"Lebanon's President Aoun Calls for National Unity, Liberating Palestinian Terri-tories." *Albawaba* (November 1, 2016), http://www. albawaba.com/news/lebanon 'spresident-aoun-calls-national-unity-liberating-palestinian-territories-899220.

"Lebanon Wants UN to Facilitate Return of Syrian Refugees." *Associated Press* (June 14, 2018), https://abcnews.go.com/International/wireStory/lebanon-facilitate-retu rnsyrian-refugees-55891878.

"Patriarch al-Ra'i: 'Syrian Refugees Threaten Lebanon Security.'" *Orient News* (December 26, 2016), https://www.orient-news.net/en/news_show/129448/0/Patri arch-al-Rai-"Syrian-refugees-threatenLebanon-security.

"Refugee Children Resorting to 'Survival Sex' to Pay People Smugglers Says UN." *International Business Times* (October, 2015), http://www.ibtimes.co.uk/refug eechildren-resorting-survival-sex-pay-people-smugglers-says-un-1525534.

"Roula Yaacoub's Husband Found Not Guilty After Beating Her to Death." *Beirut* (Novemeber 1, 2018), https://www.beirut.com/l/56670.

"Syrian Children in Lebanon Forced to Work: Report." *Al Jazeera News* (April 12, 2016), https://www.aljazeera.com/news/2016/04/syrian-children-lebanon-forced-workreport-160412051345859.html.

"Syrian President Bashar Al-Assad Wins Third Term." *BBC NEWS, World, Middle East* (June 5, 2014), http://www.bbc.com/news/world-middle-east-27706471.

"Syrian Refugee Women in Lebanon Face Abuse, Exploitation." *Agence France Press, The Straits Times* (February 2, 2016), https://www.straitstimes.com/world/ middleeast/syrian-refugee-women-in-lebanon-face-abuse-exploitation.

"Syrian Refugee Women Tell Stories About Sexual Exploitation in Lebanon." *Naharnet Newsdesk* (August, 2014), http://www.naharnet.com/stories/ar/141494.

"Syrian Women Rise Above Differences and Forge a Statement of Unity." *UN Women News* (May 23, 2016), http://www.unwomen.org/en/news/stories/2016/5/syrianwomen-rise-above-differences-and-forge-a-statement-of-unity.

"Syrians Entering Lebanon Face New Restrictions." *BBC News* (January 5, 2015), https://www.bbc.com/news/world-middle-east-30657003.

"Syrians Who Obtain Work Permits in Lebanon Risk Losing Refugee Aid." *Lebanon News, The Daily Star* (March 6, 2017), http://www.dailystar.com.lb/News/LebanonNews/2017/Mar-06/396311-syrians-who-obtain-work-permits-in-lebanon-risk-losingrefugee-status.ashx.

"Syria's Civil War Explained From the Beginning." *AlJazeera* (2016), http://www.aljazeera.com/news/2016/05/syria-civil-war-explained160505084119966.html.

"The Future of Syria: How a Victorious Bashar Al-Assad Is Changing Syria." *The Economist* (June 28, 2018), https://www.economist.com/middle-east-andafrica/2018/06/28/how-a-victorious-bashar-al-assad-is-changing-syria.

"Two-Thirds of Syrian Refugees in Lebanon 'Employed'." *Almanar TV Archive* (March 4, 2014), http://archive.almanar.com.lb/english/article.php?id=144153.

"U.S. Welcomes Lebanon Plan for Syrian Refugees." *The Daily Star* (January 4, 2013), http://www.dailystar.com.lb/News/Politics/2013/Jan-04/200934-us-welcomeslebanon-plan-for-syrian-refugees.

"Woman's Murder Prompts Mass Eviction of Syrians From Lebanese Town." *Reuters* (October 5, 2017), https://www.reuters.com/article/us-mideast-crisis-lebanonrefugees/womans-murder-prompts-mass-eviction-of-syrians-from-lebanese-tow nidUSKBN1CA18S.

UN Documents and Reports:

"1951 Refugee Convention and 1967 Protocol Relating to the Status of Refugees." United Nations, General Assembly, http://www.unhcr.org/3b66c2aa10.

"A Longing to Go Homes, in Safety and Dignity: Intentions and Perceptions of Syrian Refugees in Lebanon about their Future." *UNHCR*, Lebanon (January 2018), https://data2.unhcr.org/fr/documents/download/63310\.

"Amnesty International Annual Report 2015/2016." *Releif Web*, http://reliefweb.int/report/lebanon/amnesty-international-regrets-lebanon-s-decisionoverturn-its-open-border-policy.

"Amnesty International Regrets Lebanon's Decision to Overturn Its Open Border Policy towards Refugees and Refusal to Address Discrimination Against Women and Migrants." *Amnesty International* (March 16, 2016), http://reliefweb.int/report/lebanon/amnesty-international-regrets-lebanon-s-decisionoverturn-its-open-border-policy.

"Annual Results Report. Water, Sanitation and Hygiene." *UNICEF* (2016), 41.

"Are We Listening? Acting on Our Commitments to Women and Girls Affected by the Syrian Conflict." *International Rescue Committee, IRC* (2014), 15.

"Assessment of the Impact of Syrian Refugees in Lebanon and Their Employment Profile." *International Labor Organization* (2013), https://www.ilo.org/wcmsp5/groups/public/---arabstates/---robeirut/documents/publication /wcms_ 240134.pdf.

"Briefing Note for Countries on the 2016 Human Development Report: Lebanon." *United Nations Development Program (UNDP)* (2016), http://hdr.undp.org/sites/all/themes/hdr_theme/country-notes/JOR.pdf.

"Childhood in the Shadow of War: Voices of Young Syrians." *Save the Children* (2015), http://resourcecentre.savethechildren.se/sites/default/files/documents/chil dhood-inthe-shadow-of-war.pdf.

"Concluding Observations on the Combined Fourth and Fifth Periodic Reports of Lebanon." *CEDAW.* UN Doc. CEDAW/C/LBN/4-5 (November 3, 2015), http://docstore.ohchr.org/SelfServices/FilesHandler.ashx?

"Consideration of Reports Submitted by States Parties Under Article 18 of the Convention Fourth and Fifth Periodic Reports of States Parties Due in 2014 Lebanon." *United Nations* (May 15, 2014), https://nclw.org.lb/wpcontent/uploads/2017/10/CEDAW-Fourth-and-Fifth-Periodic-Report-Lebanon.pdf.

"Country Operations Plan." *UNHCR Regional Office in Lebanon* (2004), http://www.unhcr.org/3fd9c6a14.pdf.

Did the PLO Die in Lebanon?" *Al Jazeera*, July 28, 2009, https://www.aljazeera.com/programmes/plohistoryofrevolution/2009/07/200972855032594820.html.

"Ensuring Birth Registration for the Prevention of Statelessness." *UNHCR.* Ending Statelessness Within 10 Years (2017), https://www.unhcr.org/ke/wpcontent/uploads/sites/2/2017/11/Good-Practices-Paper-on-Ensuring-BirthRegistration-for-the-Prevention-of-Statelessness.pdf.

"Female Refugees from Syria in Iraq, Jordan and Lebanon: Lebanon Gender Profile." *United Nations Economic and Social Commission of Western Asia (ESCWA)*, E/ESCWA/ECW/2013/Technical Paper 4 (2014), 15.

"Following the Money: Lack of Transparency in Donor Funding for Syrian Refugee Education." *Human Rights Watch* (September 14, 2017), https://www.hrw.org/report/2017/09/14/following-money/lack-transparency-donorfunding-syrian-ref ugee-education.

"Food Security Sector, Monthly Dashboard." *UN Inter-Agency Coordination Lebanon* (July, 2015), http://data.unhcr.org/syrianrefugees/download.php?id=9506.

"Government of Lebanon and UNHCR, Lebanon Crisis Response Plan 2015–2016." *UNHCR Portal* (2015), 1, https://data2.unhcr.org/en/documents/download/44245.

"Growing Up Without an Education: Barriers to Education for Syrian Refugee Children in Lebanon." *Human Rights Watch* (July 19, 2016), https://www.hrw.org/report/2016/07/19/growing-without-education/barrierseducation-syrian-refuge e-children-lebanon.

"Human Rights Watch Submission to the CEDAW Committee of Lebanon's Periodic Report 62nd Session." *Human Rights Watch* (February, 2015), https://tbinternet.o hchr.org/Treaties/CEDAW/Shared%20Documents/ LBN/INT_ CEDAW_NGO_ LBN_19385_E.pdf.

"I Just Wanted to be Treated like a Person: How Lebanon's Residency Rules Facilitate Abuse of Syrian Refugees." *Human Rights Watch* (January 12, 2016), https://www.hrw.org/report/2016/01/12/i-just-wanted-be-treated-person/howlebanons-res idency-rules-facilitate-abuse.

"I Want a Safe Place: Refugee Women from Syria Uprooted and Unprotected in Lebanon" *Amnesty International* (2015), https://www.amnesty.org/download/Do cuments/MDE2417852015ENGLISH.PDF.

"I Want a Safe Space: Refugee Women from Syria Uprooted and Unprotected in Lebanon." *Amnesty International* (February, 2016), https://www.alnap.org/system/ files/content/resource/files/main/i-want-a-safeplace.pdf

"Identifying the Legislative Gaps that Need to be Filled for the Application of Security Council Resolution 1325." *United Nations Economic and Social Commission for Western Asia—(ESCWA).* (2000) on Women, Peace and Security in Selected Arab States." E/ESCWA/ECW/2015/Technical Paper.8, (March 17, 2015), women -peacesecurity-legisislative-gaps-resolution-1325-english.pdf.

"Lebanon Annual Report 2014 Highlights." *KAFA* (2014), http://www.kafa.org.lb/St udiesPublicationPDF/ PRpdf-82-635689245975040950.pdf.

"Lebanon Immigration Detention Profile." *Global Detention Project* (February 2018), https://www.globaldetentionproject.org /countries/middle-east/lebanon.

"Lebanon Security and Justice Sector Wide Assessment." *UNDP* (March 2016), file:///C:/Users/Jessy/Downloads/ SecurityandJusticeSectorWideAssessment.pdf.

"Lebanon: At Least 45 Local Curfews Imposed on Syrian Refugees." *Human Rights Watch* (October 3, 2014), https://www.hrw.org/news/2014/10/03/lebanon-least-45local-curfews-imposed-syrian-refugees.

"Lebanon: Economic and Social Impact Assessment of the Syrian Conflict." *World Bank Report*, http://documents.worldbank.org/curated/en/2013/09/18292074/l ebanon-economic-social-impact-assessment-syrian-conflict.

"Lebanon: Mass Evictions of Syrian Refugees." *Human Rights Watch* (April 20, 2018), https://www.hrw.org/news/2018/04/20/lebanon-mass-evictions-syrian-refu gees.

"Lebanon: New Entry Requirements for Syrians Likely to Block Would-Be Refugees." *Amnesty International* (January 6, 2015), www.amnesty.org/en/documents/ document/?indexNumber=mde24%2F002%2F2015 &language=en.

"Lebanon: Reveal Fate of Disappeared Syrians: Military Intelligence Detains Six Calling for Democratic Change in Their Country." *Human Rights Watch* (March 9, 2011), https://www.hrw.org/news/2011/03/09/lebanon-reveal-fate-disappeared-sy rians.

"Lebanon: Syrian Women at Risk of Sex Trafficking." *Human Rights Watch* (July 28, 2016), https://www.hrw.org/news/2016/07/28/lebanon-syrian-women-risk-sex trafficking.

"Lebanon-UNHCR Memorandum of Understanding." *Frontiers Center* (November, 2003), http://www.frontiersruwad.org/pdf/FR_Public_Statement_MOU_Nov_200 3.pdf.

"Lebanon: Waste Crisis Posing Health Risks." *Human Rights Watch* (December 1, 2017), https://www.hrw. org/news/2017/12/01/lebanon-waste-crisis-posing-he alth-risks.

"Palestinian Employment in Lebanon: Facts and Challenges: Labor Force Survey Among Palestinian Refugees Living in Camps and Gatherings in Lebanon." *International Labour Organisation (ILO), Committee for the Employment of Palestinian Refugees (CEP), United Nations Peace Building Fund* (2012), 58.

"Protection Sector, Monthly Dashboard." *UN Inter-Agency Coordination Lebanon* (July 2015), http://data.unhcr.org/syrianrefugees/download.php?id=9508.

"Pushed to the Edge: Syrian Refugees Face Increased Restrictions in Lebanon." *Amnesty International* (June 2015), www.amnesty.nl/sites/default/files/public/pus hed_to_the_edge_syrian_refugees_face_increased_restrictions_in_ lebanon.pdf.

"Q&A for Syrians Seeking Registration." *United Nations* (July 15, 2017), https://ww w.refugees-lebanon.org/en/news/88/qa-for-syrians-seeking-registration.

"Reform of the KAFALA (Sponsorship) System." *Migrant Forum in Asia, Policy Brief No. 2*, (July 3, 2013), http://www.ilo.org/dyn/migpractice/docs/132/PB2.pdf.

"Refugees from Syria: Lebanon." *UNHCR* (March 2015), 6, http://reliefweb.int/repo rt/lebanon/refugees-syria-lebanon-march-2015.

"Regional Refugee and Resilience Plan (3RP), Funding Requirements: Lebanon." *United Nations* (December 29, 2015), http://data.unhcr.org/syrianrefugees/country. php?id=122.

"Self-Protection and Coping Strategies of Refugees from Syria and Host Communities in Lebanon." *OXFAM* (July, 2015), https://d1tn3vj7xz9fdh.cloudfront.net/s3 fspublic/file_attachments/rr-lebanon-refugees-protection-300616-en.pdf.

"SGBV Dashboard." *Interagency, Lebanon* (January–August 2016), http://data.unh cr.org/syrianrefugees/working_group.php?Page=Country&LocationId=122&Id =47.

"SGBV Dashboard." *Interagency, Lebanon* (January–August 2016), https://data2. unhcr.org/en/situations/ syria/location/71.

"SGBV Dashboard." *Lebanon Interagency* (August 2016), http://data.unhcr.org/syr ianrefugees/working_group.php?Page=Country&LocationId=122&Id=47.

"States Parties to the 1951 Convention Relating to the Status of Refugees and the 1967 Protocol." UNHCR, http://www.unhcr.org/3b73b0d63.html.

"Struggling to Survive: Slavery and Exploitation of Syrian Refugees in Lebanon." *Freedom Fund* (April 12, 2016), http://freedomfund.org/wpcontent/uploads/Leba non-Report-FINAL-8April16.pdf.

"Syria Crisis Response, Situation Report." *World Food Programme, Lebanon* (September, 2015), http://data.unhcr.org /syrianrefugees/download.php?id=9670.

"Syria Regional Refugee Response." *UNHCR* (August 11, 2018), http://data.unhcr.or g/syrianrefugees/regional.php.

"Syria Regional Refugee Response, Information Portal." *United Nations High Commissioner for Refugees (UNHCR)*, http://data.unhcr.org/syrianrefugees/country. php?id=122.

"Syrian Refugees in Lebanon Surpass One Million." *UNHCR, Press Releases* (April 3, 2014), http://www.unhcr.org/533c15179.html.

"Syrian Refugees in Lebanon." *Syrian Civic Platform* (September 29, 2017), http:// www.scplatform.net/en/syrian-refugees-in-lebanon/.

"Syrian Refugees Resort to Child Labor in Lebanon." *The World Staff, PRI* (September 5, 2017), https://www.pri.org/stories/2017-09-05/syrian-refugees-resort-chi ld-laborlebanon.

"Syria's Good Neighbors: How Jordan and Lebanon Sheltered Millions of Refugees." *Washington Institute* (September 2015), http://www.washingtoninstitute.org/polic

yanalysis/view/syrias-good-neighbors-how-jordan-and-lebanon-sheltered-milli
ons-ofrefugees.

"The 2015–16 Lebanon Crisis Response Plan." *UNHCR* (December 15, 2014), http://
www.alnap.org/resource/20702,

"The Consequences of Limited Legal Status for Syrian Refugees in Lebanon." *Norwegian Refugee Council* (December 2013), 27, https://reliefweb.int/sites/reliefw
eb.int/files/resources/9687105.pdf.

"The Situation of Human Rights in Lebanon: Annual Report." *ALEF* (2015), alefl
iban.org/wp-content/uploads/2016/10/ALEF_Human-Rights-in-Lebanon_2015.

"The Situation of Human Rights in Lebanon." *ALEF, Annual Report 2017* (March,
2018), 11, https://alefliban.org/wpcontent/uploads/2018/04/annual_report_2017_
v03_-2.pdf.

"The Syrian Refugee Crisis: Labour Market Implications in Jordan and Lebanon."
European Economy Discussion Paper, European Union (2016), https://ec.euro
pa.eu/info/sites/info/files/dp029_en.pdf.

"Too Close for Comfort: Syrians in Lebanon." *International Crisis Group Middle
East Report 141* (2013), http://www.operationspaix.net/DATA/DOCUMENT/7
965~v~Too_Close__For_Comfort__Syrians_in_Lebanon_Middle_East_Report_
N141.pdf.

"Too Close for Comfort: Syrians in Lebanon." *The International Crisis Group (ICG)
Middle East Report* (2013), 9.

"Trapped in Lebanon: The Alarming Human Rights and Human Security Situation
of Syrian Refugees in Lebanon." *ALEF* (May 2016), 18, https://alefliban.org/wpc
ontent/uploads/2016/11/Trapped-In-Lebanon ALEF_PA X _ May2016.pdf.

"Trapped in Lebanon: The Alarming Human Rights and Human Security Situation of
Syrian Refugees in Lebanon." *ALEF* (May, 2016), https://alefliban.org/wpcontent/
uploads/2016/11/Trapped-In-Lebanon-_ALEF_PAX_May2016.pdf.

"Treaty of Brotherhood, Cooperation, and Coordination Between the Syrian Arab
Republic and the Lebanese Republic." *United Nations Treaty Series* (1992). 154,
https://peacemaker.un.org/sites/peacemaker.un.org/files /LY_910522-TreatyBro
therhoodCooperationCoordination.pdf.

"Uncharted Waters: Thinking Through Syria's Dynamics, Middle East Briefing No.
31" *International Crisis Group Damascus/Brussels* (November 24, 2011).

"UNHCR 2016 Regional Refugee & Resilience Plan – Funding Snapshot as of End
of 2016." *UNHCR* (December 31, 2016), https://alefliban.org/wpcontent/uploads/
2017/03/ALEF_AnnualReport_2016.pdf.

"UNHCR Country Operation Profile: Lebanon." *UNHCR* (2013), http://www.almo
nitor.com/pulse/ar/contents/articles/originals/2013/06/iraq-kurdistan-syrianrefu
gees-aid.html#

"'Unprecedented' 65 Million People Displaced by War and Persecution in 2015."
UN News Centre, http://www.un.org/apps/news/story.asp?NewsID=54269 #.
WahMY8h96bg.

"VASyR 2017: Vulnerability Assessment of Syrian Refugees in Lebanon." *World
Food Program, United Nations Children's Fund (UNICEF), and UNHCR* (2016),
http://documents.wfp.org/stellent/ groups/public/documents/ ena/wfp289533.pdf.

"Vulnerability Assessment of Syrian Refugee Men in Lebanon." *International Rescue Committee*, Lebanon (January 2016), https://www.rescue.org/sites/default/files/document/464/irclebanonrefugeemensvulnerabilityassessment.pdf.

"Without Protection: Women's Rights under Lebanese Personal Status Laws." *Human Rights Watch* (January, 2015).

"Women and the Refugee Crisis: A News Update from Lebanon." *Global Fund for Woman* (2015), https://www.globalfundforwomen.org/news-update-refugeecrisis/#.WVovCoiGPIU.

"World Report 2014 Events of 2013 2014." *Human Rights Watch*, https://www.hrw.org/sites/ default/files/wr2014_web_0.pdf. Amnesty International Focus Group Discussion (October 6, 2015), Saadnyal, Bekaa Valley.

Index

Abouarab, Said, 2
Absentees law (Syria's new property
   law of 2018), 24, 54
agency, 12, 20, 30, 33–34, 71, 86, 103,
   107, 120, 124, 127, 150, 154; Syrian
   agency, 93–96, 99, 133–34; Syrian
   women's agency, 4, 10, 44, 64, 81,
   102, 110–11, 127, 134, 150–51
aid, 21, 36, 67, 72, 74, 80–82, 85–87,
   89–90, 97, 119–20; humanitarian aid,
   1, 10, 33–34, 38–39, 43, 49, 64–65,
   67, 74–75, 77, 85, 102–7, 112–15,
   122, 127, 135–36, 142, 144, 147, 152
anti-Syrian sentiments, 2, 20
Arab Bedouins, 40–41, 103
Assad, Bashar, 4, 24, 53–54, 177–78
Assad regime, 2, 18, 21–22, 24, 32,
   52–53, 143–44
asylum, 10, 15–17, 26, 30–35, 43, 64,
   67, 74, 81, 87, 90, 93, 123, 137,
   140–43, 152; Syrian asylum seekers,
   2, 24, 31, 33, 140–41, 143, 152

Baabda Presidential Palace, 32
black-market activities, 151
blowback, 3, 108, 141–42, 150–51
border control, 16, 34–35, 48, 145
border management, 22, 34, 36, 40, 48,
   123, 129, 131

Brotherhood, 19–20, 22, 25, 51

cash-per-task, 107
Cedar Revolution, 21
child labor livelihood, 101, 121–23,
   134, 139, 151–52, 123
child marriage, 126, 131, 139, 150, 152,
   157
citizenship, 7, 16, 20, 28, 39, 45, 50–51,
   61, 77, 156
Civic Engagement and Community
   Service (CCECS), 97
Civil War: Lebanese, 3, 18–19, 21, 29,
   32, 47; Syrian, 47, 121
community engagement, 4, 70, 184
coordination, 19, 25, 42, 72–74, 89, 154
coresearchers, 8, 95–96, 99–108,
   110–11, 113, 115–17, 120–21, 124,
   127–29, 132–34, 136, 152–53

Dar Al-Fatwa, 27
decision-making power and processes,
   44, 69, 110–12
deportation, 33–36, 39, 47, 49, 73, 116,
   136, 145–48
detention and incarceration, 20, 26, 33,
   37, 41–42, 47, 116, 136, 145, 146
discrimination, 4, 27, 34, 56–57, 85,
   135, 149; gender discrimination,

185

About the Author

Jessy Abouarab is a Visiting Assistant Professor at Florida International University (FIU) with the Center for Women's and Gender Studies. She has a Ph.D. in International Relations, majoring in foreign policy and security studies in the Middle East, specializing in women's and gender studies. Her interdisciplinary academic approach is legal-normative, fostering critical thinking about gender and migration through participatory learning methods when probing the nature of questions, issues, materials, and problems under study. In addition, as a feminist Middle Eastern scholar and an enthusiastic activist, Dr. Abouarab's non-academic work includes grassroots advocacy and community organizing to increase the power, voice, and leadership of marginalized communities in advancing global justice.

www.ingramcontent.com/pod-product-compliance
Lightning Source LLC
Chambersburg PA
CBHW050652280326
41932CB00015B/2882